Documentary Editing

Documentary Editing offers clear and detailed strategies for tackling every stage of the documentary editing process, from organizing raw footage and building select reels to fine cutting and final export. Written by a Sundance award-winning documentary editor with a dozen features to his credit and containing examples from over 100 films, this book presents a step-by-step guide for how to turn seemingly shapeless footage into focused scenes, and how to craft a structure for a documentary of any length. The book contains insights and examples from seven of America's top documentary editors, including Geoffrey Richman (*The Cove, Sicko*), Kate Amend (*The Keepers, Into the Arms of Strangers*), and Mary Lampson (*Harlan County U.S.A.*), and a companion website contains easy-to-follow video tutorials.

Written for both practitioners and enthusiasts, *Documentary Editing* offers unique and invaluable insights into the documentary editing process.

Jacob Bricca is an Assistant Professor at the University of Arizona's School of Theatre, Film and Television, where he teaches classes on editing and documentary filmmaking. He has edited over a dozen feature documentaries, including the international theatrical hit *Lost in La Mancha*, the New Yorker Films theatrical release *Con Artist*, the Independent Lens Audience Award winner *Jimmy Scott: If You Only Knew*, and the Sundance Special Jury Prize winner *The Bad Kids*. His directing credits include *Pure*, which screened at the 2008 Berlin International Film Festival, and *Finding Tatanka*, which premiered at the 2014 Big Sky Documentary Film Festival.

Documentary Editing
Principles and Practice

Jacob Bricca

Routledge
Taylor & Francis Group
NEW YORK AND LONDON

First published 2018
by Routledge
711 Third Avenue, New York, NY 10017

and by Routledge
2 Park Square, Milton Park, Abingdon, Oxon, OX14 4RN

Routledge is an imprint of the Taylor & Francis Group, an informa business

Library of Congress Cataloging-in-Publication Data
Names: Bricca, Jacob author.
Title: Documentary editing : principles and practice / Jacob Bricca.
Description: New York : Routledge, 2017. | Includes bibliographical references and index.
Identifiers: LCCN 2017034743 (print) | LCCN 2017047061 (ebook) | ISBN 9781315560472 (E-book) | ISBN 9781138675728 (hardback) | ISBN 9781138675735 (pbk.)
Subjects: LCSH: Motion pictures—Editing. | Documentary films—Production and direction.
Classification: LCC TR899 (ebook) | LCC TR899 .B694 2018 (print) | DDC 777/.55—dc23
LC record available at https://lccn.loc.gov/2017034743

ISBN: 978-1-138-67572-8 (hbk)
ISBN: 978-1-138-67573-5 (pbk)
ISBN: 978-1-315-56047-2 (ebk)

Typeset in Warnock Pro
by Apex CoVantage, LLC

Visit the companion website: www.routledge.com/cw/bricca

Contents

Acknowledgments

Writing this book has let me reflect upon what I have learned from my many teachers over the years. At the tender age of 16, I was introduced to the film *Koyaanisqatsi* in a sweltering hot Chicago classroom at a Northwestern University summer program. I would like to thank the graduate student who chose to put it on the VCR—I don't remember your name, but if you're out there you can know that it changed my life.

I knew little about documentary filmmaking until I took Jonathan Mednick's "Documentary Realism" class as an undergraduate at Wesleyan University. Jonathan was an inspiring teacher whose passion for the form made a huge impression on me. Rob Rosenthal and Alex Dupuy in the Sociology department and Dick Ohmann in English were also big influences; they made me look at the world in an entirely new way.

I had several influential teachers in the editing program at the American Film Institute. Farrel Jane Levy, ACE, brought enormous patience and intelligence to our rough cut critique sessions; Howard Smith, ACE, brought curiosity and humor; Brian Chambers had a low-key steadiness that all editors need a little bit of; and Steve Cohen, ACE, brought intensity and insight ("editing is 70% psychology," he used to say fervently). I also learned a great deal about documentary editing from Keith Fulton and Lou Pepe, whose trust in hiring me to cut *Lost in La Mancha* I am still grateful for today.

In putting together this book, the patience, guidance, and support of my editor Simon Jacobs has been invaluable. Craig Huston, Fiona Otway, Michael Kowalski, Sally Rubin, and Julie Sloane all gave valuable comments that helped shape the manuscript in important ways. My longtime collaborator Jonathan Crosby gave me fantastic film suggestions, and Bill Macomber at Fancy Film provided key advice about post color and sound processes. The contributions of my University of Arizona interns Sarah Lancaster and Leslie Bosch were significant and highly appreciated, as was the extra help from students Tanya Nuñez, Adam Ciampaglio, and David Sternau. My University of Arizona colleagues Yuri Makino, Michael Mulcahy, Beverly Seckinger, Lisanne Skyler, Anna Cooper, Joshua Gleich, Brad Schauer, Barbara Selznick, Vicky Westover and Bruce Brockman are an inspiration to me on a daily basis. And I would like to thank Cecily Crebbs at Story Land, where many long hours were spent writing this book; thank you for creating such a serene place for writers in Tucson.

I would like to dedicate this book to my father, who made sure that I was surrounded by music as a child, and my mother, who gamely played along with my fantasies of being a DJ by making requests for songs on my "radio station" (i.e., a single record player in our living room). Those segues between songs that I created in my mind were my first attempts at feeling the rhythm of a perfect cut.

Lastly, I'd like to thank my wife Lisa Molomot, whose partnership in film and in life has made so many things possible, and my son Rory, whose generosity, love for life, and musicianship are an inspiration to me every day.

Introduction: The Construction of Meaning in Documentaries

Documentary editing is perhaps one of the most challenging intellectual feats on the planet. An editor begins with a mountain of shapeless footage—comings and goings of characters, interviews of varying quality, B-roll from myriad locations, hour upon hour of often uninspiring detritus—and is expected to arrive at the end of the process with a fully realized story, complete with finely tuned dramatic arcs, satisfying themes and subplots, and a carefully constructed climax. How does anyone do it?

To quote Frank Costanza from *Seinfeld*, "I've got good news and bad news, and they're both the same." On day one of the process, getting from point A to point B *is* impossible. Not even the most brilliant, experienced editor digests all that footage, sleeps on it, and comes back to the edit room the next day with a fully realized outline. It just doesn't happen.

But here's the silver lining: the impossibility of the task *can* be overcome. Documentary editing is a *process*, one that requires creativity, rigor, determination, and time—but not genius. With the right tools and approach, one can reliably start to count on those moments of inspiration that often seem so ephemeral, and plan for a workflow that will lead to strong results. This is not to say that editing a documentary is easy. An honest editor will admit that most of their projects included at least one harrowing crisis of faith. But this, too, shall pass.

When considering how to dive into this challenge, it's worth getting specific about the nature of what makes documentary editing different from narrative editing. Though successful narrative films and documentaries often share the same attributes in their finished form—a strong story structure, relatable characters, a finely tuned dramatic arc—they *start* from very different places. In a narrative film the function of every scene is carefully worked out before a single frame is shot, and in the best-case scenario the setting, staging, cinematography, costuming, and production design are all working in concert to define the meaning of each shot. There is still a huge amount of work to be done in editorial in order to shade performances, solve previously undiscovered story problems, and craft the rhythm and dynamics. But by and large, we already know the intention of every scene and the approximate purpose of every shot.

Contrast this with a documentary. Even in a thoroughly researched film with several carefully planned shoots, the purpose of a great deal of the available footage is still up for grabs. It is in the very nature of documentary film practice that *the story is created in the editing room.*

This brings us to a fundamental challenge in documentary editing, which is that every shot contains multiple attributes whose meanings are highly variable depending on context. A wide shot of a character sitting outside a school on a gloomy day could be used in many ways. We could use it purely for the existence of the dark clouds in the background, play up the sound of the thunder in the distance, and use it an establishing shot for a scene with "stormy" content inside the school. Or we could use it as an introduction to the character, cutting from this wide shot to a closer one revealing the emotions that read on her face as we begin to hear her story in voice-over (but never enter the school at all). Or we could let this shot play out and notice that the figure is tapping her toe in perfect time, and use this as the kickoff to a montage where a variety of characters move to the rhythm of a music track that grows in volume until we see her and her brethren suited up in their marching band outfits, ready to try to win it all at the state championships. Each clip of raw footage in a documentary has multiple possible meanings, each of which can be accented or diminished depending on how they are juxtaposed with other shots and scenes.

This fundamental fact about documentary is one that makes the genre's claims to "truth" a richly problematic one. Indeed, the fact that most documentarians refer to the people who populate their films as "characters" is blasphemy to some purists, who would rather refer to them as "subjects" or "participants." But using the word "character" is more honest. It acknowledges the fact that documentary editing is a highly refined form of storytelling, one that sculpts larger-than-life performances out of everyday people doing ordinary things. Jean Rouch, who borrowed from Dziga Vertov in referring to his filmmaking style as *cinema verité*, wrote with brutal honesty about this issue in his postmortem on the groundbreaking 1961 film *Chronicle of a Summer* he made with Edgar Morin:

> How do we dare speak of a truth that has been chosen, edited, provoked, oriented, deformed? Where is the truth? . . . We have only provided a few pieces of a puzzle that is missing most of its parts. Thus each viewer reconstructs a whole as a function of their own projections and identifications. [Our characters are] perceived globally by means of mere fragments of themselves.[1]

Indeed, what documentary editors are attempting to do is *exactly that*: to construct a fable out of fragments. The critic Shanta Gokhale once argued that "unless an image displaces itself from its natural state, it acquires no significance. Displacement causes resonance."[2] There is no greater joy in the life of an editor than to see a scene moved to a new spot in the cut (or a shot moved to a new spot in a scene) and suddenly see it take on new life. The content remained the same, but the alchemical mix of the ordering produced something new.

Lest you lose faith in the dignity of the project we are undertaking, or feel like you're about to sink to the same ethical muck of reality television, consider the way Rouch

FIGURE 0.1 Jean Rouch (left) and Edgar Morin (right) in *Chronicle of a Summer*

underscored the duality of documentary truth later in his essay, when he spoke of the learning process that he and Morin had gone through:

> We wanted to get away from comedy, from spectacles, to enter into direct contact with life. But life itself is also a comedy, a spectacle. Better (or worse) yet: each person can only express himself through a mask, and the mask, as in Greek tragedy, both disguises and reveals, becomes the speaker. In the course of [making the film], each [of our subjects] was able to be more real than in daily life, but at the same time more false.[3]

This contradiction of "truth" is an enduring one that we should be well aware of as we march forward; it is also one we must exploit.

* * *

This book aims to give you the tools to find purpose and meaning in your raw footage, to help you build scenes that can make it resonate, and to construct a compelling story out of those scenes. By breaking the process down into a series of specific steps, each with its own purpose and timeline, you can realize your goal of crafting a great documentary. And by hearing from some of the top editors in the field, you will learn the techniques and work practices that have seen them through many difficult edits of their own. Along the way, we will pause every now and then to consider the larger issues at

xiv   Introduction: The Construction of Meaning in Documentaries

play in the practice of documentary editing. Through patient effort, the elusive goal of reaching the finish line will begin to seem less and less like an impossibility and more and more like an inevitable result.

▶ PRINCIPLES OF DOCUMENTARY EDITING

Unfortunately, there are no hard and fast "rules" of documentary editing. If there were, I could simply list them and call it a day. Instead, there are several important *principles* that will guide us on our journey. We will return to these in the coming chapters.

1. *Contain the Chaos*

By any measure, a documentary editor is at the helm of a virtually ungovernable mess, so we must always look for ways to *contain the chaos*. At every stage, we must seek to *limit the number of variables at play*, which will let us *break the big problems down into smaller ones* and *give us reasonable, achievable goals.* If we do not apply rigorous organizational and procedural muscle to our work, it can quickly spiral out of control.

2. *Trust in Process*

Because there is no easy, straight line between raw footage and finished product, we must abandon the desire for quick fixes and instead place our trust in *process*. By engaging in each stage of the process fully, we will gain new insights, making the work of the next stage possible.

3. *Look at the Problem from as Many Angles as Possible*

Editing is fundamentally about flexibility: the ability to continually imagine a shot, scene, or sequence playing out in a different way. To make this possible, we need to be able to consistently step back from it and look at it in new ways. Through a variety of methods that will be explained as we go forward, we will give ourselves the chance to continually reset our thinking and approach the edit anew.

4. *Anchor with Narrative*

Great stories don't magically appear; they have to be sculpted and perfected. At every turn, we will be on the lookout to anchor our film with crucial elements of narrative and to embroider around those elements with subplots, supporting information, and historical context.

5. *Delay Gratification*

Narrative tension can be generated on many levels, right down to the visual progression of an individual shot. We will work in every scene and every beat to provoke audience curiosity and delay gratification in order to deliver a continually satisfying narrative experience.

6. *Define the Point of View*

No documentary is purely "objective." Figuring out how to use your footage to reflect a specific sensibility and a specific experience is one of the most important things a documentary editor can do.

7. *Favor Firsthand Experience*

There are many different types of documentary footage, and not all are created equal. We will learn how to distinguish among them, and to recognize footage that brings the audience as close as possible to visceral firsthand experience.

8. *Embrace the Unexpected*

The best documentaries are created through the application of not only rigor and organization, but also a certain level of free association. "There are times when I'm not cutting with any particular goal in mind except to see how one shot feels when it's juxtaposed with another," says editor Mary Lampson. Inspiration can come from accidents.

9. *Always Be Prepared to Walk Away*

Complacency and ego are the enemies of good editing, and the ability to remove or revamp a scene at the drop of a hat is crucial to an editor's success. As editor Aaron Wickenden points out, "I need to be very passionate about making it as good as possible, but then also have a certain detachment from the outcome. Emotionally, I have to be able to just let it go."

10. *Simplify, Simplify, Simplify*

There is a strong temptation for an editor to build scenes and narratives that are too complex, maybe because it makes us feel like we're really earning our keep. ("*That's a really complicated scene! Not just anybody could fit all this stuff into a single scene!*") But this temptation must be avoided in order to find the simplest, most direct way of getting across the required information to an audience. Maximum impact comes from an object with the most emotional density and the smallest volume.

▶ YOUR DOCUMENTARY EDITING PANEL

In preparing this book, I conducted extended interviews with seven of the top American documentary editors working today. Their insights and work practices are woven into the fabric of this book, and their quotes will help guide you on your way. In alphabetical order, they are:

Kate Amend, ACE, has edited more than 35 documentary features in her long and storied career, including the Academy Award–winning films *Into the Arms of Strangers: Stories of the Kindertransport, The Long Way Home,* and the Netflix documentary series *The Keepers.* A member of the faculty at USC's School of Cinematic Arts, she is a recipient of the American Cinema Editors' Eddie Award, and is a frequent advisor at the Sundance Institute's Documentary Edit and Story Labs.

Marshall Curry is a two-time Academy Award–nominated documentary director and editor based in New York City. His film *If a Tree Falls: A Story of the Earth Liberation Front* won the Best Documentary Editing Award at Sundance in 2011, and his 2014 film *Point and Shoot* won Best Documentary at the Tribeca Film Festival.

Mary Lampson is a veteran documentary editor known for her work on the Academy Award–winning *Harlan County U.S.A.,* the Emile DeAntonio films *Underground* and *Millhouse,* and the recent Naomi Klein climate documentary *This Changes Everything.* She is a frequent advisor at the Sundance Documentary Edit and Story Labs.

Fiona Otway is a documentary editor whose credits include the Sundance Grand Jury Prize winner *Hell and Back Again,* the Academy Award–nominated *Iraq in Fragments,* and the recent Hot Docs Film Festival selection *The Pearl.*

Geoffrey Richman, ACE, is the editor of such outstanding documentaries as the Academy Award–winning *The Cove,* the Academy Award–nominated *Sicko,* and the Sundance Grand Jury Prize Winner *God Grew Tired of Us.* He also edits narrative features; his recent credits include *Sleepwalk with Me* and the Terrence Malick film *Knight of Cups.*

Kim Roberts, ACE, is a Los Angeles–based documentary editor whose credits include the Academy Award–nominated films *Food, Inc.* and *Daughter from Danang,* as well the Kirby Dick exposé *The Hunting Ground.* She was nominated for an ACE Eddie Award in 2010 for her work on Davis Guggenheim's *Waiting for "Superman."*

Aaron Wickenden, ACE, is a multiple Emmy- and ACE Eddie–nominated editor whose credits include *Finding Vivian Maier,* the Morgan Neville/Robert Gordon documentary *Best of Enemies,* and the Steve James documentary *The Interrupters.* He is a longtime member of the Chicago documentary collaborative Kartemquin Films.

▶ NOTES

1   Jean Rouch, *Cine-Ethnography,* ed. Steven Feld (Minneapolis: University of Minnesota Press, 2003), pp. 258, 262.

2   Karen A. Foss, Sonja K. Foss, and Cindy L. Griffen, eds., *Readings in Feminist Rhetorical Theory* (Long Grove, IL: Waveband Press, 2004), p. 235.

3   Rouch, *Cine-Ethnography,* p. 283.

PART I

Setting the Stage for a
Successful Edit

1

Planning Your Schedule

It is vital when you start work on a documentary that you set realistic goals, put in place strong support networks, and carve out the hours to do a proper job. When this doesn't happen the casualties are not simply to your sanity, but also to the film itself. A schedule that is too aggressive will cause you to be less creative, less thorough, and more accepting of poor-quality work. Thus, the first stage of your editing process begins before you ever look at an image or make an edit: it starts when you plan your schedule.

▶ DOCUMENTARY SCHEDULES: HOW MANY WEEKS?

When I posed this question to our panel of editors, some of them refused to even entertain it. "If a producer asks me that question," said Mary Lampson, "I always say, 'I don't know—all I can tell you is that I work fast and hard,' and that's how I dodge the question." Fiona Otway concurred: "When people ask me how long it's going to take, I always tell them I have no idea. Until I start getting my hands on the footage it's just really hard to predict."

And yet, the real world often doesn't allow the open-ended schedules that many of us might want. So let us proceed—cautiously—to lay out some guidelines.

Kim Roberts uses a rule of thumb for estimating the editing schedule for the films she cuts: for every 10 minutes of final running time, she allows a month of editing. Thus, a 90-minute film should have nine months of editing set aside to get from initial explorations to final locked picture. Discussions with other documentary editors back this up: Kate Amend says it usually take 8–10 months for her to cut a feature doc, and Geoff Richman says he usually estimates 7–9 months. (Remember that in all of these estimations, necessary postproduction processes like sound mixing and color correction are not included.) Many American feature documentaries simply assume they will be submitting to Sundance in late September and try to start at the beginning of the year, leaving approximately nine months for the edit.

This "month per 10 minutes of running time" should be expanded slightly for short documentaries because beginnings and endings tend to take longer to construct than the middle, and these sections represent a larger proportion of the whole than in a feature. In addition, developing a tone and style for a film takes a certain amount of experimentation, and that work isn't necessarily a quicker process in a short film even though the running time is slimmer.

Factors Determining Length of Edit

▶ **Quantity of raw footage** (more footage = longer edit)

▶ **Type of raw footage** (verité footage = longer edit, interview based = shorter edit)

▶ **Quality of raw footage** (less experienced shooter = longer edit)

▶ **Use of animations and graphics** (more animations and graphics = longer edit)

▶ **Presence or absence of an assistant editor** (no assistant = longer edit)

▶ **Language** (footage that must be translated and subtitled = longer edit)

▶ **Number of producers and stakeholders** (more producers and stakeholders to sign off on the project = longer edit)

It's also useful to develop an idea of how long each step of the process may take.

Percentage of Time Devoted to Each Stage of Edit

▶ **Ingesting/organizing footage:** 5–10% of total time.

▶ **Watching/digesting footage:** 10–20% of total time, depending on quantity of raw footage. For every hour of raw footage, allow at least an equal amount of time for this viewing/digesting stage.

▶ **Making select reels/organizing footage**: 10–20% of total time.

▶ **Refining select reels/making paper edit**: 5–10% of total time.

▶ **Making first cuts of all scenes**: 10–15% of total time.

▶ **Building the first rough cut**: 5–10% of total time.

▶ **Revision and feedback process (getting from rough cut to fine cut):** 25–40% of total time.

▶ **Fine cutting**: 5–10% of total time.

It is also worth noting that some documentaries will begin editing before production is fully complete. This has positive and negative consequences. The upside is significant, because it can greatly enhance the director's ability to modify their plan while they are still shooting, and it can make every shoot that much more productive. The downside is an increase in the complexity of the media management and review operation since the material arrives in batches, and a possible loss of focus for an editor now being asked to handle several different stages of the operation at once.

Please see Appendix B for detailed case studies of the schedules for four feature documentaries.

2

Organizing Your Footage

Before any editing can take place, two things must occur. First, the media files (footage, archival stills, music tracks, etc.) must be organized on the hard drive(s). Second, the files must be brought into a non-linear editing (NLE) platform such as Adobe Premiere Pro or Avid Media Composer and organized further. Although these are tedious processes, their successful completion is crucial to a successful edit because this is where the organizational backbone of the entire project is built. Doing this right is our first way of *containing the chaos*.

▶ ORGANIZING THE FILES ON THE HARD DRIVE

There is no single, universally accepted way of organizing raw media files on the hard drive(s). Different editors develop their own practices that work for them, but the key is to have a rigorous organizational scheme and to stick with it. The following principles should be observed.

> ▶ **Create different folders for different types of media.** Interview footage should not be mixed in with jpeg stills, and music files should not be mixed up with animation files. See Figure 2.1 for a sample organizational strategy: it shows folders for **Archival** documents, sorted into separate categories for **Movies** and **Still Pics**); **Graphics+Animations** (charts, animated segments, etc.); **Music** (with different subfolders for **Temp Music** and files arriving from the **Composer**); **Sound FX; Stock Footage; VO** (voice-over); and **Raw Footage** (files generated by the cinematographer and sound recordist for this documentary, with separate subfolders for Audio and Video if sound was recorded double system.) Note the "z" in front of the name so that it drops down to the end of the list for easy access.

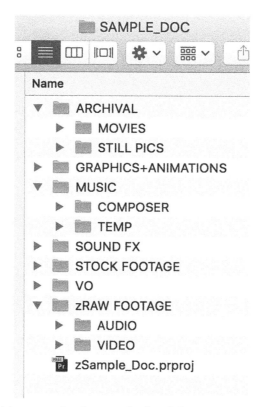

FIGURE 2.1 File folder organization on the hard drive

▶ **Create a simple and consistent way of naming the raw footage files.**
When the video clips are named with a consistent nomenclature that
includes the date (e.g., FilmName_17.12.06_001, FilmName 17.12.06 002,
FilmName_17.12.06_003, for three clips shot on December 6, 2017), then
they will helpfully sort themselves alphanumerically (see Figure 2.2). New clips
added to this folder at a later date will land at the bottom, and there is no
guesswork about when something was shot. Note the use of the underscore as
a way of separating out the different parts of the name: this is industry practice
to avoid possible PC incompatibility with blank spaces, back and forward
slashes, and other special characters.[1]

If you have a workflow that calls for preserving the original files (i.e., copying the clips
from the memory card wholesale rather than transcoding them), then placing all footage from each shooting day in its own folder is a popular choice (see Figure 2.3). In
these cases, you can name the containing folders in the same way that you would have
named the clips themselves. It is very important to note that some cameras save files
in highly specific folder structures, and these must be preserved in order for the NLE
program to be able to successfully read the files.

FIGURE 2.2 All video files placed in one folder. Note how the naming convention forces them to sort alphanumerically.

Other types of media (archival footage and stills, music, etc.) usually arrive pre-named, and the names often have a lot of variation from file to file. Instead of fighting this by trying to rename them, it's best to just leave these files alone and do the organizational work of classifying them once they're brought into the NLE. Preserving the original name is a good idea anyway because the film may need to arrange licensing, and the name of that file is a necessary piece of information to communicate to the party that provided the clip.

To keep track of which new media files have been brought into the NLE, one common strategy is to create new folders for each new date that material is added. Thus, in Figure 2.4 the new temp music that was added on June 21, 2017, was placed in a folder called 17.06.21 inside of the TEMP music subfolder. If you don't create dated folders you may find yourself struggling to identify which new files were just added, since the inconsistent naming of the files will cause them to land all over the place once copied.

FIGURE 2.3 Each set of AVCHD video files placed in its own folder on the hard drive, preserving its original folder structure from the camera. This shows four video files (00000.MTS–00003.MTS) on the second of two cards (17.12.06-1 and 17.12.06-2) that were shot on December 6, 2017.

▶ BRINGING THE FILES INTO THE NLE

Every NLE has the ability to link to your original files. If you're using Adobe Premiere Pro, DaVinci Resolve, or the old Final Cut Pro 7, this is called "importing." If you're using Avid Media Composer, this is accomplished by choosing "Link to Files," and if you're using Final Cut X, you choose the "leave files in place" option in the preferences and then import.

Often times these files are quite large, though, and system performance suffers. Many editors use proxy files as a way of solving this problem. *Proxy files* are compressed versions of the original files and are used during editing, only to be replaced at the end of the process when finishing occurs. They can be created in Media Composer from the linked files with the "Consolidate/Transcode" command (new files are then generated with new clip icons) or right from the start by choosing "Import" instead of "Link

FIGURE 2.4 New material added by date. Note how the "TEMP" folder has subfolders named by date containing all the music files added on that date. Further organization takes place within the NLE.

to Files" when first bringing in your media. In Premiere Pro, right-click on the clips, choose "Proxy" and then "Create Proxies" from the sub-menu; Premiere will use Adobe Media Encoder to create the proxies, which are automatically attached to the original clip icons. In Final Cut X, proxies can be created upon import by having the "Create proxy media" box checked in the Preferences, or by right-clicking on a clip and choosing "Transcode media…" and then selecting the "Create proxy media" option; Final Cut will create the files in the background and attach them to the original clip icons.

Creating proxy files is a type of *transcoding*, which simply means making a new video file from the old one. Some workflows call for transcoding video clips with programs like Adobe Media Encoder or Apple Compressor before they're ever brought into the NLE, often times in order to get video shot in one format or resolution to conform to the specs of the other clips. At some point these discrepancies have to be resolved, and it can either be accomplished on the front end (before editing) or on the back end (after picture lock is achieved.)

▶ RUN A TEST

When figuring out your strategy for all of this, it is essential to run a full test on your chosen workflow before getting too far into the edit. Try running the test on a handful of files (including files with different resolutions and/or frame rates as well as archival media and stills) by performing the ingestion process and putting all the clips into the timeline to see how they behave, then reconnecting the full-res media and doing a sample export. If you'll be using external color-grading and sound editing software for finishing, you should also perform a dry run of the finishing process by exporting an AAF or XML for coloring and an AAF or OMF for sound editing. Then check that these files can successfully import into your color grading and audio editing programs, with your proper full-res files (not the low-res proxies) showing up in your color grading program and the audio showing up in sync in your audio editing program.

This may sound like a lot of work, but it's much simpler to solve possible problems now rather than later on down the line, when correcting mistakes will be more difficult and costly. Although NLEs are incredibly flexible in allowing the importation of almost any kind of file, you can be in for a rude surprise when you try to accomplish an export and find that the program crashes or delivers unexpected visual results. Premiere Pro will let you import very large JPEG files, for instance, but may crash when you actually try to use them. Doing a test will answer questions like, "Will my NLE produce acceptable results if I mix different formats in the same sequence (including when I export), or will I be better off transcoding the nonstandard footage to the same codec and resolution as the rest of the footage?" Talk with the facility that will be doing the final conform, because they may have specific recommendations for transcoding or advise you to leave the nonstandard files alone so they can deal with the transcoding themselves. Most color grading facilities will run tests for you as a courtesy when setting up plans to use their services, as will most post sound facilities and freelancers.

▶ BACKING UP

There is one iron clad rule in editing: never, ever work on anything without at least one failsafe backup. This backup must be kept in a separate physical location; having a complete backup sitting in the same room as the original files isn't much good if there's a robbery or the facility burns down. When new files are coming in from the field, never erase the memory card from the camera until the files are fully transferred *and* backed up.

One organizational strategy for new media files is to add a colored tab on all material that has been fully backed up, making it obvious which files or folders still require backup. Note in Figure 2.5 how the temp music folder "17.10.12" is the only one without the tab next to it, showing that it still needs to be copied to the backup drive(s). It can be much easier to just add new folders to the existing backup(s) rather than to erase the backup hard drive and start over from scratch.

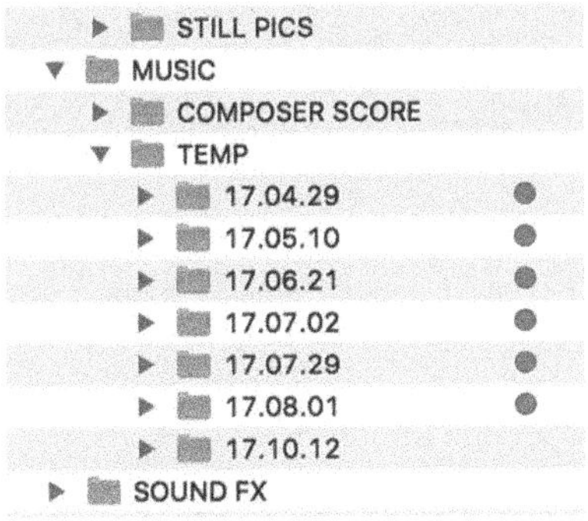

FIGURE 2.5 Using tags to mark backed up material. Note the circles next to the folders that have already been backed up.

When creating the backup, you should never allow the backup operation itself to jeopardize the project. A sudden power failure or accidental cable malfunction while copying files from your primary drive to your backup drive could potentially render *both* drives inoperable, so you should devise a system to keep these unlikely scenarios from becoming fatal. Using a small transfer drive to shuttle files between your primary drive and the backup drive is one option; maintaining a second full backup is another.

▶ ORGANIZING FOOTAGE

Once you've got all your media into the NLE and backed it up, the last major project is to organize it. When we do so, we're not just performing a technical task. We are designing a foundation for how the footage will be viewed and understood for the remainder of the edit, and our understanding of its shape and contours will be greatly enhanced with the application of an approach that is both rigorous and thoughtful. Have you ever looked at your computer and seen several dozen files populating the desktop such that it's hard to even distinguish the background? The mental stress and clutter than comes with that experience is what we're seeking to avoid.

With interview and verité footage, one strategy is simply to organize all the clips chronologically, closely mirroring the file structure on the hard drive. This is probably most common on narrative-driven verité films for which chronology is important, but is sometimes used on other films as well. Each day of shooting gets its own folder, and all the clips for that day (each of which should bear the date of production in their name) are contained within it. We are thus left with an exceedingly simple and logical window on our footage. We can see the clips laid out day by day, and quickly understand where each clip fits into the larger whole.

If you look at Figure 2.6, you will see a screen shot of how the footage was organized by our assistant editor Bill Hilferty on the 2016 Sundance documentary *The Bad Kids*,

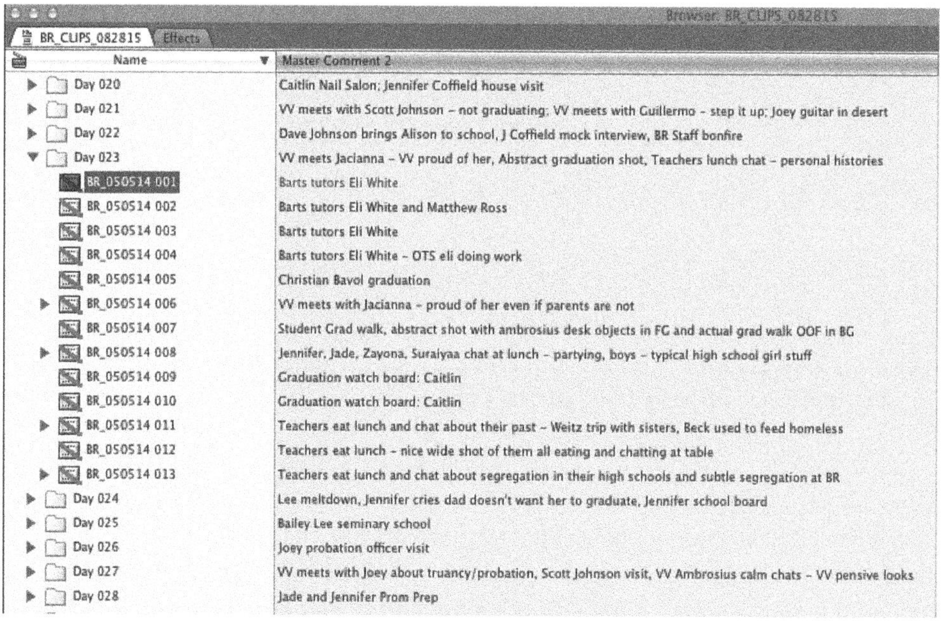

FIGURE 2.6 Clips organized chronologically in *The Bad Kids* ("BR" stands for "Black Rock," which was the working title of the film)

about hard-luck kids in a California continuation high school. In this organizational strategy, much of the "binning" (i.e., sorting the footage into various thematic categories) is left for the forthcoming select reel process. Note the information contained in the "Master Comment 2" column: the names of all characters that appear in the clip, along with a very brief description of what happens. Regardless of how your clips are organized, it can be a big boon to have some logging information attached to them, which can be searched as needed in order to find specific clips.

With the expenditure of a little more labor, one can further organize the metadata into separate fields so it's easier to read and access. Looking at an expanded view of the *Bad Kids* metadata in Figure 2.7, you will find that we had separate fields for logging notes (first column), location (second column), and characters (third column).

If there was a scene that took place in the back room and we were looking for an appropriate cutaway, a search in the Location column for "back room" could easily yield a bevy of useful clips. What's more, if we were looking for a cutaway of a certain character, we could do a more advanced search that would yield all clips that took place in the back room with that character on a particular date. Creating more fields also has the side benefit of reducing the amount of information that needs to be entered into each, making all of them easier to read. Here in Final Cut Pro 7 we used the "off-the-shelf" columns (i.e., Master Comment 1, Master Comment 2, etc.) and adapted them for our own purposes, but you can create custom categories in Premiere, and Media Composer

Browser: BR_CLIPS_082815

BR_CLIPS_082815 | Effects

Name	Master Comment 2	Master Comment 1	Master Comment 3
▶ 🗀 Day 020	Caitlin Nail Salon; Jennifer Coffield house visit		
▶ 🗀 Day 021	VV meets with Scott Johnson – not graduating; VV meets with Guillermo – step it up; J		
▶ 🗀 Day 022	Dave Johnson brings Alison to school, J Coffield mock interview, BR Staff bonfire		
▼ 🗀 Day 023	VV meets Jacianna – VV proud of her, Abstract graduation shot, Teachers lunch chat –		
🎬 BR_050514 001	Barts tutors Eli White	Back Room	Eli White, Bartz
🎬 BR_050514 002	Barts tutors Eli White and Matthew Ross	Back Room	Eli White, Bartz, Matthew Ross
🎬 BR_050514 003	Barts tutors Eli White	Back Room	Eli White, Bartz, Matthew Ross
🎬 BR_050514 004	Barts tutors Eli White – OTS eli doing work	Back Room	Eli White, Bartz
🎬 BR_050514 005	Christian Bavol graduation	Hallway	Christian Bavol
▶ 🎬 BR_050514 006	VV meets with Jacianna – proud of her even if parents are not	VV's office	VV, Jacianna Powell
🎬 BR_050514 007	Student Grad walk, abstract shot with ambrosius desk objects in FG and actual grad w Hallway		
▶ 🎬 BR_050514 008	Jennifer, Jade, Zayona, Suraiyaa chat at lunch – partying, boys – typical high school gi Weitz room		Jennifer Coffield, Jade, Suraiyaa, Zayona
🎬 BR_050514 009	Graduation watch board: Caitlin	Front Entry	Caitlin
🎬 BR_050514 010	Graduation watch board: Caitlin	Front Entry	Caitlin
▶ 🎬 BR_050514 011	Teachers eat lunch and chat about their past – Weitz trip with sisters, Beck used to fe Hill Room		Weitz, Beck, Larson, Hill
🎬 BR_050514 012	Teachers eat lunch – nice wide shot of them all eating and chatting at table	Hill Room	Weitz, Beck, Larson, Hill
▶ 🎬 BR_050514 013	Teachers eat lunch and chat about segregation in their high schools and subtle segre Hill room		Weitz, Beck, Larson, Hill, Alexander, VV
▶ 🗀 Day 024	Lee meltdown, Jennifer cries dad doesn't want her to graduate, Jennifer school board		
▶ 🗀 Day 025	Bailey Lee seminary school		
▶ 🗀 Day 026	Joey probation officer visit		
▶ 🗀 Day 027	VV meets with Joey about truancy/probation, Scott Johnson visit, VV Ambrosius calm		

FIGURE 2.7 Clips with multiple fields of metadata on *The Bad Kids*

has even more advanced capabilities in this regard. Final Cut X works instead with keywords, and has powerful and flexible sorting capabilities.

Some editors swear by the use of this metadata; others mostly do without it. Kim Roberts, for instance, remarked that "I've tried that on some projects, and it always seems to fall apart. It takes so much labor to make it happen and then you have several different people logging, interns coming and going, and it just never quite seems to work." Whether or not it's worth spending the resources to create this metadata depends on one's own personal proclivities, the labor resources available to the project, and the number of other tasks that might have to take precedence. The rigor of the select reel process (coming in the next chapter) will ensure that even if you do not do create metadata, you can still have a well-organized project.

▶ ORGANIZING ARCHIVAL MATERIAL

When organizing archival material, one often wants to provide a more robust organizational structure for the clips than existed on the hard drive. As an example, take a look at the clip organization within the Archival section of the 2015 film *Best of Enemies* in Figure 2.8.

Here you can see the strong level of organization at the clip level for the archival footage. Every clip or subclip lives within a subfolder that gives editor Aaron Wickenden a strong sense of the context. There is a subfolder for archival footage relating to Gore Vidal's childhood and family, for instance, and one for footage related to William F. Buckley's post-debate life. On this film it was the job of the assistant editors to log the

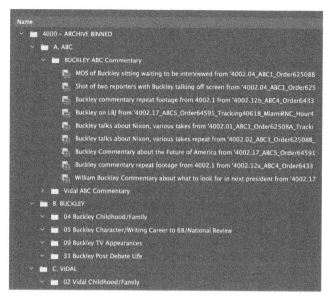

FIGURE 2.8 Binned archival footage clips from *Best of Enemies*

archival clips and break them up into subclips so they could be sorted into these categories. It was also their job to name the clips with a short description of the contents, along with a reference to the original clip that they came from. The ability to immediately track the origin of the footage back to its source is critical for an archival-heavy film like this once, given the licensing agreements that need to be made with the rights holders.

▶ ALTERNATE "BINNING" STRATEGIES

Some editors like to go further with the organization of the files, and choose to do further "binning" by dividing the clips up by footage type, character, event, or some combination of all these. With this strategy, the naming and organization of the bins becomes highly relevant and consequential.

Precious Knowledge, a 2011 documentary I edited for Eren McGinnis and Ari Palos about the fight over the controversial Mexican American Studies program in the Tucson public school system, provides a useful example. As you can see in Figure 2.9, there were 10 major categories into which all the footage was divided: Classroom (containing verité footage organized class by class); Students (interview footage); Faculty (interview footage); Student Activities (verité of extracurriculars taking place on campus); B-Roll; History (interview footage about the history of discrimination against Latino students in public schools); The Fight (a combination of interview, verité and archival footage related to the political battle over the Mexican American Studies classes); Music; Sound Effects; and Pics (archival stills).

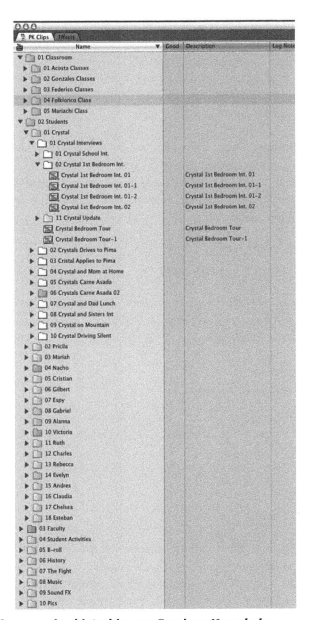

FIGURE 2.9 Clips organized into bins on *Precious Knowledge*

There are a lot of idiosyncrasies here: some categories are defined by topic (History, for instance) while others are defined by character, and still others are defined by footage type (Pics, for example). This organization would likely drive some editors crazy because different types of footage were intermixed in the same folder. But this organization made sense because of what I understood about the nature of the project and the initial hunches the directors and I made about its eventual structure. Every editor's organizational system will be different; it's the creation of the system itself that is the important thing.

Also note the numbering system, which we used to rank the relative importance of the subcategories. 01 Crystal, for instance, was more likely to become a major character in our eyes than 11 Ruth, 15 Andres, or 17 Chelsea, who were further down the list. As our understanding of their relative importance evolved, we changed the number prefixes attached to the folders. This type of system provides another layer of information that doesn't require changing the names of any clips.

We also used a coloring system for the folders. Green meant that the clips inside it had been fully reviewed and integrated into select reels (which we will get to in Chapter 5), orange meant that it had been partially integrated, and red meant that it had not yet been integrated. Many editors are fond of these color-coding schemes to remind them what state a clip or sequence is in.

▶ DOCUMENTS YOU WILL NEED

Documentaries are not created from raw footage alone. As you move through the process, it is extremely helpful to have a set of the following documents that can help you *view the problem from multiple angles.* (See Appendix C for examples of all of these documents.)

▶ Cast of characters with pictures

When you are first diving into a film the number of characters can be overwhelming, so having a printed document that identifies each character by name with a corresponding close-up shot can be extremely useful. This can also eliminate the need for repeated calls to the director, who probably has better things to do than to remind you of who is who in the film.

▶ Written transcripts

While nothing substitutes for watching footage in real time, reading transcripts is a crucial way of seeing patterns in your footage that are harder to spot when you're locked into a time-based medium. They take less time to digest than raw footage, and they can be highlighted, word-searched, and easily made into a "paper edit" by cutting and pasting. Perhaps most important, as the process moves toward rough and fine cuts they can be consulted to find specific words and phrases, greatly improving efficiency. I have successfully edited films without transcripts, but it made things harder at every stage of the process. Don't settle for paraphrased versions of what is said; word-for-word accuracy is key.

▶ Updated continuity

A continuity is a simple text document listing each scene of the film, along with a one-line description of its contents, in the order in which they currently reside in the cut. Having such a document taped to the wall or accessible in a binder nearby is an invaluable way of seeing the structure of your film from a bird's eye perspective. This document must be kept up-to-date in order to be of use: a great job for an assistant editor or an intern. Saving old versions that correspond to specific cuts is also a good idea, as is using Google Sheets to create the document so the updates can be seen instantly by collaborators working in remote locations. Color coding the scenes by character or topic can help you see how the structure of the film is developing.

▶ **Index cards for sketching structural ideas and keeping continuity**

The desktop NLE can be an incredibly restrictive tool at times. Its interface is entirely two-dimensional, and you are confined to working within a screen environment. What if you could actually pick up your scenes and move them around at will on a huge table or wall? Some of the best tools are the old-fashioned ones, and index cards are a reliable staple of most editing rooms. Each card represents one scene or sequence of scenes, and can be color-coded by character and pinned to a large bulletin board or taped to a wall. Taken as a whole, they represent the full structure of the film, often with a "graveyard" section to the side holding scenes that have been removed from the cut.

▶ **Diagramming software for sketching structural ideas**

Some editors have embraced this high-tech version of the old index card. Apps like draw.io, Cacoo, and especially LucidChart and Inspiration have gained converts as tools to help sketch structural ideas quickly, especially for productions where the editor and director may be working in separate cities. While they lack the three-dimensional advantage of index cards, they have the ability to save many different scene orderings so that they can be instantly compared, and can quickly display all of the cards of a single topic. "I use it as if it were a set of notecards," says documentary filmmaker Jamie Meltzer (*True Conviction*), "but since it's online I can share ideas and structures with editors I'm working with remotely."

▶ **NOTE**

1   Go here for a list of characters to avoid in file names: www.mtu.edu/umc/services/digital/writing/characters-avoid/.

3

Everyday Work Practices

Before we enter into the nitty-gritty of editing, it will be useful to briefly delve into the subject of work habits. Think of the following suggestions like you would tips about daily exercise or eating right: healthy habits that will increase the chances of a long life for your film. Editing is intense mental labor that can easily feel overwhelming, so arming yourself with appropriate tools and eliminating clutter from your work environment is crucial to thinking clearly. Again, we are trying to create the optimal conditions for mental clarity by containing the chaos.

▶ WORK IN STAGES

The chapters that follow will lead you through a series of stages that will advance your edit from initial viewing all the way to locked picture output. But for these stages to be useful, you need to *fully complete the work of one stage* before moving on to the next. As a rule, for example, you should avoid creating highly refined versions of one part of your film before completing initial rough cuts of the other parts.

The reason for this is more fundamental than just a fastidious desire for orderliness. A truism of documentary editing is that one's understanding of individual scenes is highly dependent on their context within the larger whole, both on the structural level and as it relates to rhythm and pacing. So your flashy cut of one scene will likely need to be completely rebuilt once you realize that the scene actually is more about character B's reactions rather than character A's statements, or that the whole scene needs to play out much more deliberately now that it's being used to build up tension rather than to release it. Working evenly throughout your cut can save huge amounts of time that might otherwise be wasted by fine-cutting scenes before their true purpose is known. As Kate Amend notes, "you can spend too much time on making a scene good, because you might find out later that what that scene needs to be is completely different from what you first thought."

There are exceptions to this rule. Sometimes you need to explore the potential of a scene in some detail in order to complete a "proof of concept" about how it can function. Doing so may allow you to understand how other scenes need to relate to it, or to give you a feeling for the rhythm and dynamics of the film that other scenes can match to.

Kate Amend gives an example of another reason for cutting a scene very early in the process from her work on *The World According to Sesame Street*, a 2006 documentary about the challenges of producing international versions of *Sesame Street*:

> I'd been watching dailies and making notes for four weeks and hadn't edited any-thing, and then I came across a scene where the first shipment of Muppet costumes arrived in Bangladesh for the crew. They had been working with "mock puppets" for weeks, so when they opened the crate and each person was given their own Mup-pet their excitement and emotion jumped off the screen. I stopped everything and said to myself, "I'm cutting this scene." I spent a couple hours on it, and I brought everybody in the room and showed it to them and everybody cried and was happy. Sometimes you just have to treat yourself!

Despite these kinds of exceptions to the rule, completing each stage of editing evenly throughout the body of the film will save you time and will bring you more quickly to a thorough understanding of the material's emotional and narrative possibilities.

▶ FOCUS

When we sit down to watch a documentary, what does that world feel like? Roomy and expansive? Taut and tense? Exhilarating? As we will discuss in Chapter 10, one of the fundamental things an editor is responsible for is pacing, and in order to properly define the pace of a documentary we have to separate ourselves from the ubiquitous distractions that populate our everyday lives. How can we expect an audience to build patience for the slow build of a carefully crafted story if we don't have that patience ourselves?

Thus, we need to find ways of creating a buffer between the world of the editing room and the rest of our lives, where the distractions from text messages and pings from Facebook and Twitter are so ubiquitous. Consider turning off your phone and looking into apps that restrict your Internet access for prespecified periods of time.[1] Editing is hard work, and it becomes that much harder when you're trying to fit it in between multitasking on several other fronts.

We also want to find ways of treating the work that happens in the editing room with a certain level of reverence. For some people (myself included), dressing up to go to work is surprisingly effective, especially if you're working alone in a home office. For others, keeping strict work hours is key. Find a way to create a feeling of sacredness for what you're doing in the edit room; it will give you the mental clarity needed to create a well-realized world of experience for your audience.

▶ THE VITAL IMPORTANCE OF TAKING BREAKS

Whether we admit it or not, most of us have a masochistic relationship to work. If we're not killing ourselves trying to achieve our goal, then we must not be trying hard enough! But an abundance of new psychological research backs up what experienced editors have known for a long time: taking breaks and limiting work hours is vital to getting things done.

University of Illinois psychology professor Dr. Alejandro Lleras explains that the brain's capacity for problem-solving decreases if one spends too much continuous time focused on the same task, and likens this to a similar phenomenon in visual and aural perception in which the brain gradually stops registering a sight or sound if the stimulus remains constant over time.[2] Painters are well aware of this phenomenon, and speak of the need to "rest their eyes" every now and then in order to see the colors they're putting down on canvas in an accurate way. "We propose that deactivating and reactivating your goals allows you to stay focused," Lleras explains.

In practical terms, this means that taking a 5- to 10-minute break every hour or two is a good idea. You don't necessarily need to put yourself on a stopwatch, but try to get familiar with that feeling of sluggishness or frustration that may creep up on you. When you find yourself bogged down on a particular scene, or unable to get a good read on how to reshuffle a series of shots in a montage, take a break. This can be the hardest time to do so, because you want to feel the reward of completing a difficult task. But editing is all about trying to see problems from a new angle, so giving your brain a break is crucial. You will almost always be more productive in the long run by taking this route rather than trying to stick it out and hoping for divine inspiration.

Another reality of the cutting room is that you only have a certain number of truly productive hours in the "gas tank" every day. After six or seven hours of intense work your productivity may lag, and even the breaks may not revive you. Rather than trying to fight nature, structure your days so that you're at your cutting desk during your hours of peak productivity and then leave when your planned workday is done. Of course, there will be times when deadlines will make such limited work hours laughable—just as there will be times when you're on a roll and stopping work would be counterproductive—but the general rule applies. Think of editing as active, physical activity: the best athletes have strict sleep schedules as well as tough workouts.

▶ DUPLICATE AND ARCHIVE: LEAVING A TRAIL OF BREADCRUMBS BEHIND YOU

For those of us who were old enough to have cut film on a flatbed or edited video on a tape-to-tape system, the flexibility and speed of today's NLE systems are nothing short of miraculous. But the ability to edit multiple versions of a scene doesn't mean much if you don't have a work process that takes full advantage of it.

One crucial work habit is to adopt a practice of "leaving a trail of breadcrumbs behind you"; that is, regularly saving copies of your sequences so you can return to previous versions. Even if you never use these old sequences, just knowing that your work is saved creates a feeling of freedom that can encourage experimentation. But this can create as many problems as it solves if you have so many versions that they become difficult to navigate. As Marshall Curry notes:

> With *Racing Dreams*, we tried to be methodical and make a new version every day with our assistant editor. But we found that when we would want to go back to something specific, it was hard to find because there were so many versions that had been saved. If you make them less frequently, you know exactly which one is which.

Thus, you need to find a sweet spot that preserves old versions of your work without creating too many choices. There is no one "right" way to do this, but here are some suggestions and options to consider that are based on common practices among documentary editors.

Practice 1: Save Versions of Cuts (Essential)

When putting together a scene or sequence, work on it until you have a finished a version that reflects your ideas to that point, then set it aside. When you screen it (either alone, with the director, or in a screening), take thorough notes. When you come back to it ready to make changes, duplicate the sequence and start cutting with the new version. Give the new version a new name (v.2, for instance, if the older one was v.1). Repeat this process with future versions, giving the new cut a new number each time.

Exactly when to move on to a new version is a gray area. As Marshall Curry says:

> There is no rigid system, but if I feel like it has been a while and I have made a lot of changes since my last version, then I make a new version. Or if I have an idea that is going to require ripping up a sequence then I create a new version before I do it. That way if it turns out to be a bad idea I can revert back to the previous version.

Sometimes I'll append a note to the version name, explaining in plain language what makes the new version different. So, for example, it'll be "Rough Cut 14 without love" if I'm making a version that cuts out the love story.

The exact numbering convention on any edit is less important than *having* a convention and sticking to it. Personally, I like to create versions that ascend from v.1.0 to v.1.1, v.1.2, v.1.3, etc., and then only move to v.2.0 when it feels like the edit has moved to a new level of maturity or when that edit is one that will be screened for feedback with an audience. This way, the numbering convention carries some meaning all by itself (tenths for smaller milestones, whole numbers for larger ones). This method has the added benefit that the numbers don't seem to get too large. By the time the film is done it may have reached v.11.6, but while the total number of versions completed is exactly the same as if it was named v.73, it has the psychological feeling of being more disciplined and contained.

Practice 2: Updated Continuities (Highly Recommended)

This was mentioned in the previous chapter: it can be extremely useful to save versions of your written continuity that correspond with the major archived cuts. This way, when you're looking back on Rough Cut v.3.0, you not only have a sequence to refer to but also a continuity that you can quickly scan to evaluate its structure. This also makes possible quick word searches on scene names within the continuity to identify the placement of a particular scene within a particular cut.

Practice 3: Save Versions of Individual Scenes (Works for Some)

By the time you get deep into the editing process, you will likely have several versions of each of the major scenes of the film strewn across the various cuts. While it's possible to find them by searching the continuities or scanning the sequences, some editors also like to save versions of the scenes within a separate bin of the project. With this method, every time you complete a new version of a scene, you copy/paste it into a sequence and save that sequence within a bin marked with the name of the scene. Thus, you can go to your "Scenes" folder and look in the "Heather Contemplates Leaving Her Job" bin to find four previous versions of the scene, ready to view instantly.

The downside of this practice is that it creates additional work, and it increases the size of the NLE project file. Some editors don't find the benefits of this practice are worth the expense of its complications.

▶ SCRAPS SEQUENCES AND ALTERNATE SHOTS

As you're editing, you are likely to have extra fragments of scenes that you may wish to hang onto, at least temporarily. For instance, in the course of cutting a scene in which an interview subject describes a harrowing ordeal with an insurance claim, you may be on the fence about whether to include a portion that shows her rifling through her boxes of

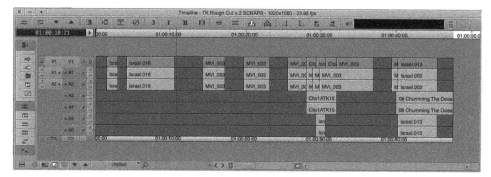

FIGURE 3.1 A sample scraps sequence

documents. These three extra shots aren't important enough to warrant saving a whole new version of the scene, but you want to set them aside for the time being instead of deleting them. A great solution to this problem is the "scraps" sequence, which includes little bits and pieces of things from here, there, and everywhere. Simply park these shots in the scraps sequence—you can always go back and find them there.

I tend to create a scraps sequence for each of the scenes that I cut. Thus, in the bin for the "Randy discusses options with his lawyer" scene, I would have saved all versions of the scene as well as one scraps sequence named "Randy discusses options with his lawyer SCRAPS." It's pretty easy to step through a scraps sequence to find what you're looking for, and by removing extra material that would otherwise be sitting untidily at the end of your sequence it creates a cleaner work environment.

Once the process moves beyond initial cuts, I also have a scraps sequence for my rough cut. Every now and then I try to look through it and clean out any elements that are no longer necessary to save.

Another way to hang onto certain options in your edit is to place them as inactive tracks in your sequence. For instance, you may start with one cutaway shot but then find a better cutaway to replace it. But is it better? There may very well be a reason to return to the old option down the road. Solution? Simply leave the alternate shot on a video track underneath the current shot, placing the old one as a disabled shot on V1 while the current shot sits enabled on V2. With this practice, you will again avoid the need to save an entirely new version of the sequence just for one minor change, and you will have quick access to the alternate shot down the road.

▶ **THE DIRECTOR-EDITOR RELATIONSHIP: WORKING TOGETHER AND WORKING ALONE**

When the relationship between a director and an editor is a good one, anything is possible. The creative ferment takes projects to unexpected places and can lift a film to new heights. So what makes these relationships work?

The word you will most often hear when speaking to documentary directors and editors is *trust*. Directors have often spent several years of their lives gathering the footage for their film, so it is an act of extraordinary faith to share it with someone else. Will the editor understand their intentions? Will they make sure to catch every gem and hold on to every good idea? Will they be honest about their opinions without taking over the project?

You should remember that part of your job as an editor is to play diplomat and psychologist, not just technician and artist. Most directors appreciate an editor who can give strong opinions while remaining clear about the chain of command, who can offer words of encouragement when morale is low, and who can internalize the director's own intentions and make them her own. Beyond that, establishing a level of trust that allows forceful, sometimes passionate arguments about issues in the film without jeopardizing the relationship is vital. "Just creating a sense of openness and trust in communication, where people feel they can express themselves freely without hurting anyone's feelings, is important," says Fiona Otway. "That can be really challenging because we all have our own egos invested in the work, and you have to be able to express conflicting ideas, confusion, and even your own insecurity." As Kim Roberts notes:

> I've cut four films for Robert Kenner, and I feel very comfortable with him in terms of discussing things, arguing about things, and trying things. But when I work with a director who I haven't worked with before, it's like going back and dating again after you've been married to somebody. It feels like, "I can't just say 100% what I think because you might be offended." It takes a while at the beginning of the relationship to build that trust.

Operating with a strong level of professionalism is also key to a trusting relationship. Expectations should be clearly set with respect to working hours and the duration of the commitment, and there should be a deal memo signed by editor and producer so that these things are spelled out in writing. It goes without saying that spending large amounts of time on social media in the edit room is a no-no, and the editor must understand that it's their role to be fully prepared for a work session with a director by having everything prepped and ready to watch without delay. (Waiting 20 minutes for large sections of a sequence to render at the start of a scheduled editing session is not acceptable.)

Likewise, there are subtle cues about the pecking order of an editing room that should be observed. I once saw an assistant editor nearly get fired for showing up for work the first day, putting his feet up on the desk, and generally acting like he owned the place. Neither should an editor do this, for it signals a lack of understanding of boundaries. A workplace should be a neutral space where decorum allows everyone to do their best work, regardless of whether it happens to be in the editor's own home or in an editing facility. Directors have final say over artistic decisions, and when push comes to shove it's their prerogative to determine how an editor spends their time (which scenes to cut, what to accomplish, etc.). But in a good working relationship, a director will seek out an editor's counsel about almost everything: how to tackle a particular problem, how long it will take to accomplish a particular phase of the editing, what music to try.

As should be abundantly apparent, communication is perhaps the one common ingredient in all successful collaborations. The editor should be asking the director, "how do you like to work," and the director should be asking the editor the same question. The more that each party is able to articulate their preferences and proclivities, the quicker the route to a successful, fluid collaboration.

* * *

From a practical standpoint, what does the editor need from the director when the project begins? Editor Fiona Otway describes her initial conversations with the director like this:

> I'm trying to extract their understanding of their own story. So part of what I want to know is why they wanted to make the film on the most basic level. What drove them to this topic? How did they get sucked in to it? How did they decide that they were going to set out to do this and invest so much time and energy and resources into it? And what happened along the way that was unexpected? How did that change their thinking about the film?

Aaron Wickenden thinks about it this way:

> I try to get the director to just describe the film to me, in their own words, and I take really detailed notes about the things that they seem to get excited the most about. We take a lot of time and they spell out the entire film for me, basically give me a verbal version of the treatment. I've found that to be really helpful, just to make sure not only that I'm hearing the director's vision but that they also feel that they've communicated it to me.

As both Otway and Wickenden explain, the editor is trying to internalize the intentions of the director. It is vital to know which scenes the director considers crucial, which scenes are also important but perhaps incomplete, and what supplementary materials (graphics, etc.) are anticipated. An editor also needs to know what the schedule and budget allow for in terms of follow-up interviews, acquisition of additional B-roll, creation of animated graphical elements, and the like.

Once these initial conversations are complete, the editor needs some time alone to start sorting through things. This on-again, off-again pattern of working together/working alone makes up the backbone of an editing work schedule. Often a director will check in once or twice a week to see the first drafts of scenes that are being cut and to make comments, or it may be a few weeks in between meetings. Then once a rough cut is in place, the director's involvement usually becomes more frequent. A "to do" list of items is created collectively, and the editor takes anywhere from a couple hours to several days to complete them. Then, collective work sessions of anywhere from a couple hours to a few days' time will be convened, during which a new "to do" list is created, and the process starts all over again.

Directors benefit from these breaks because it keeps them fresh and because it gives them time to focus on other business that is usually ongoing—fundraising, additional shooting, etc. Editors benefit from the time alone because such solitude is usually a condition of strong editing work; the more people there are in the editing room, the slower the work proceeds. Editor–director teams should be wary of getting mired in endless problem-solving sessions that yield few results; usually this indicates a need to move on to a different problem for a while.

▶ NOTES

1   David Nield, "8 Tools to Help Block Out Online Distractions," Gizmodo.com. June 20, 2014. Web.

2   Diana Yates, "Brief Diversions Vastly Improve Focus, Researchers Find," *Illinois News Bureau*. news.illinois.edu. February 8, 2011. Web.

PART II
Finding Patterns

4

Viewing and Digesting

After bringing all your footage into a project, organizing it, and having initial discussions with the director, the next thing to do is to watch all of your footage. Yes, *all* of it. Let's stop right here and appreciate the time investment this represents. With a film that contains 160 hours of raw footage—not at all unusual these days—we're talking about spending *four weeks* just digesting it. This is precious time that could theoretically be spent doing something else.

But let's consider *why* we would contemplate sinking so many hours into this step. When we watch raw footage, we start to become attuned to its rhythms, its patterns, and its strengths and weaknesses. A picture of the whole of the film starts to form in our minds, even if it is a jumbled and confusing one at first. More important, whether you recognize it or not, *your brain is absorbing everything you view*. This is crucially important because by spending the time now, you're giving yourself a chance to make a greater range of associations at a later point down the road. Ten weeks hence, when a thought pops into your head about how to solve a problem—"What about putting that clip where Dani looks off into the distance *here*?"—you will be happy you did.

This first pass should be unhurried and free of assumptions. It is crucial to put aside the need to *do* anything with your footage and leave yourself free to just *watch* and take notes. Starting with this intention lessens the pressure we inevitably feel and helps us focus our attention on the strengths and subtleties of the footage itself. What do you see when you view these images? Do you *feel* anything? As editor Kate Amend says:

> I'm looking for the most compelling material, the most emotional material, the most dramatic material, so I'm really responding to everything from the gut and making

notes of things that I'm drawn to and that I'm moved by. If something makes me laugh I'll take a note of it. I've been known to cry watching dailies.

You might be excited by a particular look on a character's face, an exceptionally beautiful composition, an animated exchange that seems to have resonance beyond its literal meaning, or an interesting visual juxtaposition. Editor Aaron Wickenden is looking for "moments that I'm surprised by, moments I'm pulled in by that seem emotional." Whatever it is, make a note of it in whatever way works best for you—on paper, in a spreadsheet, or in a metadata field in your NLE. The simple act of writing it down will help further imprint this clip in your brain, and if you've done your project organization work properly it will not be hard to find even if the notes go missing.

This first viewing is not to be treated casually, because you will never again see the footage for the first time; this is your best chance to watch it in the way that your audience might. Of course, a large part of the meaning will eventually come from the context you put it into, but the raw materials do have some inherent qualities of their own. Remember that you will end up leaving most of what you watch on the cutting room floor, so do not be alarmed if only a small portion of the footage excites you.

As a parallel step, read your transcripts. (Yes, all of them.) You can read a transcript of an interview at a much faster rate than you can watch it, and while seeing the words on paper gives little indication of whether the footage is emotionally compelling, it does help clarify the topics being covered, and can be much easier to organize. Whether you take this step before viewing your footage or after, have your highlighter ready and mark any sections that seem particularly relevant.

If possible, the director should be present for this entire phase as it gives them a chance to characterize which portions of the footage they find particularly important, to muse about how things might fit together, and to quickly answer the questions that you will inevitably have. Mary Lampson describes her approach in this way:

> I like sitting with the director and watching the footage because that's the time when I as the editor absorb what the director's intent is, and what the movie really is about on some deeper level. And then I can react to what is actually on the screen and what I, as the editor, perceived that the audience would read on the screen, which might be different from what the director sees. If the director has shot 400 hours and it's not possible to sit through all of it with them then I need to at least have an extended conversation with them when I'm done watching it.

As Lampson notes, if the director was not able to watch all the footage together with you then it's important to debrief and discuss when *you* have finished watching it. Don't be discouraged if there are very few structural ideas at this point. The next steps are designed to bring those to the fore.

5

Making Select Reels

Before we dive into the nitty-gritty of the select reel process, let's take a step back to reflect on the nature and purpose of documentary filmmaking. When a filmmaker begins a project, they identify a particular topic by looking at the world from a particular point of view. Their curiosity leads them to highlight a specific aspect of social life and bring it to the surface in order to draw their audience's attention to it.

As editors, we have the exact same mandate: to use *our* powers of observation to seize upon particular words, phrases, themes, objects, and visual juxtapositions that jump out at us and to bring them together with other moments to make meaning out of them. Thus, one of the key things we're looking for is *patterns*, and one of the key skills of the documentary editor is the ability to perform *pattern recognition*.

Frederick Wiseman, who edits his own films, has developed a brilliant career by making works that reveal beneath-the-surface patterns in the institutions he trains his camera on. By placing a frame around the activities in a particular location or institution (*Hospital, Zoo, High School, Juvenile Court*) rather than around a particular character,

FIGURE 5.1 *Juvenile Court* **(Frederick Wiseman, 1973)**

the commonalities between the behaviors of different individuals rise to the surface. Albert and David Maysles accomplished a different version of the same thing in their 1975 classic *Grey Gardens*, which was a study in the repetition and evolution of various patterns of codependent behavior between Edith Beale and her daughter. And while the creation of those lacerating media segments on *The Daily Show* showing one politician after another repeating the same moronic phrase is aided by a sophisticated server-based technology called SnapStream,[1] it is the insight of an observant individual noticing the pattern in the first place that makes it possible.

One of the main activities of the documentary editor, then, is *observing a pattern and making use of it.* The trick at this stage is how to use the select reel process to aid us in the finding of these patterns.

▶ CREATING SOURCE-BASED SELECT REELS

What is a select reel? It's basically chunks of raw footage that have been cut into a sequence because there was something to recommend them. It's the "good stuff." Most editors will create a select reel for the footage from each shoot, whether that shoot is an interview or a morning's worth of verité shooting or a chunk of archival material. The specifics of the film will dictate how the source material is divided up, but basically you want to be able to quickly look at a select reel sequence in order to see all of the best material from that part of the raw footage, putting a short title card in front of each section that describes the clip. Geoff Richman goes about it like this:

> It's different for each film, but generally it's by shoot or location. And then for each of these chunks of footage, I lay out a select reel. If it's a huge amount of footage then I'll do two passes—select A and select B—where I whittle it down a little bit more. And then I organize the clips on the timeline by action or topic of conversation and I'll put big titles on the timeline and big gaps between the sections. It's easier to have this overview because five hours of footage on a shoot is incredibly overwhelming and it's just impossible to see what's what in five hours. But once you've trimmed it down to three hours, if those three hours are organized nicely on the timeline, it boils down to 10 actions or topics of conversation, which makes it much easier to see.

Thus, as you work your way through the footage, you essentially make a better organized, somewhat condensed version of it that lives within a set of *sequences* rather than as a series of clips spread across multiple folders. By the end of this step, you will have all your footage viewable in reels rather than in clips, and be able to look at the titles for a quick reminder of what the clips contain. You may want to put a star (or two or three) in the description to instantly mark it as something of particular interest, as shown in Figure 5.2.[2]

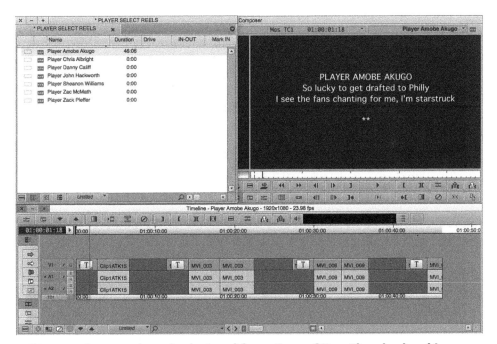

FIGURE 5.2 A source-based select reel from *Sons of Ben*. The play head is parked on a title card describing the interview clip that follows. The two asterisks at the bottom of the description designate this clip as one of particular interest.

Note that Richman performed a crucial second step when he made his "select B" reel: he started organizing his footage by *topic*. This is the next stage in the select reel process.

▶ CREATING TOPIC-BASED SELECT REELS

The jumble of select reels you've now assembled represents a project with a lot more structure than you had before, but it is still a mess. Your reels may not have any clear relationship with one another, and the fact that you've whittled things down doesn't erase the fact that the footage in each section is still full of digressions and excess detail. Yet the work you've done makes possible the next step, which is to apply the same "sifting" process you used on the raw footage to the select reels themselves.

Start watching your select reels. They will be long and the work will start to get tedious, but this time around you don't necessarily need to watch every single minute of every clip. You only need to watch long enough to decide how this clip should be categorized. Your goal here is to copy and paste some portion of this footage into new select reels that are *topic* driven rather than source driven. Thus, all of the footage of Topic A that came from Shoot 1 might be combined with Topic A footage from Shoots 2, 3, and 4, and from Archive Reel 1, for instance.

How do you come up with the topics in the first place? The interviewer may have asked a similar set of questions in every interview, so you have a pattern defined by multiple answers that cover the same subject matter. Or the topic may be more abstract: in *The Bad Kids* there was a certain faraway look of despair that we noticed on the faces of some of our teenage subjects that we ended up putting into a select reel called "Holding On For Dear Life." Or in an observational doc a topic can simply be a scene, and you can create a reel for the most compelling material from that scene.

There are no "bad" ideas at this point, so when a pattern suggests itself create a reel— and also copy in the clip that inspired the idea. It's important to note that we don't need to figure out *how* to use this material yet—it's enough just to recognize the pattern. As Mary Lampson states, "it's fine not to have a clue what the answer is, because it's all a process of exploration and surprise and finding things you didn't know were there." Let me offer some examples to help you get a feel for what you're looking for.

In *Precious Knowledge* our first topic-based select reels were relatively simplistic ones based on what students and teachers had said about the program. As seen in Figure 5.3 one big reel was called "What they get out of the classes," which was organized into different subtopics like "Improvement in specific skills," "Motivation to participate/ community service," and "It's a second home," each of which had several clips in it.

But as the editing went on, it was the reels that had greater thematic and moral complexity that ended up being even more useful. Categories like "Hate/Love/Fear" contained

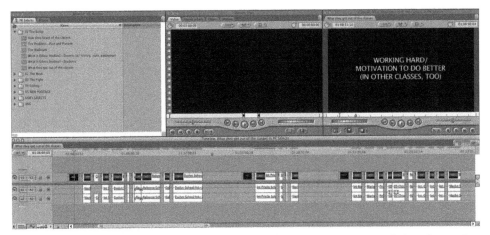

FIGURE 5.3 A topic-based select reel called "What they get out of the classes" from *Precious Knowledge*. Note the longer title cards at the beginning of each section defining the subtopic. Play head is parked on "Working Hard/ Motivation To Do Better" subtopic.

material that dealt with the difficulty activists faced in trying to live by their own non-violent, "love thy enemy" ideals when they were simultaneously so angry at their opponents. Other categories like "Indoctrination?" contained not only interview material from the opponents of the program but also verité scenes from the classroom that these opponents might have interpreted as the teachers' endorsement of a specific political ideology. Putting this material in the same select reel led directly to certain sections in the final cut that explored these topics.

On *The Bad Kids*, providing a sense of the regular rhythms of the school was important to the directors' vision, so we devised select reel categories to highlight those things (see Figure 5.4), and the final film uses many of these repeated actions.

Principal Vonda Viland greets the bus outside the school every morning when it arrives ("VV Greeting Bus"), and these bus arrivals ended up functioning as bookends at the beginning and ending of the film. Once school begins, Ms. Ambrosious makes regular calls to students who had been absent in previous days ("Ambrosious Calls For Attendance"), the flag is raised outside the school ("Flag Raising"), and late arrivals have to clock in ("Late Clock In"). At recess, Vonda collects unwanted containers of milk and redistributes them to students in need ("VV Redistribution of Food"), and these shots became the raw material for a quick montage. As the select reel process moved forward, it became clear that Vonda had a particular method of dealing with discipline issues ("Discipline"), and those scenes ended up being crucial for building two different scenes. When students graduated, they walked down the hallway ("Grad Walks") in a touchingly modest ceremony that was used in three different scenes in the film.

FIGURE 5.4 Topic-based select reel folders in *The Bad Kids*, each of which contains one or more select reels

Another instructive example comes from the select reels for my 2008 short documentary *Pure* (Figure 5.5).[3] This film deconstructs many visual tropes of the action movie genre, from the ubiquitous foot chases and car chases ("Running and Running Past" and "Car shot at, ducking down") to more subtle tropes like the look of a hero as the camera tracks around him before he goes off to settle a score ("Vengeful Looking" or "Watchful Looking"). Once you watch enough action films, you start to notice that there is an awful lot of white debris flying around ("Glass Breaking/Water Splashing"), climbing and descending of stairs ("Going Up"/and "Going Down"), quick entrances and exits ("Doors"), and of course lots of stuff related to guns ("Arming Up," "Two Guns In the Air," "Guns Going Off").

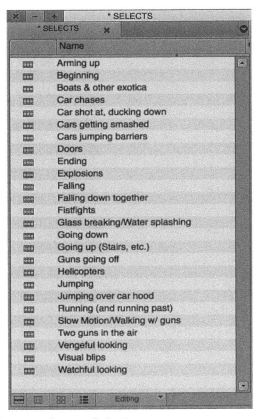

FIGURE 5.5 Topic-based select reels in *Pure*

▶ NOTES

1   Nicole Dieter, "Inside the Secret Technology That Makes 'The Daily Show' and 'Last Week Tonight' Work," splitsider.com. March 25, 2015. Web.

2   If you're using Final Cut X, you can create topic-based select reels by coming up with a new keyword and then attaching it to specific sections of the raw clips. Then when you select the keyword in your browser, all instances of its use will instantly pop up. Adding a description in the "Note" metadata column can substitute for the title cards that you would otherwise create in a sequence. Final Cut Pro X takes some getting used to for new users, but its powerful capabilities are worth considering when choosing an NLE.

3   *Pure* is available to view online at: https://vimeo.com/12133254.

6

Refining Select Reels

After you've gone through all your select reels and created your topic reels, take some time to watch through one of the new topic reels. At first it will likely feel bloated and uninspiring. Just because a bunch of things are happening related to the same topic doesn't instantly make them revelatory. In fact, the very repetition of the theme may have the opposite effect of making it feel like your subjects are beating the topic into the ground. But have patience and keep watching; the magic of this process is that with the newfound clarity of being able to see these clips side by side instead of scattered throughout zillions of hours of footage your instincts will start to get sharper about what is truly relevant and how these clips relate to each other.

As you watch, look for opportunities to correct or improve upon the short name you've given to each clip in the title card that precedes it, as well as to cut out sections where the subject strays from the topic. For particularly compelling clips, you can raise them to the V2 track to indicate their special status. And at this stage you can also make some judgments about clips that are simply not as compelling as the rest; for example, they're boring, or they've got a picture or sound defect that makes them weak. Place them in a new category at the end of the sequence called "NG" (the universal phrase for "NO GOOD"). By sticking them here they will be out of your way, but still easily accessible.

You may also find that some of your clips have been mis-categorized and are not in the proper topic reel. Go ahead and move these into a more suitable reel. Additionally, you're likely to find a few reels that are so similar to each other as to make distinctions between them meaningless, so combine them. For instance, is there a real advantage to keeping around a separate reel for "morning at the bar" and "afternoon at the bar"? If the film is a poetic meditation on the passage of time in a single location, then the distinction is crucial. But if the film is about a character who just happens to spend some hours in this one location, then the answer is probably no. Remember our *contain the chaos* principle: refining and eliminating categories can be a small but important way of adding a little bit of brain power to every step you take from this point forward.

If possible, also take the time to apply some organizational muscle to the reels by placing them in folders so that you can start to see how they relate to each other. This initial sorting can help turn a mass of a few dozen select reels into a more manageable series of folders, each with several reels inside.

On *Precious Knowledge* there were select reels based on characters as well as events and topics. As you can see in Figure 6.1, the reels in the folder "02 The Meat" ended up being

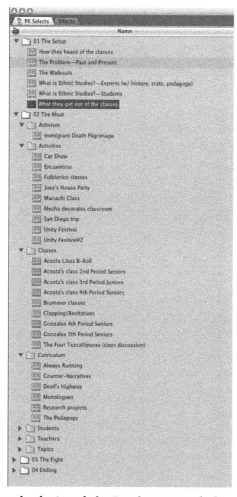

FIGURE 6.1 Topic-based select reels in *Precious Knowledge*

sorted into seven categories: "Activities," "Activism," "Classes," "Curriculum," "Students," "Teachers," and "Topics." The reels under "Activities" are fairly easy to identify: they're simply events that took place, defined by place and time. Other categories like "Classes" were repositories for the best footage that took place in the classrooms of particular teachers.

It's important to note that not all documentary editors create their select reels in the same way. Geoff Richman, for instance, does a lot of the categorization work within his initial source-based select reels, and does not create topic-based select reels until later in the process once a rough cut exists. And some editors will skip the source-based select reel step and go straight to topic reels if the clips themselves have been binned and categorized.

Whatever the exact process used, all successful documentary editors employ *some kind of rigorous sorting/sifting process* in order to turn the chaos of the raw footage into something that is easier to navigate and that reflects the imprint of their interpretive powers. These select reels will become the building blocks of your edit in the next steps.

▶ DRAWING INITIAL CONCLUSIONS ABOUT YOUR NARRATIVE FROM YOUR SELECT REELS

By looking at all your select reels, you now have the guts of your film in a more compact and organized form. You can look it over and try to come to some initial conclusions about where your film is headed.

The first major thing you want to determine is *what are the strengths of this material?* Of course, everything that ended up in one of these reels had something to recommend it or it would not be here. But taking an honest view of it, what are the elements that truly stand out as compelling? It's at this point that you form stronger instincts about what kind of film you can create.

If your footage has lots of great landscape imagery and a few compelling characters but not much progression in the stories, you are better off shading the film as an atmospheric "portrait" than a high-stakes drama. If your footage has one or two great characters whose stories develop in dramatic ways but was not shot in a particularly cinematic fashion, you are better off creating a character drama that sticks to the point of view of its protagonists. Great editing is at least as much about sensitivity and accommodation as it is about bending material to your will; you will make a better film if you and the director are realistic about the strengths and weaknesses of the footage.

The second major thing you want to do is to try to make some initial theories as to the organization of the film. By looking at a completed set of select reels, one ought to be able to see the thematic contours of the film as well as hints of possible narrative progression, and some of your select reels may be sufficiently refined that they can become the building blocks of your rough cut. While the goal in this sorting/sifting process is not to edit any sequences yet, it does lay the foundation for the cutting in a powerful way and makes the task ahead more manageable.

Returning to *Precious Knowledge* in Figure 6.1, note that another layer of interpretation has been added to the organization of the select reels by placing them into metacategories of "01 The Setup," "02 The Meat," "03 The Fight," and "04 Ending." This arrangement was determined after a full second pass through the select reels, once an idea for an overall structure had been conceived. In "The Setup" the audience is shown what the classes are about ("What is Ethnic Studies"), how students come to enroll in them ("How they heard of the classes"), as well as some history to give context ("The Problem—Past and Present" and "The Walkouts"). "The Meat" is a big category comprising a fuller rendering of what would be presented in "The Setup," and "The Fight" is where the political drama starts to play out once the Superintendent for Public Education announces his intention to shut the classes down.

In the final film we digressed from this structure liberally (routinely grabbing footage from "The Meat" and using it in the section dominated by footage from "The Fight," for instance), so the categories can be fluid. The point is to build a mental map of the footage that reflects your intentions, not to lock oneself into a particular narrative order.

▶ A FORK IN THE ROAD

At this point you have come to a fork in the road in the cutting process. With the mass of footage fresh in your mind and some major organizational work complete, you can now move on to the next phase of cutting scenes and assembling your rough cut. But which comes first?

You now have a bit of a chicken and egg issue. You want to dive into cutting scenes, yet the function of the scenes may not be clear enough yet to really know how to cut them. On the flip side you want to piece together an initial rough cut, but it's hard to know how to order the scenes if they're just a bunch of unedited clips.

A common plan of attack is to simply start with what you know. There will be some scenes that you will have identified as being crucial and compelling, so you can begin editing those. Then there may be another section for which you already have some good ideas brewing, so cut those scenes and put them in order. After cutting all the stuff you're confident about, you can try your first baby steps at building a rough cut—slugging in title cards in place of scenes that you haven't cut yet. That ordering process will bring more ideas, which will let you push forward with cutting more scenes, and so on.

Another strategy is to build a paper cut—stitching together a structure by shuffling around selections from the transcripts—and use the paper cut as a blueprint to put together an initial rough cut right away. This is well suited to interview-heavy films whose logic is primarily driven by the spoken words of the subjects. In this scenario, great attention is paid to reading and rereading the transcripts. Yet another strategy is to make a first cut of every scene, and only at that point start putting them on the timeline to see how they play beside each other.

No matter which road you take, you will inevitably find yourself shifting back and forth between the tasks of cutting scenes and building structure, so read these next two sections ("Part IIIa: Constructing and Refining Scenes" and "Part IIIb: Building the Rough Cut") as parallel paths that are both heading in the same direction. "Constructing and Refining Scenes" should inform your thoughts on how to achieve the rough cut, and vice versa.

PART IIIA
Constructing and Refining Scenes

▶ **INTRODUCTION**

Motion pictures cast a spell on us. When a film is "working," it transcends its origins as a series of disconnected moments and feels instead like a seamless experience, a smooth roller coaster ride that pushes us through space and time in a dynamic and satisfying way. Up through the 1950s, the language of editing in mainstream Hollywood filmmaking to achieve this effect was remarkably conservative. "There was almost a formulaic way of presenting films," says editor Carol Littleton in *The Cutting Edge*, a 2004 documentary about film editing. "This film language was very strict, and in editorial terms there were rules that one felt could not be broken." "A master shot had to come first," elaborates the legendary editor Dede Allen, "and then if you had an over-the-shoulder shot you used the over-the-shoulder shot, and you never went to the close up until you had done the whole dance coming from far to close." This consensus was blown apart by the arrival of the French New Wave. Audiences quickly became comfortable with jump cuts as a legitimate style choice, and since that time wave upon wave of revisions have been made to the "rule book."

But even before the French New Wave, tolerance for deviation from the "rules" had always been greater in documentaries, perhaps in part because their claim to authenticity lay in the very "rawness" of their style. As Louise Spence and Vinicius Navarro say in their book, *Crafting Truth: Documentary Form and Meaning*, "we think of handheld camera, obscured views, and overlapping sound as markers of documentary truth. . . [Unbalanced] compositions, and an aesthetic of visual and aural clutter are easily read as signifiers of immediacy, instantaneity, and authenticity."[1] Indeed, one look at *Nanook of the North* (1922), which some cite as the world's first documentary feature, shows a style that is rougher and less bound to a linear notion of time and space than most of the narrative films of its era.[2]

Regardless of their difference from narrative films, the way most documentaries are edited is not fundamentally different from narrative films. Both types may employ omniscient "voice of God" narrators (think of the similarity between David Attenborough narrating the *Planet Earth* series and the narration in the Coen Brothers' *O Brother, Where Art Thou?*), or they may choose to let the characters themselves do the narrating (the small boy Mohammed narrating his segment of James Longley's 2006 documentary *Iraq in Fragments* or Travis Bickle narrating *Taxi Driver*). They both use title cards to impart information to the audience (the opening to *Star Wars*, for instance). Both feature musical scores and the use of sound sweetening to emphasize particular elements of on- and off-screen activity. Both may use classical "invisible" editing to hide the presence of the filmmaker and make the cuts feel seamless and fluid, or to build specific sequences with a series of jump cuts. Both attempt to build a satisfying arc. The difference, as Bill Nichols points out in his seminal book *Introduction to Documentary*, is mostly in what we assume about the *source* of the footage—it came from historical reality in documentaries rather than being shot on a set with actors—and in the differing institutional structures that support each kind of filmmaking and confer meaning upon it.

* * *

What does editing look like in documentaries today? Speaking broadly, it falls into three basic categories, presented here in order of how much they have in common with traditional narrative editing.

▶ **Traditional "verité" editing** (similar to narrative "continuity" editing).

Here, a documentary editor follows the conventional rules of continuity editing (i.e., so-called invisible editing) to construct the illusion that the discontinuous shots are actually taking place in continuous time. In the logic of the film, the elapsed time of the scene is the same amount of time that passed for the characters as they experienced it in the story.[3] As mentioned earlier, there are fewer "rules" to this type of editing than there used to be, but some basic conventions apply.

▷ Establish the geography of the scene somewhere near the beginning (i.e., use an establishing shot or a wide shot showing the context of the characters within their environment).

▷ Cut between shots of similar sizes (medium to medium, close-up to close-up, etc.) whenever possible, rather than cutting arbitrarily from one shot scale to another.

▷ Determine the point of view of the scene, then cut to match. For instance if our main character is Julie we should be cutting to other shots *off of Julie's glances*, and paying very close attention to how the scene affects *her*. (For two great examples of scenes built on the point of view of a single character, watch the first five minutes of *Born into Brothels* and *Iraq in Fragments*. In both films, extreme close-ups on the faces of children are used as the motivating element for the scenes.)

▷ Pay attention to the emotions that read in people's faces, and especially in their eyes. The eyes are the most expressive part of the body, and the tiniest gesture can have enormous emotional content. (See same examples above.)

▷ Construct a narrative and emotional "arc" for the scene that culminates in some kind of climax, resolution, or new question at the end. If possible, save close-ups for the climax so they have more power.

▶ **Montage editing** (similar to narrative montage editing).

Nearly identical to montage editing in narrative films, this is a series of images, usually buttressed by music, that are linked to each other by a common theme, event, or series of events.

▶ **Evidentiary editing** (specific to documentaries).

Bill Nichols first coined the phrase "evidentiary editing" in his 1991 book *Representing Reality*.[4] He defined it as editing in which images act to explain or validate the spoken words heard underneath. Here, the documentary interview (or at least the audio taken from the interview) acts as the anchoring element. The cutaways have a relationship mostly to the words, and need not necessarily have any further relationship to each other. The passage of time is arbitrary, because we are overtly jumping between one topic and the next via the anchoring interview. Most people are familiar with this type of editing from Ken Burns films and "issue" documentaries that rely heavily on interviews.

▶ NOTES

1   Louise Spence and Vinicius Navarro, *Crafting Truth: Documentary Form and Meaning* (New Brunswick, NJ.: Rutgers University Press, 2011), p. 32.

2   Thank you to Bill Nichols for consultation on this.

3   This means that some moments may be cut to "fly by" while others may be stretched out for emphasis.

4   Bill Nichols, *Representing Reality: Issues and Concepts in Documentary* (Bloomington: Indiana University Press, 1991).

7

Evidentiary Editing
Building Interview-Based Scenes

We will start with "evidentiary editing," which is the easiest to master. As previously mentioned, this term was coined by author Bill Nichols to refer to a very common "mode" of editing that uses interviews (or at least the audio generated from interviews) as the anchoring element in sequences that describe a concept or tell a story. The words from the interviewees are supplemented and gently reinforced by images that provide "evidence" for their claims. Evidentiary editing can be interwoven with verité editing and used for sections as short as a few seconds or as long as an entire film. While this term is an academic one and isn't commonly used in the professional world, it nonetheless provides a good way of thinking about how this most common type of documentary cutting works.

▶ CONSTRUCTING THE FRAMEWORK: ANCHOR WITH AUDIO

The anchoring elements in evidentiary editing are the interviews themselves, and it's with these clips that you should start. Our workflow for interview-based material dictates that we determine the *verbal* content of our scenes before we address the *visual* content. This is because it is far easier to construct your scenes by *anchoring with audio* than with any other method. Essentially this means that we are going to figure out the text of the scene first (i.e., what is said, and in what order) and only later solve the problem of making it visually appealing. (Some people refer to this first cut as a "radio edit" since it is about words rather than pictures.)

There are couple key reasons why we anchor with audio. First, if we spend valuable time making the scene work visually at the outset by looking for cutaways and fashioning custom-made transitions, much of this work is likely to be wasted since a large portion of it will eventually be removed or rearranged. Second, it helps us focus on the logic of the *ideas* anchoring the scene, rather than getting distracted with the more complex associations made possible by the visual cutaways.

As you start to lay out a scene like this, you can draw directly from the clips you have assembled in your select reels, and then chisel them down from there. Ultimately you're looking to make a flow of ideas that feels fluid and inevitable. One person's comment will lay the groundwork for the next, as if every voice were in the same lively salon, building off each other's statements or piping up to raise an objection at precisely the right moment.

Try a first stab at ordering the clips, then play the sequence out and figure out whether the ideas are flowing logically or not. Are there redundant sections that can be eliminated? Might it work better to start with a statement which is now near the end? As we devise a flow through the various ideas brought up by the interview subjects, we need to be careful to take the most direct route, eliminating distracting elements and always remembering to *simplify, simplify, simplify*.

As an example, look at the left column of Figure 7.1, which shows a sequence of clips from a hypothetical advocacy film on the topic of illegal immigration. There are three main topics ("Difficult to enter legally," "Crossing is dangerous," and "Migration is difficult to police") and a handful of examples for each. In this jumble of ideas, we have asked our audience to transition between the three different subjects six times even though there are only eight clips. That's a lot of throttling back and forth, and is a recipe for a confused and exhausted audience. With a little rearrangement, as seen in the right column, the number of times we change topics could be reduced to just two.

Going a step further, let's consider the potential to carefully progress through ideas in a way that takes into account not only the *content* of each clip but also where it *leads*. Every clip has an ending; if you can match the content of the ending to its natural match in the beginning of another clip, you can create a cut with less friction, and now that we have the clips grouped by subject this level of detail is easier to spot. For instance, take a look at the three "Crossing is dangerous" clips in the reordered sequence on the right in the same Figure 7.1. What if the clip "thieves prey on migrants" (third from the bottom) ends with the following sentence: "Migrants are in an incredibly vulnerable situation, and the thieves know this and take advantage of it. You're out there in an unfamiliar place, completely out of your element." This would segue perfectly into, "It's easy to get lost, and it's so hot that you can really only last for about a day without water," which is how the preceding "dehydration happens quickly" clip begins. Thus, we would swap the order of these two "Crossing is dangerous" clips.

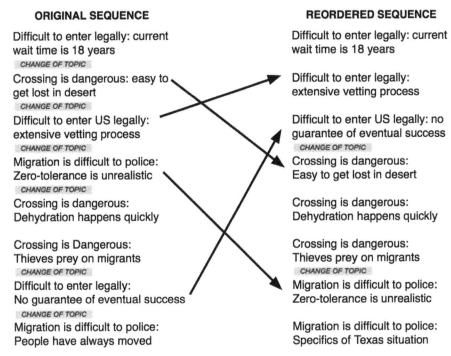

FIGURE 7.1 Reshuffling clips to improve flow

Looking at our sequence further, we could also reverse the order of the two "Migration is difficult to police" clips at the end so we could close with the "zero-tolerance is unrealistic" clip. A broad statement about the futility of zero-tolerance approaches to immigration policy will probably function as a nice concluding statement, while a clip about the specific situation in Texas may be too parochial to serve this function.

Be advised that this kind of shuffling sometimes creates new problems that have to be worked out with additional pruning and shuffling. Repeated passes of problem-solving are par for the course.

For a nice example of a smooth flow of ideas in a finished documentary, let's take a look at a section from the 2015 Kirby Dick documentary *The Hunting Ground* in which Harvard Law student Kamilah Willingham has just finished describing an incident in which she had been sexually assaulted by a fellow student.[1] Note how the end of each person's comment sets the stage for the next one to continue the story.

APRIL WILLINGHAM, KAMILAH'S MOTHER

It seemed pretty clear that he had assaulted both of them while they were unconscious. I absolutely presumed that Harvard would do right by Kamilah.

KAMILAH WILLINGHAM

I went to the Dean of Students office, and she said, "I just want to make sure, above all else, that you don't talk to anyone about this. It could be bad if people started rallying around having him removed from campus." And I was like, "well, he is a predator, and he's dangerous, and that's exactly what I want." We both had the right to legal representation. My lawyer was pro bono.

COLBY BRUNO, VICTIM RIGHTS LAW CENTER

She was a phenomenal client. She really told her story with a great deal of confidence.

KAMILAH WILLINGHAM

I went into the hearing and even the professors were, like, did I give him the wrong message with our friendship and that he misunderstood our friendship? The response was, "No, because sex was never part of that friendship. And if it was ever going to be introduced, when I was awake would be a good time for that." I'm getting questions like, "why didn't you fight him?" He's 6' 3", over 200 pounds, I was unconscious or just coming to, and could barely take control of my own body, but why didn't you fight him? There was this extreme reluctance to believe me.

DANIELLE DIRKS, AUTHOR, "CONFRONTING CAMPUS RAPE"

Campus administrators are overly concerned about false reporting. You look at the statistics about false reporting, it's much, much smaller than what people estimate it to be.

SUSAN MARINE, FORMER ASSISTANT DEAN OF STUDENT LIFE, HARVARD UNIVERSITY

The data about false rape claims is that they're a tiny minority of all claims ever made.

COLBY BRUNO, VICTIM RIGHTS LAW CENTER

Rape and sexual assault have the same percentage of false reports that any other crime has in our country.

DAVID LISAK, CLINICAL PSYCHOLOGIST

The best research around the world on false reports would put the percentage somewhere between two and eight percent. Which means 90 percent, but more likely 95 to 98 percent of reports are not false.

The first comment from the mother makes the transition from the time of the assault itself into the moment when Kamilah reports it. Then Kamilah moves events forward to the hearing and subtly introduces her lawyer, who never needs to be formally introduced because the context is so clear. The lawyer speaks for a moment and hands the stage back to Kamilah to continue with another anecdote from the hearing itself. Then the film makes a clever leap from Kamilah's last line ("there was this extreme reluctance to believe me") to Danielle Dirks' commentary on false reporting, which offers an interpretation of *why* the administrators might be reluctant to believe the victim. The remaining clips then debunk false reporting as a valid concern.

Now, if it seems like the way these people discuss the subject at hand is little too perfect to have been possible in the raw interviews, that's because it is. Many of the quotes are, in fact, composed of fragments of sentences taken from a variety of moments in the same interview, stitched together with the use of b-roll cutaways (in this case shots of the Harvard campus) or with cuts from wide to close-up shots. Take a look below to see all the cuts (noted as forward slashes) in the audio. The highlighted portions in **bold** are the lines actually delivered onscreen.

APRIL WILLINGHAM, KAMILAH WILLINGHAM'S MOTHER

It seemed pretty clear / that he had assaulted / both of them / while they were unconscious. / I absolutely presumed that Harvard would do right by Kamilah.

KAMILAH WILLINGHAM

I went to the Dean of Students office, and she said, / "I just want to make sure, above all else, **that you don't talk to anyone about this. / It could be bad for everyone if people started rallying around having him removed from campus." And I was like, "well, he is a predator, and he's dangerous, and that's exactly what I want."** / We both had the right to legal representation. My lawyer / was pro bono.

COLBY BRUNO, VICTIM RIGHTS LAW CENTER

She was a phenomenal client. **She really told her story with a great deal of confidence.**

KAMILAH WILLINGHAM

I went into the hearing and / even the professors were, like, did I give him the wrong message with our friendship and / that he misunderstood our friendship? **The response was, like, "No, because sex was never part of that friendship. And if it was ever going to be introduced, when I was awake would be a good time for that."** / I'm getting questions like, "why didn't you fight him?" **He's 6' 3", over 200 pounds, I was unconscious or just coming to, and could barely take control of my own body, but why didn't you fight him?** / There was this extreme reluctance / to believe me.

DANIELLE DIRKS, AUTHOR, "CONFRONTING CAMPUS RAPE"

Campus administrators are overly concerned about false reporting. / You look at / **statistics about false reporting, it's much, much smaller than what people estimate it to be.**

SUSAN MARINE, FORMER ASSISTANT DEAN OF STUDENT LIFE, HARVARD UNIVERSITY

The data about false rape claims is that they're a tiny minority of all reports ever made.

COLBY BRUNO, VICTIM RIGHTS LAW CENTER

Rape and sexual assault have the same percentage of false reports that any other crime has in our country.

DAVID LISAK, CLINICAL PSYCHOLOGIST

The best research around the world on false reports would put the percentage / of false reports / somewhere between two and eight percent. / Which means **90 percent, but more likely 95 to 98 percent of reports are not false.**

It takes quite a bit of work to edit your clips down into a form where they function like in *The Hunting Ground*, but the process starts with the very simple task of laying several clips out, side by side, and seeing how they flow together. Sometimes the end of one clip transitions perfectly into the beginning of another, and sometimes it takes a bit more work to accomplish this easy flow. This is why we're always on the lookout for what I refer to as "hinge clips" or "pivot clips."

▶ FINDING "HINGE CLIPS"

One of the joys of a well-edited documentary is the way in which it moves you effortlessly from scene to scene, topic to topic, and event to event. A section will showcase a satisfying anecdote from a talking head interview, and the subject will then (as if by magic) end on a phrase that perfectly introduces the next topic. In a strong film, it should feel as though the disparate characters are all telling the same story, even though it's really the director and editor telling the story through the editing.

I prefer to think of the transitional elements that make this kind of storytelling possible as "hinge clips" because they allow an effortless pivot, facilitating the smooth and seamless redirection of the audience's attention. These clips are almost never planned in production; they have to be discovered and excavated in the editing room.

For instance, when we needed to swing the discussion in *Precious Knowledge* from the history of Chicano movements for educational equity in the 1960s back to present-day efforts, we were fortunate to find U.S. Representative Raul Grijalva remembering his days with the movement. "Like any group of young people, our expectations were high," he states. "In these next four or five years we're going to fundamentally change the way this world is, and how we're treated. . . . Obviously, we're still at that." That last phrase, an acknowledgment that the work is far from complete, let us segue to a title card discussing the efforts in the early 2000s to address the achievement gap.[2]

As you review your own footage, be on the lookout for these moments when the characters make a pivot from one subject to the next.

▶ STITCH TOGETHER THE SEAMS WITH CUTAWAYS

The *Hunting Ground* example is made possible with the strategic use of cutaways. Ask any documentary editor what they need to make their work easier; the response is very likely to be, "More cutaways!" Cutaways allow two clips from different moments to be joined together as if they were one. Watch any documentary: anytime you're not actually *seeing* the person who is speaking on camera, it's a fair bet that the cutaway is allowing a new sentence to be formed or two different ideas to be joined together. In a very real way, all documentary editing is the process of hopscotching from one anchor clip to the next with the help of cutaways.

On the most basic level, then, cutaways accomplish one thing: they eliminate jump cuts. But cutaways also provide the "evidence" implied in the term "evidentiary editing," proving to your audience in a more visceral way that what is being talked about is true and has a physical presence in the real world. At their best they do this in a subtle and emotionally satisfying way.

Consider a moment in *Happy Valley*, Amir Bar-Lev's 2014 film about the Jerry Sandusky sexual abuse scandal at Penn State.[3] We see a classic talking head interview shot of attorney Andrew Shubin as he lays out the remarkable circumstances under which Sandusky gained custody of a young boy named Matt who lived in his community. "From the beginning, Jerry expressed a desire to try and adopt him . . . and Jerry began making deliberate moves to separate him from his family," says Shubin. At this point, we see a chilling shot of a grown man's hand grasping the arm of a little boy who is smiling but running away from him, and as the shot widens out, it reveals that it's an archival photo of Sandusky's hand grasping young Matt's arm. The shot does much more than bridge the gap between this statement and the one that follows. Crucially, it adds a visceral sense of foreboding.

Or take the moment in *20 Feet from Stardom* when we see archival footage of the Ikettes performing onstage as part of Ike Turner's band.[4] The segment begins with former Ikette Claudia Lennear recalling her joy at having been selected by Turner, but then takes a critical turn when USC Critical Studies Professor Dr. Todd Boyd says, "Ike saw himself as a pimp, and he saw his singers . . . as his hoes." By this point, we are cutting back and forth between shots of Ike Turner onstage and his Ikettes dancing, and we see the images in an entirely new way: the pure exuberance of the first set of images gives way to a darker and more complex reality as we start to look at the body language of the musicians onstage and note the power relationships between them. These examples illustrate the fact that mixing interview footage with cutaways is like performing alchemy: it can yield an entirely new emotion that would not have been possible if either element had been used on its own.

When cutting from your interview shot to the cutaway, there's an important but often overlooked consideration of *when* to cut out. Whereas in narrative cutting it is common to cut from one side of a conversation to the other in the middle of a line, in evidentiary editing it often makes sense to wait for a character to finish their sentence or to cut on a pause. As Aaron Wickenden notes, "I look for people's mouths and always like to edit with a person's mouth closed if possible before they start opening their mouth up again." Using the pause as a cut point can give a subtle but significant emphasis to the points that are being made, and makes the cutting flow rhythmically with the dialogue.

It's also crucial to work on the *exact* placement of shots. Sliding a cutaway shot just a few frames forward or backward can make a huge difference in how impactful it will be. If you use a cutaway too early your audience will be confused because they're still digesting the information coming from the voice-over about the previous topic. If you wait too long to go to the cutaway you have "Mickey Mouse" editing, which feels obvious and a little bit juvenile, as if we were watching someone's show and tell session. The sweet spot is right in the middle, where new visual information is keeping the audience on their toes without making them work too hard. If you're unsure about where to cut, just try moving the clip back and forth a bit to see what the result is. Even after many years of cutting documentaries I still slide cutaways back and forth to audition what the effect will be.

Note that the term "cutaway" is sometimes a bit of a misnomer, as "evidentiary editing" often features much more cutaway footage than actual interview footage. Instead of being anchored on an interview shot and making brief visual diversions for the occasional cutaway, editors often construct whole scenes out of cutaway material.

▶ SMOOTHING EDITS

Once you've put your audio quotes in order and stitched them together with cutaways, you may still find that things feel jumpy. This is often because of sudden, unintended changes in the audio track. To fix them, it's important to understand something about human perception: while most of us no longer face mortal threats to our safety on a daily basis, our perceptions are still tuned in such a way as to alert us to the sudden noises made by potential predators. Even the most annoying sound will tend to fade into the background of our consciousness if it is constant, but *sudden* changes in sound immediately draw our attention. This can be used to one's advantage if you're trying to provide a sudden jolt to your audience. More often than not, though, you're trying to do the opposite. As you're looking to make your cuts smoother and draw less attention to them, remember that your audience doesn't immediately distinguish between the picture and the sound as separate elements. Rather, they will assume that a series of shots joined together in a scene all happened in the same place at the same time so long as the background sound remains constant. Here are some simple rules to follow.

Avoid Cutting Picture and Sound at the Same Time

You can make huge strides toward hiding your cuts by simply moving your picture cuts to be *asynchronous* with your sound cuts. This way the picture cut will feel smoother because it's happening over a continuous piece of audio, and when there is a change in the texture of the audio your audience will be less likely to notice it. Bottom line: if there is any difference in the background audio between your tracks, your timeline should not show any top-to-bottom straight lines across the video and audio tracks (as in Figure 7.2), but rather a checkerboard look (as in Figure 7.3).

Add "Bad" Sound to Smooth Out Cuts

If just moving your sound cuts away from your picture cuts is insufficient to hide the changes in background audio, try hiding the bad sound *by adding more of it* (see Figures 7.4 and 7.5). This may seem counterintuitive, but it often works like a charm.

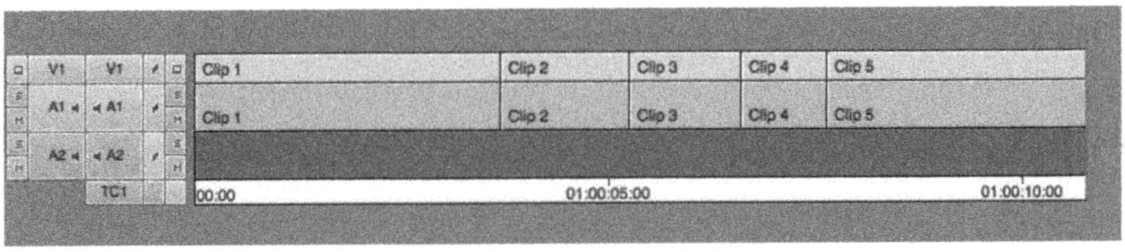

FIGURE 7.2 Sound and picture are cut straight across (likely to produce jumpy cuts)

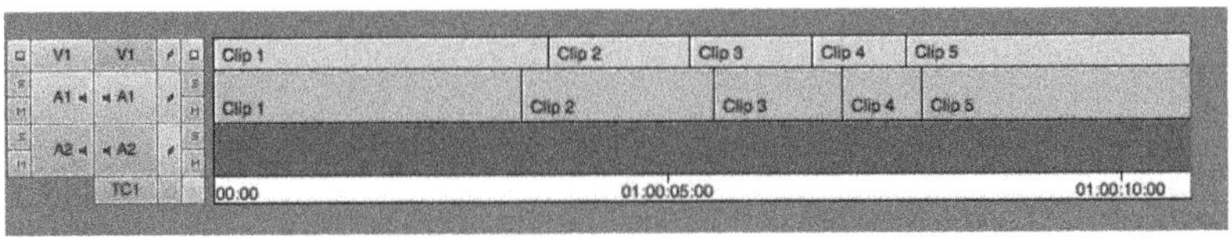

FIGURE 7.3 Sound and picture are cut asynchronously (likelier to produce smooth cuts)

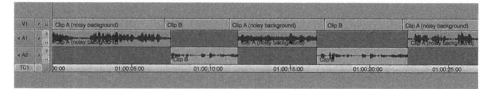

FIGURE 7.4 Noisy background on Clip A produces jumpy audio transitions

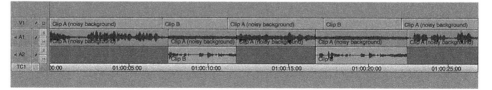

FIGURE 7.5 Added background noise on A1 eliminates jumpy audio transitions

Let's say Clip A has a noisy air conditioner in the background, but Clip B is clean and relatively free of background noise. Place all uses of Clip A on the A1 audio track, and all uses of Clip B beneath it on the A2 audio track. Then find the longest stretch of uninterrupted noisy "room tone" air conditioner noise (with no dialogue) from Clip A to fill in the gaps on A1. You will no longer notice big changes in the background, and can later add filters to clean up the noise.[5]

Avoid Cutting on Loud, Sudden Noises

There are some cases where you get accidental coincidences between sound and picture that work to your detriment. Any loud, sudden noises—even if they come from an unrelated source—will call attention to your cuts if the cuts happen to fall on them. It is amazing the number of times I've had a sound effects track contain a stray noise that has accidentally coincided with a picture cut and made it feel jumpy.

Stay Away from Blinks

Just as you'll tend to have smoother edits when you let your characters finish their sentences, also pay attention to when people blink. If the small, sudden movement of a blink appears right next to a cut, it feels like there was a subtle connection between the two, and the cut may feel "harder" and more noticeable. A blink is a minor form of disruption exhibited by your human subjects; whether your audience perceives it consciously or not, a cut that happens right at the blink is often a bad idea.[6]

▶ NOTES

1   The transcribed portion that follows occurs between 16:52 and 19:08 in *The Hunting Ground*.

2   This transition occurs at 9:37 in *Precious Knowledge*.

3   This section of *Happy Valley* begins at 12:45.

4   This scene begins at 27:00 in *20 Feet from Stardom*.

5   Note that this is just a temporary solution made for the purposes of the rough cut. The sound editor will later need to perform noise reduction—and potentially further editing—on these clips to get everything to blend together seamlessly.

6   Murch makes the case in *In the Blink of an Eye* that cutting on blinks in narrative editing can be a great choice. This is a complex issue, but I have personally never found blinks to be helpful in documentary editing, because they constitute a new "microbeat" (see Chapter 9), and I usually want to let a microbeat play out in full before making a cut. Walter Murch, *In The Blink of An Eye: A Perspective on Film Editing* (Los Angeles: Silman-James Press, 2001).

8

Verité Editing
Building Observational Scenes

Now that you know a bit about the evidentiary editing model, let's move on to the harder nut to crack: verité editing. Verité scenes, which feature footage of spontaneous conversations and activity happening in front of the camera, are more difficult for one simple reason: you are trying to make all the clips feel like they happened in continuous time. When one character speaks followed by another in a verité scene, not only do the ideas have to flow smoothly but we also have to believe that the radically foreshortened dialogue actually occurred as shown. And yet, the *process* is exactly the same as with evidentiary editing, starting with the mandate to *anchor with audio* by going through the material and figuring out *what should be said*. In addition, we will look for bits of nonverbal communication to help tell our story, and we will later look for cutaways to make it all cut together.

▶ BUILD UP OR TRIM DOWN: TWO OPTIONS FOR FINDING "THE GOOD BITS"

After you've identified a portion of verité footage that deserves to be cut as a scene, you've got two basic options for getting it down to size: building up or trimming down. In the first approach, you mark "in" and "out" points in the raw footage in the source monitor and transfer only the "good stuff" to the timeline. This approach is likely preferable when you already have a clear idea of why the material is relevant, and you already know pretty much what you want from it.

Over time I have grown to prefer the second approach, which is to bring the entire chunk of verité into a sequence and start whittling away at it. This approach is better for material that seems vaguely useful but is bloated, because it's often easier to tell when something *isn't* working than when it is. Where does the conversation go off track into irrelevant digressions? *Cut!* Where does the cinematographer point the camera at the ground and turn off the sound? *Cut!* After a couple passes on the material, it will be easier to identify the irrelevant material and to get rid of it.

▶ INVISIBLE OR SELF-REFERENTIAL?

Before we go any further, there is a fundamental issue with verité footage that must be addressed. Every documentary develops a strategy with respect to whether it operates with any kind of self-referentiality or self-consciousness. Are we made aware of the camera, or does the film instead try to pretend that it's not there?

Films operating in a purely "observational" mode will remove all references to the camera or the filmmaking, treating the flow of images as a transparent window onto a pre-existing world, regardless of how much intervention was actually involved. This is easy enough to do: one simply cuts out all footage of the filmmaker talking from behind the camera and interacting with the subjects, and all moments in which the subjects seem aware that they are being filmed. The tutorial video on "Invisibility" available on this book's companion website shows exactly how this works. In footage from my 2006 documentary *Indies Under Fire: The Battle for the American Bookstore*, Santa Cruz Borders bookstore manager Kris Arnett stands and looks out the window onto a group of protesters who are making their opposition to Borders known. She contemplates them for a moment in a wide shot and then, unprovoked, states in a close-up that she respects their opinion and hopes to one day win them over. In the raw footage you can see that her utterance was actually a response to a question that I asked her off camera: "What do you think of the people protesting outside?" With careful cutting, my intervention was eliminated and the scene plays like a thoughtful reflection by someone who was moved to comment by the sheer drama of the moment.

The observational ideal was championed by 1960s documentary pioneers like Frederick Wiseman, D. A. Pennebaker, and Robert Drew.[1] Their filmmaking style also tended to exclude interviews, narration, and title cards, minimizing the overt editorial intervention of the filmmaker and drawing attention to details like Jackie Kennedy's hands fidgeting during a campaign event in Drew's *Primary* (Figure 8.1).

The opposite approach is to fully acknowledge the intervention of the filmmakers. This was the *cinema verité* ideal championed by Jean Rouch in *Chronicle of a Summer*, in which the filmmakers boldly and unapologetically interacted with the subjects and the subjects talked about how they were being portrayed. In this framework, references to the camera can seem to "[confirm] the authenticity of what we see and hear,"[2] as Spence and Navarro note, and the intervention of the filmmaker is not a distraction at all but rather another marker of "truth."[3] In the Maysles' *Grey Gardens*, for instance, many of

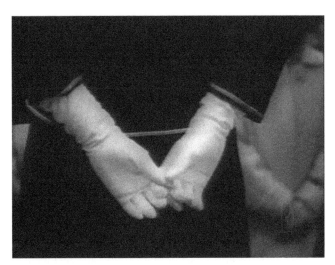

FIGURE 8.1 Jackie Kennedy Onassis fidgets with her hands in a scene from Robert Drew's *Primary*

the most poignant moments come out of Little Edie's interactions with camera operator Albert Maysles, in which she flirts with him, confides in him, and generally makes him part of the family. (The term *verite* has since become a more general term used to refer to unscripted events happening in front of a [usually handheld] camera, and it is this definition that we will use in this book.)[4]

Other films successfully operate somewhere in the middle, and may occupy the observational space but include some moments that acknowledge the camera when the reasons for inclusion are compelling. Good examples include the scenes in *Harlan County U.S.A.* where director Barbara Kopple interacts directly with mine foreman Basil Collins by asking for his ID,[5] and when cameraman Hart Perry's camera is thrown to the ground in a scuffle with a strike breaker.[6] Another less austere stripe of the observational ideal will contain verité footage and also interviews—but only the *voice* (and not the picture) from those interviews. In this framework what we *see* is entirely verité footage, but the filmmakers leave themselves a direct channel to the characters' experience by letting us inside their thoughts via aural reflections. James Longley's *Iraq in Fragments* adopts this strategy, as does Peter Nicks' *The Waiting Room*. This way, the filmmaker can provide backstory and context without visually reminding the audience that they intervened in the characters' lives by interviewing them, thus preserving the integrity of the observational ideal while also giving the filmmaker greater latitude.

When attacking your verité scenes, be aware that by the time the film is finished it will need a coherent strategy when it comes to these issues. We will return to this subject in a more substantive way in Chapter 10.

▶ MICROBEATS: SCULPTING HUMAN BEHAVIOR ONSCREEN

In fiction filmmaking a lot of care has been taken to sculpt dialogue that has a particular flow, with opening salvos, specific interruptions, zippy one-liners, and concluding statements. Then the actors refine these beats and give them a living rhythm in their performance. But in documentary, it's up to the *editor* to isolate, identify, and create the beats. As you continue to look at the scene, you'll be trying to home in on the *specific* parts that can make it sing.

Take a clip from the short documentary *Never Been Kissed* about a young gay man named Soukey and his search for his first romantic relationship.[7] In the final scene, after our protagonist has concluded that meeting guys on hookup apps like Tinder may not be the best path forward, we see him discussing his conclusions with the filmmaker at a restaurant. In the raw footage, he talks for a while about his experience, then announces, "I'm done with the apps." His phone vibrates and he looks down at it briefly before looking back at us and reiterating his stance: "I'm done with the apps."

The meaning of this clip is entirely dependent on which portion is used. If it's included in its full duration, it would likely play as a straightforward declaration: Soukey has not found what he's looking for and is going to cancel his accounts. Yet in reality Soukey is ambivalent, and this is reflected brilliantly in his very quick reaction to the phone vibrating. So if the editor cuts right after Soukey's eye has been drawn to his phone (but before he returns his gaze to the camera), it creates a humorous and clever ending that suggests that even though he *says* he's "done with the apps," he may not be so sure. This fits better with the comedic tone of the film, and silently poses the question: if he's really done with the apps, why does he find it so impossible to ignore the signals of his smartphone? (Please see the tutorial video on "Microbeats" available on the companion website to watch the scene in full.)

To discover microbeats, it can be useful to look at great film and stage acting. Every memorable performance is made up of a series of beats, and the best actors deliver these beats in a highly sculpted way that somehow also manages to seem completely natural and spontaneous.[8] If you look at the scene in *Glengarry Glen Ross* when Jack Lemmon is asked to leave the home of a potential customer after delivering an unsuccessful sales pitch, you'll find several recognizable beats (Figures 8.2–8.5).[9] Lemmon is desperate for the sales commission and he has been working every angle he can think of to get this man to consider signing up for a parcel of land. Lemmon parries the man's rejections with increasingly insistent counterproposals and even sees if an insult might do the trick—"I don't want to tell you how to handle your wife!"—but eventually the man makes his final answer clear. "No, no, *no!* Do you understand? Thank you, no." (*Beat.*) Lemmon looks at the man, who will not return his gaze. (*Beat.*) Once the man does glance at him briefly, Lemmon looks away and then edges to the door being held open for him. (*Beat.*) The rain is coming down outside, and he turns for one last look, this time with an expression of bewilderment and hurt. The only thing left to do is to turn and leave.

FIGURES 8.2–8.5 Jack Lemmon facing rejection in *Glengarry Glen Ross*

These beats are also to be found in real-life performances by documentary subjects, but when we first apprehend a section of video, it often looks dull and unexciting. Nothing much seems to be happening, and it's unclear how or why the moments contained herein can be useful. But by watching a clip over and over we can start to pick apart its potential "in" and "out" points and see it as a series of distinct beats that could be plucked, harvested, and utilized in specific ways, and then joined together with cutaways.

A beat might be as short as a second or two, or it can be quite long, and one larger beat can contain several smaller beats within it. Look at an early scene in *The Iron Ministry*[10] and you will see a 90-second clip of a man onboard a train who is engaged in the action of rolling a tobacco cigarette to put in his pipe (see Figures 8.6–8.9). He takes several long looks across the train car in between each stage of the process, but continues rolling the tobacco the whole time. After he stuffs the cigarette into the pipe and lights it he finally looks in the other direction, at which point the director cuts to the next scene. Because of the continuous action of the cigarette rolling, the entire 90 seconds counts

FIGURE 8.6 A man looks intently at something off screen while rolling tobacco in *The Iron Ministry*

FIGURE 8.7 The man continues staring

FIGURE 8.8 After a long while, he finally lights the tobacco in his pipe

FIGURE 8.9 And finally looks away

as one complete beat, even though each look up from the cigarette could probably be used as a separate beat if there was a reason to do so.

Being aware of microbeats can open up possibilities for humor. A punchline becomes a punchline largely because of its status as the last utterance in the performance, and by editing a clip to conclude on a specific line, humor can be created. Consider a scene halfway through *The Waiting Room*, Peter Nicks' 2012 documentary set in the ER unit of an Oakland, California, hospital and edited by Lawrence Lerew.[11] The charismatic and empathetic nurse CJ is castigating a new patient for his use of foul language. "Stop all that cussing!" she says to him, giving him a stern but loving lesson as she takes his blood pressure. After admonishing him some more, she pauses as if trying to put two and two together, and asks with utter sincerity, "Are you a Scorpio?" The line is unexpected, and brilliantly funny. If the film had allowed her speech to carry on beyond this line it would not have had the same power, but edited in this way it becomes a laugh line.

Remember that shots themselves have beats as well, even if they contain no human subjects or obvious human drama. When a person or object crosses the frame in the foreground and then leaves frame, that action (starting with the empty frame and ending with the empty frame) could be a beat. At 1:05:30 in *The Iron Ministry*, an absolutely amazing shot develops as the camera is pointed out the window of a moving train. The shot begins with the frame being completely taken up by giant apartment buildings, transitions to reveal a highway, and then develops into a shot of a single motorcycle rider taking center stage. The traffic then slowly obscures the rider, and finally the apartment buildings fill the frame again. The entire section feels like one complete beat because of the bookending function of the apartment shots.

▶ BODY LANGUAGE

Great documentary film dialogue can be thrilling and satisfying but actions often speak louder than words. As you're viewing your footage and trimming it down, make sure you stay open to the fact that the best moments may be nonverbal.

Examples abound. Near the close of Chris Hegedus and Jehane Noujaim's 2001 documentary *Startup.com*, Kaleil Tuzman and Tom Herman, the two founders of the floundering Internet company govWorks.com, go to the circus with Tom's young daughter. It's a wordless scene composed of only three shots and no dialogue. Nothing needs to be said because the way the two men's bodies are positioned says it all: they are sitting side by side in cramped arena seats but are angled away from each other, as if the last thing they want to do is to speak.

In *The Bad Kids* one of the three main stories revolves around troubled teen Lee and his girlfriend Layla. They have a son together and are trying to make their relationship work, but Lee is often consumed by jealousy for her academic achievements. At a ceremony at which she is being given an award, Lee abruptly gets up and leaves, laughing derisively on the way out. In the following shot, not a word of dialogue is spoken but the meaning is crystal clear. We see Layla through a window, a sad, faraway look on her face. Lee walks right by her, a friend in tow, then exits frame. He comes back into frame going the opposite direction, still refusing to give her the time of day, and Layla, dejected, walks out of frame trailing behind him. Everything about their relationship is evident in this single shot: Lee treats Layla poorly, but she is resigned to it.[12]

One of the most devastating scenes at the conclusion of *Lost in La Mancha* is one in which director Terry Gilliam views dailies from his ill-fated shoot in a low-rent Madrid office building (see Figure 8.10).[13] He stands next to the projector, wordless, with a look of defeat that speaks volumes. Gilliam is normally a talkative character, so seeing him

FIGURE 8.10 Terry Gilliam in *Lost in La Mancha*

silent represents a startling change, and we can't help but compare his behavior to that in the beginning of the film when hope and excitement ran through his veins and he babbled constantly. Here, the dynamics of his behavior are working to tell the story for us. (We will have more to say about dynamics in Chapter 14.)

▶ VERITÉ CUTAWAYS

Once you have a reasonable idea of the content of the scene and have included the relevant beats of action, dialogue, and nonverbal body language, it's time to start stitching it together with cutaways. At their core, they serve exactly the same smoothing/joining function as they did in our evidentiary editing scene. The trick is to find cutaways that feel natural and appropriate. Listening/reaction shots are often good, and hopefully the camera person has shot a fair number of them so you have a choice of several. Cutting out to a wide shot that is either wide enough to obscure the lack of sync or has the speaking character with their back to the camera is another choice. Or a detail shot of something else that appears in the location—a sign on the wall, for instance—can work if it fits the theme. For scenes in moving cars, a shot out the window of the passing landscape is almost always effective.

Take a look at Figure 8.11 for an example of just how much of a verité scene is often covered in cutaways. This is a scene from *Precious Knowledge* in which the film's three main characters are introduced to some of the concepts of their Raza Studies classes in an outdoor assembly. All of the clips on V1 are sync clips in which we see the person who is speaking onscreen. Everything on V2 is cutaway material.

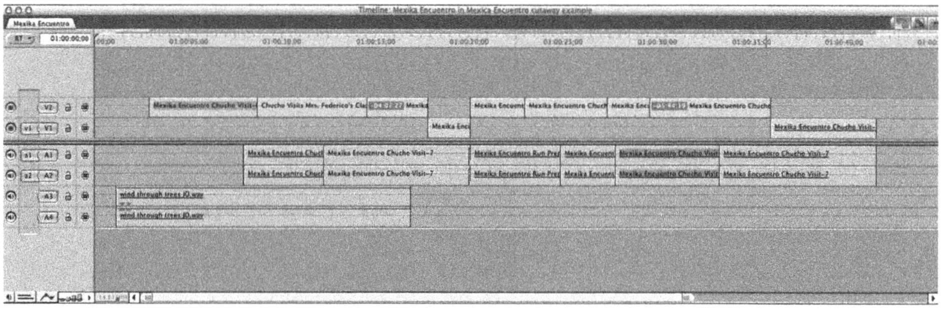

FIGURE 8.11 Cutaways dominate a verité scene in *Precious Knowledge*. All cutaways are seen on the V2 track.

As you can see, the majority of the scene is actually covered in cutaways. The words that the speaker is saying are not unimportant, but the real reason this scene exists is to show all three main characters absorbing the information and silently reacting to it. Cutaways can be fabulously expressive, sometimes much more so than the shot of the person who is actually speaking.

Once in a blue moon, it's actually necessary to construct a scene entirely out of cutaways in order to shoehorn in a passage of audio for which no usable sync picture exists. A terrific example of this comes from *Grey Gardens*, the landmark 1976 film about the Beatles, a mother and daughter pair living in semi-seclusion in a crumbling East Hampton mansion. The editing team of Susan Froemke, Ellen Hovde, and Muffie Meyer decided it was imperative to find a spot for the backstory of a secondary character named Tom Logan, a "pseudo-carpenter/maintenance man/cook/caretaker"[14] who lived with the Beatles for nine years. But for the majority of the scene the camera had not been rolling, and all that existed was the dialogue. So the first 38 seconds is constructed entirely out of cutaways: a tight shot of some questionable-looking appetizers that Little Edie is offering around the room, a medium of Big Edie listening while Little Edie speaks, a shot of Little Edie with her back to the camera, a tight shot of Big Edie playing with a flower in her hands, a shot of Little Edie with her eyes downcast listening to her mother, etc. The scene plays beautifully.[15]

(For a demonstration of the cutting of a simple verité scene from start to finish, please go to the *Documentary Editing* companion website and look for the "Cutting a Verité Dialogue Scene" video.)

▶ WORKAROUNDS FOR INSUFFICIENT CUTAWAY MATERIAL

What if you're stuck in a scene where you need to make an edit but you simply have nothing to cut away to? There is almost always a solution, so here are some things to try:

Combine Cutaways to Use Them More Efficiently

Sometimes the lack of a cutaway is simply due to the fact that the existing cutaways haven't been used strategically enough. By reshuffling them, you can solve the problem (see Figures 8.12 and 8.13).

Zoom in on the Existing Shot to Create a New One

If your film is shot in 4K and you are delivering in HD, you likely have significant latitude to resize images. But even if you're shooting in the same resolution that you're delivering in, a zoom of 20% or so is usually tolerated by the quality control departments at cable and network broadcasters. More than 20% may get you into trouble because your images can appear to have soft focus and may be noisy. However, if your film's visual style is sufficiently rough, or you have no other external forces calling the shots, you can often achieve tolerable results with as much as a 50% reframe and get yourself out of a jam.

Reuse a Cutaway You've Employed Earlier

It's surprising how well this can work. You would think that an audience would immediately spot the reused shot, but if it has enough visual complexity in it and it's used discreetly you can often get away with it. In my personal documentary *Finding Tatanka*, I used the exact same cutaway shot of my sister Laura folding her laundry only 25 seconds after I had already used it in the same scene, and in every single test screening it passed unnoticed.[16]

Use a Very Long Visual Prelap to the Next Shot

In this scenario, you cut to the incoming shot several seconds before the subject begins speaking on camera, letting the dialogue with all the audio edits from the current scene

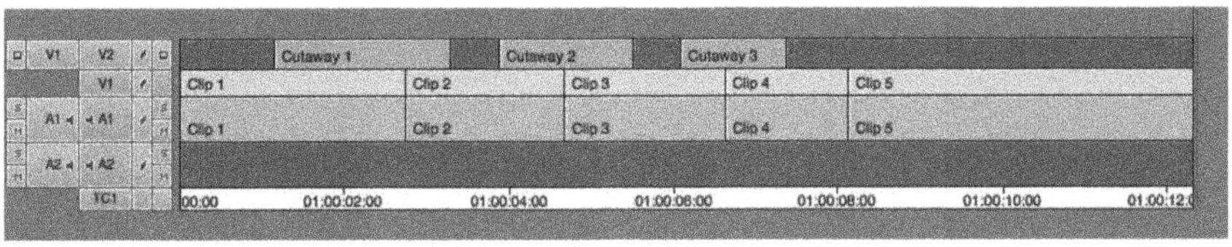

FIGURE 8.12 Inefficient use of the cutaways on the V2 track—too much cutting back and forth, no cutaway available to hide the jump cut between Clip 4 and Clip 5

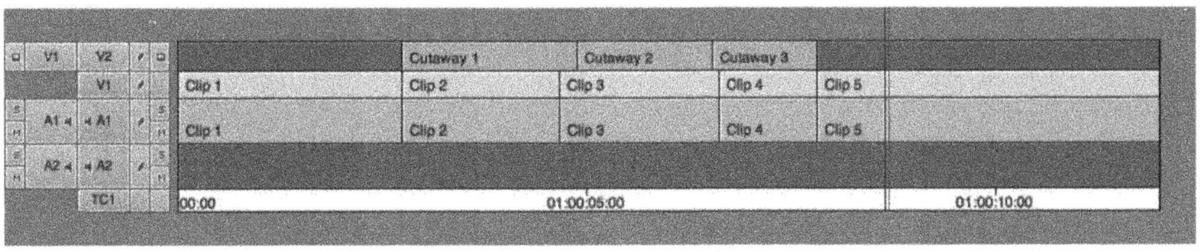

FIGURE 8.13 Cutaways on V2 have been consolidated

continue underneath. This technique has become more common lately; it works well when you don't mind having a slightly unconventional "multilayered" feel, and when you have footage with a long pause at the beginning to use in the incoming shot. Witness a key moment in the Ray Johnson biopic *How to Draw a Bunny* when you see gallery owner Richard Feigen staring silently off into space.[17] He begins speaking even though his mouth is not moving, saying, "I stopped showing [Ray's] work because I couldn't get any." Four seconds later, he raises his head and begins speaking on camera, saying, "because Ray would ask you to do all kinds of crazy things," as if he's just continuing his sentence.

A variation on this technique simply uses a piece of interview in which the subject is not speaking as the cutaway.[18] At 53:20 into *The Waiting Room*, you will find a very well-executed version of this technique. A patient with painful bone spurs in his back has a lengthy conversation with an accounting representative from the hospital regarding payment for his ER visit. As the conversation makes a turn toward its conclusion and the patient realizes the financial burden he's just assumed, three successive shots of the patient listening (and looking progressively more worried) are shown, even as his dialogue continues.

Use a Jump Cut

Jump cuts are not always a deal-breaker, and can be used very effectively if executed well. The trick to selling a jump cut is to get the rhythm right, and making the flow of words across the cut feel as if they continued as if nothing has happened. Witness the moment at 26 minutes into *The Central Park Five* when suspect Raymond Santana recounts his experience of being interrogated by Detective Umberto Arroyo on the night when a shocking rape and beating took place in New York City's Central Park. "And then this guy pulls up a chair next to me and starts to yell right in my ear," he says. A jump cut is made, and without skipping a beat, he continues his story: "So I have Arroyo here yelling at me, blowing smoke in my face, and then I have this guy on my side and he's yelling at me, and then they're like. 'You f**king did it . . .'" The story is so compelling and the delivery is so natural that we barely notice that two jump cuts have been made before the scene is through.[19]

For another great example, witness the frequent use of jump cuts in the celebrated 2016 ESPN Films documentary *O.J.: Made in America* (see Figures 8.14 and 8.15). In scene after scene, jump cuts are used to get from one point in a talking head interview to another. The image is resized, but always by less than 25% (which is not enough to turn a medium into a close-up), so even though the image is not a pure jump cut it still functions as one. Once again, the rhythm justifies the use of this technique, along with the fact that the technique is used so consistently that it simply becomes part of the style of the film.

FIGURES 8.14–8.15 A jump cut in *O.J.: Made in America*

▶ MAKING AMALGAM SCENES

In some cases an even greater level of flexibility is offered by the raw footage: one that will allow not only the use of one-off cutaways to join material, but will actually allow the merging of multiple scenes filmed at different times into a new one.

Consider in Figure 8.16 the first teachers' meeting scene in *The Bad Kids*.[20] Because production took place over two years with the same subjects repeating similar actions over and over again in the same locations, we took the opportunity to build this scene out of an amalgam of moments that happened over a large stretch of time. Footage taken from a shoot in January 2015 is shown on V1/A1, footage from May 2014 is on V2/A2, and footage from February 2015 is on V3/A3.

The scene begins with footage from January 2015 of Vonda introducing the concept of "adopt a student" and Ms. Hill saying, "did we find out what's going on with Jesse?"

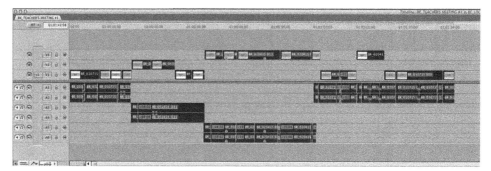

FIGURE 8.16 Footage from three different shoot dates combined in an amalgam scene in *The Bad Kids*

Vonda's response ("yes, he and his mom has been evicted . . . ") comes from a meeting that happened in May of the previous year, and then two cutaways are shown that come from the original January material. Miss Alexander pipes up with a story about a student named Maurice which comes from a meeting in February 2015, at which point the scene returns to the January 2015 material before going to a cutaway from February 2015 and concludes with more shots from January 2015. By the time the scene is over, both picture and sound elements have been plucked from three different shooting days that were as much as eight months apart, but the effect is of one continuous conversation.

Another example can be seen in the press conference scene that takes place at the outset of the landmark 1967 documentary *Don't Look Back*.[21] Bob Dylan gets off the plane in London to throngs of excited fans and immediately we find ourselves in some kind of a press staging area, where he is being peppered with questions. The interview continues on, but by the time it's over we've somehow moved venues to a hotel suite somewhere. The frequent use of extreme close-ups and the question-and-answer rhythm binds the two (or three?) scenes together, which play as one continuous scene.

▶ INTEGRATING AUDIO FROM UNRELATED SCENES

As you work on your scenes, you may find yourself wanting to integrate lines of dialogue or sections of interview material that don't seem to have a natural fit elsewhere. The elements in question may make your scene too long if used in a standard way, or they may be tiny bits of information that are necessary for the audience to know but would be boring to include as full interview/verité bites. This is exceedingly common.

In solving this problem, the important thing to remember is that *anytime a subject is not facing the camera is a potential moment to include an offscreen line of their dialogue.* Just as we are accomplishing the merging of discontinuous clips with a cutaway, we can also accomplish the addition of relevant lines whenever the opportunity arises.

Look at the opening of *The Waiting Room*. After establishing the location of the hospital and listening to the head nurse give a brief announcement to the room of patients waiting their turn to be seen, we see a series of short vignettes, each lasting 5–10 seconds. A young woman looks around and tries to count how many people are ahead of her in line; a woman explains to the guy next to her that her friend has something "stapled into his head"; an Asian couple at the counter explain to the receptionist that they don't speak English. At this point, we see an African American man walk away from the camera, a cell phone to his ear, as he says, "Oh man, I'm trying to get some help for my knee. My insurance ran out so I'm here today, but it's a process though, you feel me?" (see Figure 8.17). Given the context, it feels as though he must be speaking to a friend or loved one over the phone, but in fact this is a piece of interview material that's been grafted onto the picture in order to accomplish a succinct description of his malady and to keep with the verité-dominated style of the film. Here, audio from one source is joined with pictures from another source so that the amalgam can fit the filmmaker's chosen mode of address for the sequence.

A more complex example comes from the 2002 documentary I edited, *Lost in La Mancha*. As Terry Gilliam's production of *The Man Who Killed Don Quixote* has started to fall behind schedule and go over budget, the film's producers raise the idea of firing the film's First Assistant Director, Phil Patterson, as a way of righting the ship. The first part of the conversation between Gilliam and the producers was captured by the documentary crew in a hotel lobby, but its conclusion happened in a private room and was not recorded.

In order to piece the scene together and give the audience the feel of fully witnessing it, the directors found a sound bite from an interview with Gilliam in which he recounts, "I said to the producers, 'Well if Phil goes then I might as well go, too, because Phil has

FIGURE 8.17 Lines are inserted over a shot of a man with his back to the camera in *The Waiting Room*

FIGURE 8.18 Bernard Bouix reacts to Terry Gilliam's stolen offscreen line in *Lost in La Mancha*

been one of the few people holding this thing together.'" We chopped off the words "I said to the producers" and inserted the rest into the hotel lobby scene, as if Gilliam was actually speaking to the producers in the moment.[22] The stolen interview bite fits in perfectly over shots of the producers reacting (Figure 8.18) since Gilliam *was* giving them an ultimatum that they understood perfectly well, and a satisfying scene was born.

▶ MIXING EVIDENTIARY AND VERITÉ EDITING WITH THE "POP-IN" MOMENT

It's a type of scene we've all seen hundreds of times before: a character in a documentary speaks over verité material, narrating an experience they had or discussing how they feel about a particular topic. When they take a break from speaking, we "pop in" to that apropos verité moment, which takes over at full volume to illustrate the idea. This is a cross between evidentiary editing and verité editing, with the verité moments functioning as short interludes in a scene that is otherwise dominated by voice-over. The very ubiquity of this style masks some of its complexity, so let's dig deeper.

One good example comes from the Kirby Dick film *The Invisible War*, edited by Doug Blush and Derek Boonstra. The scene starts out in verité, as we witness U.S. Coast Guard veteran Kori Cioca's husband playing with their daughter at home.[23] They play for about nine seconds, and then we start to hear her husband's voice: he speaks about what a great mom she is as the scene continues with the sync audio track pushed to the background. We then resume full verité and witness Kori demonstrating her parenting skills with their daughter for about seven seconds before the sync audio dips again so that her husband can continue his narration. The ideas are guided by the voice-over, but at strategic moments the verité assumes center stage.

In the video tutorial "The Pop-In Moment" on the companion website, you will find a dissection of this technique as used in a scene from *Aging Out*, Roger Weisberg's film about foster care children confronting adulthood [24] (Pop-in verité moments are in **bold**.)

▶ Daniella Anderson walks down the street and enters a building, while the narrator says, "Daniella moved into her first group home at age 16 after being severely abused by her father. Since then, she's moved a dozen times, most recently to a special group home in Manhattan for pregnant girls in foster care called Inwood House." (19 seconds)

▶ **Daniella sits down at a table next to a young woman with a baby, and says, "Hi Grace, how ya doin'?" (5 seconds)**

▶ Daniella (voice-over): "For a long time I pondered over what decision to make" while camera pans from Daniella to her friend's baby. (5 seconds)

▶ **Daniella in verité: "She's so precious." (2 seconds)**

▶ Daniella (on-camera interview): "I felt like, 'I'm a freshman in college, I'm going to be able to work, I'm going to be able to do all these things,' and, boom, here's a responsibility." (10 seconds)

▶ **Daniella is seen next to her boyfriend Visna; she laughs. (3 seconds)**

▶ Daniella continues her thoughts in voice-over.

In this scenario, the film has given the audience a dynamic experience, shifting back and forth between hearing about a character with various forms of voice-over (which dominates the scene) and "popping in" for select moments of verité that illustrate the ideas being put forth in the voice-over. By seeing this "evidence," the audience feels like they've gotten an experiential taste of what the person is talking about.

▶ NOTES

1 Wiseman's first film, *Titicut Follies*, contains harrowing scenes with one character, Jim, who stares directly at the camera for long periods of time. In general, though, Wiseman's films take an observational approach.

2 Louise Spence and Vinicius Navarro, *Crafting Truth: Documentary Form and Meaning* (New Brunswick, NJ: Rutgers University Press, 2011), p. 19.

3 For a particularly outrageous example of this kind of strategy, check out the scenes of filmmaker Joanna Arnow working with her editor, who sits at his editing desk stark naked, in her highly enjoyable personal documentary *i hate myself :)* (2013).

4 Many passionate ideological battles over the relative merits of *cinema verité*, *direct cinema*, and the like were once fought in the 1960s and 1970s, but noted observational filmmaker Frederick Wiseman saw much of it as overheated posturing. In a 1971 interview he referred to *cinema verité* as "a pompous, overly worked, bullshit phrase" Frederick Wiseman, *Documentary Explorations: 15 Interviews with Film-makers,* G. Roy Levin, ed. (Garden City, NY: Doubleday, 1971), p. 318.

5 The ID scene runs from 52:07 to 52:50 in *Harlan County U.S.A.*

6 Perry's camera is thrown to the ground at 1:04:34 in *Harlan County U.S.A.*

7 Directed and edited by Elen Tekle and Stacy Howard, *Never Been Kissed* is available online at: https://vimeo.com/148516087.

8 In his book *Film Directing Fundamentals: See Your Film Before Shooting*, Nicholas T. Proferes defines an acting beat as "a unit of action committed by a character." He goes on to say that "there are literally hundreds of these acting beats in a feature-length film. Every time the action of a character changes, a new acting beat begins." As you will see later in this section, my term "microbeats" is somewhat less precise and more flexible, given that they are determined by their utility in the editing process. Nicholas T. Proferes, *Film Directing Fundamentals: See Your Film Before Shooting* (London: Routledge, 2008), pp. 25–26.

9 This exchange can be found at 39:10 in *Glengarry Glen Ross*.

10 This scene from *The Iron Ministry* begins at 9:13.

11 This scene begins at 44:50 in *The Waiting Room*.

12 Lee gets up and walks out at 46:31, and the scene concludes at 47:06, in *The Bad Kids*.

13 This scene from *Lost in La Mancha* occurs at 1:20:40.

14 BJK. "Other Staunch Characters." Grey Gardens Online. greygardensonline.com. Web, 2009.

15 The cutaway portion of the scene runs from 47:39 to 48:17 in *Grey Gardens*.

16 This clip is used at 57:17 and again at 57:42 in *Finding Tatanka*.

17 This moment occurs at 11:02 in *How to Draw a Bunny*.

18 Another example of this technique can be found at 1:05 in *How to Draw a Bunny*.

19 Another well-executed jump cut sequence can be found at 35:40 in *The Central Park Five*.

20 This scene runs from 22:05 to 23:35 in *The Bad Kids*.

21 This scene runs from 5:18 to 8:55 in *Don't Look Back*.

22 This scene can be found at 1:04:55 in *Lost in La Mancha*.

23 This scene from *The Invisible War* begins at 7:55.

24 This scene from *Aging Out* begins at 17:50.

9
Building Montages

A montage can be a hugely valuable element in a documentary. It can move us quickly through an era, giving us a feel for the "essence" of a time period without having to play it out in longer scenes. Or it can draw attention to the news coverage on a particular topic, raising the profile of the issue and making a point of its importance in the public eye. Or it can highlight the common themes or shared experience of a variety of people, building the case for a particular rhetorical point through repetition of themes, words, and phrases. Regardless of the specific function of the montage you're building, there is one common denominator: a successful montage *exploits patterns*. We've already explored how finding patterns is a fundamental part of documentary filmmaking in general; it is even more true of the montage, in which these patterns are distilled and refined into tiny chunks of meaning that flow into each other.

A textbook example of the "move through an era" montage is the venture capital sequence in *Startup.com*.[1] Like most montages, it's driven by music, in this case a cover of the Motown hit "Money (That's What I Want)." Coming off of a scene showing the last in a series of failed attempts to close a venture financing deal, govWorks.com cofounder Kaleil Tuzman states to his partners, "I'm tired of this sh**; I just want to raise the money and do the [expletive] thing." Then begins the montage:[2]

▶ Establishing shot of Hearst New Media Center (1 second)

▶ Man in suit shakes the hand of Kaleil's partner as Kaleil looks on (2 seconds, 22 frames)

▶ Kaleil gestures to a group of businessmen while making a presentation (1 second, 9 frames)

▶ Establishing shot of Flatiron Partners sign (1 second, 19 frames)

▶ Kaleil goes through a revolving glass door (2 seconds, 15 frames)

▶ Establishing shot of Sandler Partners sign (1 second, 3 frames)

▶ Wide shot of NYC's Central Park (1 second, 15 frames)

▶ Kaleil shakes the hand of a businesswoman (2 seconds, 11 frames)

▶ Three shots of Kaleil gesturing in a presentation room (1 second, 2 frames; 1 second, 7 frames; 1 second, 22 frames) (See Figures 9.1–9.3)

▶ Reaction shot of a businessman smiling (1 second, 10 frames)

▶ Kaleil smiling (1 second, 16 frames)

▶ Nighttime shot of NYC out of an airplane window (3 seconds, 4 frames)

▶ Kaleil passed out on an airplane seat, nighttime (2 seconds, 2 frames)

▶ Kaleil stretching on an airplane, morning (1 second, 25 frames)

▶ Shot of San Francisco International Airport as seen from a moving car (2 seconds, 7 frames)

▶ Kaleil walking through San Francisco International Airport (1 second, 21 frames)

▶ Three shots of Kaleil as seen from the outside of different conference rooms, making his presentation (3 seconds, 4 frames; 2 seconds, 20 frames; 1 second, 19 frames)

▶ Kaleil hugs his business partner Tom (1 second, 20 frames)

▶ Tom and an associate run to catch a subway (1 second, 26 frames)

▶ Three shots of Tom and Kaleil standing together among their partners, celebrating (2 seconds, 22 frames; 1 second, 12 frames; 1 second, 15 frames)

▶ Close shot of Kaleil shaking hands with someone (1 second, 8 frames)

▶ Shot of California freeway traffic as seen from inside a moving car (2 seconds, 26 frames)

▶ Shot of palm trees as seen from inside car (1 second, 11 frames)

▶ Shot of Kaleil and partners exiting Kleiner Perkins venture capital firm, smiles on their faces (7 seconds, 4 frames)

FIGURES 9.1–9.3 Kaleil Tuzman gesturing in a *Startup.com* montage

As the music fades out and the montage concludes, we join Kaleil in the back seat of a car on his cell phone, saying, "We closed 10 million of the deal yesterday."

In these 30 shots that play out over 63 seconds, note how small moments serve to summarize larger sets of actions and how shots often play out in series of three. There are three signs, three shots of Kaleil gesticulating, three shots of Kaleil making his presentation, and three shots of Tom and Kaleil enjoying themselves with their partners. Three is the magic number for montages as it shows a pattern without beating us over the head with it.

This montage serves the purpose of summarizing the actions of a few months' time and brings the story forward to the next phase, where govWorks.com has raised the necessary funds to start hiring. But while simply showing a single verité scene of Kaleil closing the deal could have moved the story to the same place, it would have provided none of the blood, sweat, and tears that make us root for the protagonists and raise the stakes on the eventual success or failure of the company. Seeing how hard Kaleil has worked makes his cause more sympathetic.

A montage can also be a much shorter affair, quickly summing up a point with the rapid-fire repetition of a concept or phrase. At about a third of the way through *20 Feet from Stardom*, we find this short montage:

Claudia Lennear (offscreen):	"The English rock scene was just a phenomenon."
Darlene Love:	"They were trying to sound black."
Claudia Lennear:	"Most all of them tried to sound black."
Darlene Love:	"And the only way they could get that sound? They had to use *us* to get that sound."
Claudia Lennear (offscreen):	"Like Led Zeppelin, for example. Robert Plant. Or even Joe Cocker."

Note how the phrase "trying to sound black" is repeated and how the validity of the concept is cemented by this repetition, even as the film moves quickly to advance the topic to its next big stopping point—in this case, the personal experience of Merry Clayton being a part of Joe Cocker's band.

▶ MEDIA MONTAGES

Repetition is also part of the media montage: a series of news broadcasters flood the screen in quick succession, each of their statements echoing the one before. At the base level, this kind of montage shows that whatever event is depicted is worthy of media attention, and therefore adds gravitas to the proceedings. These clips can also quickly summarize a concept or event in a way that we might otherwise have to do with narration.

The standard playbook for creating a montage like this is to identify the nugget of news, and then repeat it a few times in clips from different news sources. The first clip or two should be the longest, and give the most context for the information. Each subsequent mention of it should be shorter, and can also develop the concept and/or elaborate on it, ending with a final statement, which can again be longer.

The "we take these allegations very seriously" montage from *The Hunting Ground* is a textbook example of this.[3]

Unidentified university administrator #1: "Any allegation of sexual assault is something that we at the university take very seriously."

Reporter #1: "ASU issued a statement that stated in part that Arizona State University takes all sexual misconduct complaints very seriously."

Reporter #2: "The university says it's taking these allegations very seriously."

Unidentified university administrator #2: "We take all incidents very seriously."

Reporter #3, quoting UCLA administrator: "We take these accusations very seriously."

Reporter #4, quoting Occidental College statement: "We take reports like this very seriously."

Reporter #5, quoting Wesleyan University administrator: "They take all reports very seriously."

Unidentified voice, quoting statement from James Madison University: "James Madison University takes the safety and well-being of our students very seriously."

There is a lot of repetition in here; in a different context one might argue for slimming it down. But in this case the astounding similarity of the statements over a large number of different institutions is precisely the point, and the quantity is thereby justified. "Thank goodness you have these PR departments where everybody is spitting out the same phrase, because that gives us something that we can cling to to have a little bit of humor!" states *Hunting Ground* coeditor Kim Roberts.

Contrast this with the extremely short media montage about the phrase "eco-terrorism" in *If a Tree Falls: A Story of the Earth Liberation Front.*[4] It lasts all of seven seconds but it gets the point across beautifully. After a line of narration stating, "In the media, and in the courtroom, the question is debated," we see the following clips, each with a different slice of reporting from different television news outlets:

CLIP 1: "Eco-terrorism: terrorist acts by radical groups. . . "

CLIP 2: "Eco-terrorists"

CLIP 3: "Eco-terrorism"

CLIP 4: "Environmental terrorists"

FIGURES 9.4–9.6 The "we take these allegations very seriously" montage in *The Hunting Ground*

Another highly effective example comes from *O.J.: Made in America*. Legal analyst Jeffrey Toobin sets the stage for the montage by stating, "There was no Internet, there was no MSNBC, there was no Fox, there was *one* cable news network, and CNN covered the case gavel to gavel. This case was *everywhere*."

We then see partial clips from a variety of sources, which are cut off midstream with the added sound effect of an old-fashioned click of a television dial:

Tom Brokaw:	"The Simpson trial by any standard is a very, very big news stor . . . "
Dan Rather:	". . . In this country, the O.J. Simpson mur . . . "
Peter Jennings:	". . . O.J. Simpson trial toda . . . "
Matt Lauer:	"There are some big decisions to report today in the O.J. Si . . . "
Sam Donaldson:	"More on the O.J. Simpson story tonight on Nightline, and tomorrow night on 20/20!"

We forgive, of course, the fact that even in 1995 most viewers would have been switching channels with a cable remote rather than an actual dial on a television set, and that Peter Jennings and Sam Donaldson were both on the same network and would thus have not been seen in such close proximity to each other by someone flipping channels. This is a *simulation*, heightened by a skillful use of added sound effects, and gives an overall impression that the story is, indeed, everywhere.

When creating media montages, also consider whether you want the audience to look at the clip at face value (with little critical perspective about its origin or its ideological bent) or with more scrutiny. In *The Central Park Five*, New York City Assistant Chief of Detectives Aaron Rosenthal begins the film by giving a summary to a television news crew of a brutal rape that has been committed in Central Park. But the film's editor Michael Levine had access to the original unedited tapes; before Rosenthal begins, you hear him say to the camera person, "Ready?" The camera person replies in the affirmative, then Rosenthal proceeds. The difference is subtle but powerful: by including not only the clip itself but also the lead-up to it, we witness the authorities actively *performing* their roles for the media. Depending on your feelings about police, you may or may not feel more skeptical of Rosenthal having seen this, but regardless of interpretation it does give the moment a liberating "behind the scenes" feel. Even if you only include tiny bits of moments like this, you can change the audience's understanding of its context and cultivate a new level of scrutiny in their attitude toward it.[5]

Consider also that the audio and video portions of media clips can be broken up and used independently. In *Happy Valley*, a series of slow-motion shots of newscasters performing their stand-up intros outside a Penn State football game is the visual backdrop for a series of audio segments plucked from these same broadcasts.[6] By separating out the two streams of information and aestheticizing the visual through slow motion, a slightly dreamy and contemplative effect is achieved, inviting the audience to subtly question the whole affair as a bit of a media circus.

Or one can utilize media clips in such a way as to integrate them into the narrative as a sort of background "atmospheric" element. *The Central Park Five* deftly sketches the tragic events of April 19, 1989, blow-by-blow, and at one point in the story it's important that we understand that all five boys have been apprehended. But instead of bluntly cutting to a news anchor talking head, the film instead inserts the *audio* from such a clip ("The police now have five teenagers in custody") softly in the background over visuals of the precinct where they are being held. Here the film has taken the opportunity to let the information float into our consciousness subtly, as if we heard it almost by accident in a city that was inundated with media reports about it rather than having to jolt us out of the moment to a different visual environment.

▶ NOTES

1   This montage from *Startup.com* begins at 27:52.

2   *Startup.com* was shot at 30 frames/second.

3   This montage takes place between 35:24 and 35:49 in *The Hunting Ground*.

4   This montage takes place from 1:13:17 to 1:13:24.

5   The classic 1992 film *Feed*, directed by Kevin Rafferty and James Ridgeway, consists entirely of excerpts of satellite-feed footage of politicians and newscasters prepping and puffing themselves up just before their interview goes live. Jehain Noujaim's wonderful 2004 film *Control Room* is also concerned with this staging of opinion, and makes a powerful statement by showing behind-the-scenes moments from Al Jazeera's coverage of the Iraq War.

6   This montage runs between 2:04 and 3:43 in *Happy Valley*.

PART IIIB
Building the Rough Cut

► INTRODUCTION

> There's a writer named Anne Lamott who says in order to get started you have to write really shitty first drafts. And I think the same applies to documentary. When you have this massive amount of footage, you have to come up with your initial outline of how you think it's all going to come together. I know that whatever I come up with first is not actually going to be what works. But you just have to come up with your first big guess and be okay with the fact that it will fail, because you'll learn something from that.
>
> —Kim Roberts, ACE

There are several moments in the documentary editing process where the enormity of the task can easily overwhelm even the most seasoned practitioner, and building the first rough cut is often one of those times. It is very easy to become paralyzed by the endless number of choices that one could make about the flow of scenes, but every editor should take solace in the fact that they are not alone. Indeed, as legendary editor Mary Lampson relates:

> There's some times when I'm trying to put my first rough cut together where I say to myself, "Okay, what the [expletive]?" I have absolutely no idea how to make it

work. It used to really panic me and made me freeze up when I was younger. And so what I've learned is to just walk up the stairs to where my cutting room is on the second floor of my house and just sit down and start. The anxiety can be paralyzing, so just start cutting and put one thing after another. Just follow your gut and play with it.

Lampson's advice is solid: one has to *trust in the process* and just start putting scenes into a sequence (or index cards into an order on the floor) until a first rough cut appears. This cut is likely to be messy and awkward, but once you have it you will be able to see your work in a new way, and a new set of ideas will emerge.

At what point should you take this step of putting a rough cut together? For a documentary with at least some interview material, many editors find that the quickest way to build their rough cut is to start with the aforementioned paper edit. By cutting and pasting printed sections of the transcripts and using 3 × 5 cards to represent other scenes, you can create an initial, trial-run structure and then carry it out on the computer. As Kate Amend states:

> There are times where the director and I make 3 × 5 cards of the scenes and then put them up on the bulletin board—act one, act two, act three—and come up with the structure before we even start cutting.

Other editors are much more deliberate. Geoff Richman has a very organized, systematic approach in which he first refines all his individual scenes and only then makes the jump to building the rough cut:

> I call the first versions of my scenes ".1 scene edits." They are really just pared down select reels, and that's like the "radio edit" of the scene. And then .1b or .2 would be like a watchable version of that select layout, where I have cutaways and things are cut down to actually be playable for someone other than myself. So, my .1b's or .2's will just accumulate and once I have enough of those, then I'll lay them out for what I think the structure of the film should be.[1]

Mary Lampson wants to always be open to the more idiosyncratic connections between different parts of the material, and thus leaves herself open to building bits of potential rough cut material during the select reel stage:

> When I'm watching selects, if I have the impulse I'll jump out and change gears completely and just play with the material. And I actually begin to "cut" but not with the mind-set that I'm building an assembly. I'm just looking for patterns and trying to keep from getting trapped in a very linear way of thinking.

Regardless of which method you choose and how early in the process you start to build a rough cut, the important thing is to start *somewhere*. The following chapters delve into the many considerations one faces: choosing the type of footage to employ (Chapter 10);

how to master narrative logic (Chapters 11 and 12); how to work with supplementary elements like music, graphics, and titles (Chapter 13); and how to work with pacing, rhythm, and dynamics (Chapter 14).

▶ NOTE

1   A "radio edit" is a rudimentary first cut of a scene without any cutaways. It is so named because it works for sound but not necessarily for picture.

10

Choosing and Framing Footage

In Part IIIa we discussed the mechanics of how to put together documentary scenes. Now we need to look a little deeper at the relative value and potential function of the different types of footage that might be available to us. If we're choosing between describing an event via talking head interviews, showing it with verité footage, depicting it in reenactments, or summarizing it in a title card, how do we decide which way to tell our story? Every film will proceed according to its own logic, but let's start by positing that we should *always try to bring the audience as close as possible to firsthand experience.*

▶ A HIERARCHY OF EXPERIENCE

> I've found that the closer you can get to the source and the closer you can get to the event itself, the more interesting the footage is.
>
> —Aaron Wickenden

Look at Figure 10.1. It is a "hierarchy of experience," with the types of footage that have the most direct link with our characters' experiences listed at the top, and those that require an audience to hear about events secondhand listed further down.

Verité footage lets our audience see something play out directly in front of them—we witness the events ourselves. Archival documents are also direct links to experience but

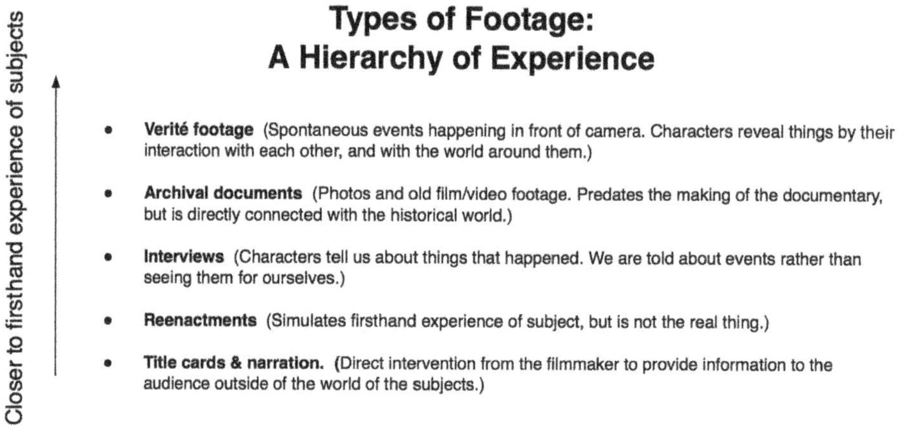

FIGURE 10.1 Types of footage classified by how close they come to firsthand experience

took place in the past. Interviews must *tell* us about something that happened through words rather than pictures in an account that is, by definition, after the fact, so they are further down the list. Reenactments help us *imagine* how something played out but can't quite have the same value as verité because they are staged for the camera. Narration and title cards are even further from that firsthand experience.

As you consider the various ways that a moment could be portrayed, a documentary editor would usually *favor firsthand experience* and use footage higher on the list so that they can let the audience experience the world through the eyes of their subjects.

As editor Kim Roberts notes:

> If you can tell it in verité, then the audience feels like they're the ones discovering it for themselves. That's the best way to get any information, because you've left something for the audience to figure out. If you can't do it that way, you might use a combination of verité and an interview where somebody is giving you their personal experience. Then there are moments when you just have to literally *tell* the audience a piece of information you want to get across with a title card, but you try to at least balance it out by having a lot of those higher quality discovering-it-for-yourself scenes.

In films where multiple types of footage are used, the climax almost always plays out in verité. Indeed, the powerful climax from Joshua Oppenheimer's groundbreaking 2013 film *The Act of Killing* plays out in a verité scene, and nothing substitutes for the moment when Heidi is asked for money to help her family at the climax of Gail Dolgin and Vicente Franco's *Daughter from Danang*, which also plays out in verité.[1] And while the "evidentiary editing" style is perfectly workable and tons of great documentaries have been made using it, it is almost always more credible when buttressed by scenes that play out in verité.

▶ A HIERARCHY OF INTERVENTION

Consider the chart shown in Figure 10.2. It is a "hierarchy of intervention" with the types of footage listed in order of how much intervention from the filmmaker is shown. Note in the chart that as soon as an interview occurs we've broken the spell of nonintervention because the subject is obviously answering a question from the filmmaker. Also note that using just the audio from the interviews (as suggested in Chapter 8) can be a subtle compromise, since we are never *visually* reminded of the artificiality of the scene. And an informal interview that's conducted while a character is going about the business of their day may be less intrusive than a formal interview that removes them from their world and puts them in front of a studio backdrop. Title cards and narration are furthest down the list, as they are a direct editorial intervention from the filmmaker *telling* the audience something. If we can tread lightly to avoid reminding the audience about the artificiality of the experience, there may be a greater chance that they will let down their guard and enter the world we're constructing for them. On this scale, verité footage again wins the day.

▶ THE LIMITS OF VERITÉ

Yet for all its many advantages, verité footage has some fundamental limitations. Crucially, it cannot let you into the *inner* psychological life of a character. If we forego any

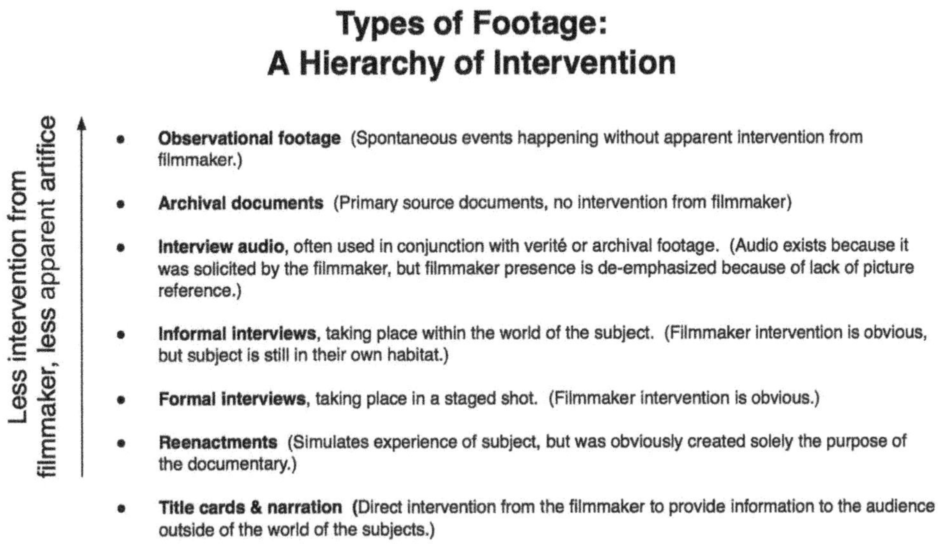

FIGURE 10.2 Types of footage classified by how much intervention from the filmmaker is felt by the audience

kind of intervention into the character's life we may cede the ability to hear them reflect upon their *own* experience. Note the challenges faced by editor Fiona Otway and directors Jessica Dimmock and Christopher LaMarca on their 2016 documentary *The Pearl* about a group of transgender women in the Pacific Northwest:

> The directors of *The Pearl* were really interested in telling a story that had no voiceover, and no interviews. Additionally, they wanted to normalize the idea of what a transgender person is by shooting a lot of footage of the women doing everyday, mundane things. We wanted it to be the purest, most observational film possible and yet it was a story about transgender women who are *hiding* their identities and dealing with feelings, thoughts and emotions that are very *internalized*, and would thus be opaque to the audience. How could we get a window into their thoughts and feelings? We had a challenge to keep to the directors' intended style while also being able to hear directly from the characters via voice-over, which let us know that their experience is actually very *different* from somebody else's experience. In the end we had to bring in a lot of offscreen voice-over to help the viewer understand where these characters were coming from and what they were going through, because it just wasn't clear from their actions and behaviors in the visuals.

Here we have a great case of a team wrestling their way through the pros and cons of different types of footage. In the end, they bent their original preference for a purely observational film to the reality that without interview audio (used as voice-over), the audience would have been shut out of crucial emotional information that helped make the film compelling.

Verité footage can also be of limited value when a film needs to summarize events or relay a specific piece of information. Consider the case of *Lost in La Mancha*. The directors' initial intention was to avoid "voice of God" narration at all costs because it broke the spell of nonintervention and initially seemed at odds with the considerable strengths of the verité footage. But this approach quickly proved too restrictive: there were moments when a brief bite of narration could neatly set up a scene or explain a detail that would have been too cumbersome to engineer otherwise. The directors were able to secure the talents of Jeff Bridges as narrator, whose connection to Gilliam as star of his film *The Fisher King* made his presence feel organic, and whose low-key drawl added a tonal element that would have otherwise been missing.

It's also important to note that elements like formal interviews and reenactments, which are in disfavor on the aforementioned charts, can be used to explore stylistic and thematic territory that would be impossible with verité alone. Errol Morris' *The Thin Blue Line* is a brilliant, groundbreaking film composed largely of these two types of footage. By offering overtly stylized reenactments and disconcertingly centered compositions with the subjects looking directly at the camera, Morris created a film that worked simultaneously on a number of levels: compelling true crime thriller, exposé on a gross miscarriage of justice, gorgeous aesthetic object celebrating its own artifice.[2] *The Act of Killing* is another film that would seem to blow apart the value systems behind the charts, especially the "intervention" chart. It features reenactments as the foundation of its story, and never lets us forget about the presence of the camera. Indeed, it uses the participation of the subjects in the production of the reenactments as a way to reveal the "truth" about their relationship with the 1965–66 massacres in Indonesia. What do the choices taken by the protagonists in trying to represent their own experience say about them and the society they belong to?

Thus, let's come around to a third chart (Figure 10.3) that attempts to give a more complete view of the pros and cons of different kinds of footage. Note that in many cases certain qualities are listed as both potential advantages *and* potential disadvantages, since it is the precise nature of their framing and juxtaposition that will bring meaning to them. (For instance, the intervention of the filmmaker betrayed by the use of reenactments is a plus in a film like *The Act of Killing* but could be a minus in another film framed as a pure verité doc.) A director may or may not have figured out a complete

Types of Footage:
Potential Advantages and Disadvantages

	Advantages	Disadvantages
Observational footage (Spontaneous events happening without reference to camera.)	• Direct, firsthand link to character's experience • Minimal reminders of filmmaker presence	• Must interpret character's experience solely by their outward appearance; no insight into private feelings
Participatory footage (filmmaker interacts with subjects on camera)	• Direct, firsthand link to character's experience • Interaction between filmmaker and subjects brings about dynamic situations and fresh insights into "truth" • Obvious intervention by filmmaker draws attention to the artifice of the enterprise	• Obvious intervention by filmmaker draws attention to the artifice of the enterprise
Archival documents (Photos and old film/video footage.)	• Direct, firsthand link to historical experience	• Potentially limited ability to conform document to film's style; may need to preserve original attributes in order for it to have integrity
Interview audio used to supplement verité or archival footage	• Can provide intimate account of personal experience • Audio contains fewer reminders of filmmaker presence than using full interview with video	• *Tells* us about events/actions rather than *showing*. We must take their word for it • By definition, it takes place after the fact
Informal interviews taking place within the world of the subject	• Can provide intimate account of personal experience • Can provide supplementary information about characters through environment • More 'natural' than formal interview	• *Tells* us about events/actions rather than *showing*. We must take their word for it. • By definition, it takes place after the fact • Filmmaker intervention is obvious
Formal interviews taking place in a staged setting	• Can provide intimate account of personal experience • Staging can give distinct aesthetic style to film	• Less 'natural' than informal interview • *Tells* us about events/actions rather than *showing*. We must take their word for it. • By definition, it takes place after the fact • Filmmaker intervention is obvious
Re-enactments	• Can bring subject's experience alive via visceral images • Filmmaker intervention can raise interesting questions if used carefully	• Filmmaker intervention is obvious, drawing attention to artifice of the enterprise
Title cards and narration	• Can quickly summarize information that would otherwise be too cumbersome to provide with observational footage	• Not "cinematic" • Editorial voice announces itself too loudly; unsubtle

FIGURE 10.3 Comprehensive chart showing potential advantages and disadvantages of different types of documentary assets

strategy for how to best exploit the resources available to them when the edit begins, and indeed the framing of a film often evolves through a process of trial and error. A film may choose to include the director as a character in the film, for instance, because it adds a crucial element of drama to the proceedings. (See the analysis of *My Kid Could Paint That* in Chapter 17 for a great example of this.) Or the opposite may be the case if the director's presence distracts from the drama with the main characters. Whatever the particulars of the individual case, the real trick in editing is to use your assets in a coherent, consistent, and creative way.

▶ **NOTES**

1   Or the moment when Tressa sends a text to her talent agent saying, "I'm done with porn" in a crucial sequence in *Hot Girls Wanted* (also in verité). The exception proves the rule in Robert Drew's *Crisis*, where the climactic showdown between Robert F. Kennedy and Alabama Governor George Wallace feels like somewhat of a letdown because the actual moment is not caught on camera.

2   It is important to note that Errol Morris has always resisted interpretations of *The Thin Blue Line* that pitch it as a kind of *Rashomon* equivalent, or as a postmodern argument for the ultimate unknowability of "truth." He is heard on Episode 9 of Barry Lam's *Hi-Phi Nation* podcast denouncing the dangers of this kind of relativism ("The Ashes of Truth." *Hi-Phi Nation*, April 18, 2017).

11

The Fundamentals of Narrative

The fundamentals of documentary storytelling are simple. Whether an audience consciously recognizes it or not, they expect to see three things: *characters*, *conflict*, and *progression*. Every documentary will utilize these three elements in different ways, and may emphasize one element more than the others, but they are always there.

▶ CHARACTERS

As you're trying to determine which characters will emerge as primary ones and which will be left on the cutting room floor, a simple fact stands clear: great documentary subjects have undeniable charisma and presence. They draw your attention. To use an old-fashioned term, they *hold the screen*. Think of Michael Moore, especially in his earlier films: love him or hate him, his sense of comic timing is genius and his sense of outrage is real. Think of Timothy Treadwell in *Grizzly Man* (Figure 11.1), whose very specific obsession/delusion was imbued with so much love and longing. Think of the wives of the coal miners of *Harlan County U.S.A.*, whose sense of conviction was so unmistakably strong. Think even of the chain-smoking psychiatrist in Frederick Wiseman's *Titicut Follies*, whose discussion with an admitted pedophile at the top of the film is so undeniably weird. Even in this film, which has no "lead characters" per se, there are still choices to be made about who to feature and who to push to the background.

▶ CONFLICT

Your characters will remain somewhat inert if they don't have something to push against, so *conflict* is the friction that creates heat for your film. Successful documentaries *set up*

FIGURE 11.1 Timothy Treadwell in *Grizzly Man*

a challenge at the beginning that shows a distance between what their characters have and what they want. Think of the NBA aspirations of William Gates and Arthur Agee in *Hoop Dreams.* Think of the need for Ravi Patel to marry in *Meet the Patels.* Think of the distance between the pastoral ideal of how we would like our food to be produced with its industrial reality in *Food, Inc.* To put it bluntly, without conflict we have anthropological recordings. With it, we have documentaries.

▶ PROGRESSION

Conflict alone doesn't produce a story. For that to happen, we need to have narrative development, or *progression.* We have been trained by years of movie and TV watching to assume that an action in one scene will have an effect on the ones that follow, and your audience wants to feel like they're moving forward rather than standing still. Thus, if you have sufficient footage with your characters over a period of time, you must sculpt their evolution and create a satisfying arc for them.

Remember that this development is a *construction.* If we were to watch all 10 hours of raw footage from one person's story, there would be so many competing subplots and conflicting bits of information that it would feel like a long and boring slog rather than an "arc." It's your job as an editor to use the power of omission to get this to happen in a satisfying way.

To summarize, you need to (1) identify your main character(s), (2) define their central conflict (*What is it that they're struggling against? What do they need/want?*), and (3) figure out how that struggle evolves over time and how it concludes.

▶ OTHER WAYS OF CONSTRUCTING PROGRESSION

Narrative progression isn't only created by developments in what *happens to* your characters; it can also come from how the *audience's understanding of them* develops.

In *Cartel Land*, our central character is Dr. José Mireles, leader of the Autodefensas in Michoacán, Mexico, who spearheads a movement to wrest control of the streets from the Knights Templar drug cartel. At the outset he is a homegrown hero, a kindly and charismatic 55-year-old pediatrician with rugged good looks, a heartwarming commitment to his wife and family, and an almost superhuman bravery. But as the film progresses, we learn more and more about his movement of organized vigilante groups that gives us pause: some of his compatriots are committing questionable acts and using their newfound power in unsavory ways. The line between right and wrong seems increasingly blurred. Then, Mireles' personal integrity is questioned in a stunning scene in which we see him flirting in a car with a much younger woman.[1] By way of explanation, his wife says in an interview soon thereafter, "Maybe the power gave him more opportunities to have affairs, because she isn't the only one. He's had women all his life; that's his problem."

FIGURES 11.2–11.3 Dr. José Mireles in *Cartel Land*. Kindly and charismatic, he is a family man and a folk hero at the start of the film. But he is later seen flirting with a much younger woman, and our view of him changes.

Given this statement, it's almost certain that his infidelities were known to the film-maker early in the filming process, and other scenes hinting at its manifestations were almost certainly available. But by waiting to reveal this information, director/editor Matthew Heinemann and his other editors Matthew Hamachek, Bradley J. Ross, and Pax Wassermann create an *arc of audience experience* even if it's not truly an arc of the character himself developing and changing. Somewhat miraculously, this ends up being just as satisfying. (For an example of this strategy applied to a short film, see my analysis of the film *Skip* in Chapter 18.)

A similar kind of development takes place with our understanding of Jerry Sandusky's relationship with his adopted son, Matt, in Amir Bar-Lev's *Happy Valley*. Near the beginning of the film we are made aware of the 45 counts of child sexual abuse that Jerry stands accused of in his capacity as a football coach, but we don't know whether anything inappropriate happened between him and Matt. Matt describes how he was taken into the Sandusky home as a boy and made to feel a part of the family, and all of the advantages that this afforded him. But he then adds a provocative statement: "I was loyal to the family, I wasn't going to betray him . . . and yet in the end, here I sit, betrayed by them all." While we are unnerved by the potentially creepy implications of his comment, we don't know the nature of the betrayal nor the full story of his experience. It is not until much later, fully 47 minutes into the film, that we learn that he, too, was molested by Sandusky.

This revelation is itself teased out in a careful way. "After the first day of the trial," Matt says, "I went into my bathroom and I looked in the mirror. I had to look at my own reflection and say, 'am I going to remain the coward that I have been, or am I going to risk everything and tell the truth,'" prompting us to wonder: *what is his secret?* Did he see the abuse of other children, or was he a victim as well? Finally, news reports drop that Matt, too, alleges abuse at the hands of his adopted father, Jerry. As in the *Cartel Land* example, the fact was there the entire time but the filmmaker created progression by drawing out its reveal.

It is not an accident that Andy Summers appears to be alone at his large Los Angeles home in the opening to *Can't Stand Losing You: Surviving the Police*, and that we never see him with a companion until the final five minutes of the film.[2] One of the main foci has been the pressures that being in the band put on his relationship with his wife, and we are inspired to wonder whether his marriage survived the rock n' roll lifestyle portrayed in the film. The payoff comes at the end when we are finally informed of their reconciliation, but this would carry little reward if their companionship had not been absent from the screen until then. Again, perspective is constrained, then liberated in a way that creates an arc of our experience.

One can also create an arc out of the audience's evolving understanding of the documentary's own artifice. Sarah Polley's *Stories We Tell* engages us with extensive use of reenactments, but they are not identified as such until the final 20 minutes of the film. We have instead been led to believe that these are pieces of archival footage, as we join

FIGURE 11.4 Filmmaker Sarah Polley directing a reenactment in *Stories We Tell*

her on her journey to find the true identity of her biological father. Having grown to trust the images, it's a shocking and satisfying development when this trust is broken and a new understanding is revealed, because it intersects productively with the film's theme: the stories that families tell about their history in order to elide uncomfortable truths.

* * *

In conclusion, it is essential to *limit* the audience's understanding at the outset. Information must be restricted; perspective must be constrained. These limitations inspire curiosity and generate desire. Giving less at the outset has several advantages, among them making sure you have more cards left to play as the film progresses, as well as sharpening the film's focus so that the audience's attention is not overloaded. Then you release the information in a precise and calculated manner, doling it out in small quantities at strategic moments like the drip of a faucet for a thirsty supplicant.

▶ TEXT AND SUBTEXT

All great films have the text (what the film is about on the surface) as well as a deeper subtext (what it's really about underneath). Ultimately, it is the subtextual elements of a film that will make it memorable.

In *Startup.com*, the drama on the surface concerns whether the internet startup govWorks.com will succeed, but the really meaningful story is about how the longtime friendship between founders Tom Herman and Kaleil Tuzman is tested and whether it will survive. In scene after scene, we see the love and camaraderie between the two men, but also the differences that may eventually doom their friendship. Tom takes a Zen-like view of the business, and repeatedly notes that even if the company fails the two of them will still have good lives and bright futures. Kaleil listens to this and is

FIGURE 11.5 Tom Herman and Kaleil Tuzman in *Startup.com*

silently outraged, taking it as a sign of Tom's inferior level of commitment to the cause. The subtextual drama between them rises as the battle to save the company also builds. Finally, at the end of the film, the subtext becomes the text as they discuss their relationship openly.

In *The World According to Sesame Street*, the surface drama is about whether the Sesame Workshop's plan to start up *Sesame Street* shows in Bangladesh, Serbia, and South Africa will succeed or fail against a formidable list of logistical constraints and challenges. But the subtext is more interesting, as we come to learn that the barriers to progress are often cultural and political, rather than financial or logistical. Emissaries of the Workshop are working not just to build literacy, but also to build tolerance and civic institutions in environments that are often hostile to them. The backlash of American politicians to the inclusion of a Muppet character with HIV/AIDS on the South Africa show serves to strengthen the point that the United States is not immune from this truth.

The Act of Killing is a devastatingly effective exposé of the impunity with which Indonesian war criminals still operate in the country, but its real subject is far more profound: what is the capacity of the human body (and soul) for self-delusion? Can the perpetrators of these horrific crimes ultimately live with themselves, or will the truth of what they did eventually consume them?

Building subtext is crucial for a film to have resonance beyond its surface topic, so keep your mind open about how you might create it as you look through your footage and put together your rough cut.

▶ EXPERIMENTATION

The approach to editing that I've presented thus far is one that values rigor, organization, the exploitation of patterns, and the single-minded pursuit of narrative drama.

But there is a danger in assuming that everything can be accomplished on the basis of pure logic. Some of the most satisfying moments in any film are the unexpected ones, and the ones that defy easy explanation. Humans are deeply contradictory creatures and the world sometimes works in bizarre ways; to scrub a film of all idiosyncrasies is to do a deep disservice to our art.

This is why it is important to experiment with lots of different ideas at every stage of the process, including when one is building the rough cut. As you grind forward in a quest for a logical narrative, remember that it can be useful to take a few moments to put some shots up against each other that have only *indirect* relationships (rather than direct ones), or to try out a scene order that may be a little unconventional. The magical thing about editing is that the results of these experiments are deeply unpredictable.

As Mary Lampson says:

> I think perfection is overrated. I've seen films that have been really, really good but imperfect. In a doc, the director didn't have total control. So if you artificially try to impose "perfection" onto it in the form of a happy ending or a too-simple conclusion you can lose something vital.

We will explore nontraditional documentaries that push narrative concerns to the background at the end of the next chapter.

▶ NOTES

1   This scene takes place at 1:17:40 in *Cartel Land*.

2   Summers' remarriage is revealed at 1:14:25, and we see him with his family at 1:14:50. The end credits roll at 1:19:05.

12

Working with Narrative

A documentary has a beginning, a middle, and an end. Each section has a special function, and must be approached in its own way.

▶ THE FIRST SCENE

The first scene of a documentary is a special moment. It's the only time in your film when you really have a blank slate. Your audience has no expectations beyond the ones that made them buy a ticket or click to stream the film online. While the first 5–15 minutes of a feature carry the burden of getting a certain amount of critical information on the table, the first scene itself is a place where teasing an audience with something idiosyncratic can be really rewarding. Thus, when you're building your rough cut you want to be on the lookout for footage where the *lack* of context can be productive or where your film can speak in purely visual terms.

Some films take this idea of provocation quite literally—look at the opening of *Finding Vivian Maier*, which begins with eight successive shots of silent interview subjects looking puzzled. On the ninth shot, an unnamed woman in a red sweater utters the word "paradoxical," and thus begins the utterance of a series of single-word descriptors for Maier, all of which make her seem intriguing and mysterious.

A close cousin to this approach is to inspire audience curiosity with a character's reluctance to speak about it. The first scene of Sarah Polley's *Stories We Tell* includes several clips of her subjects talking about how little appetite they have to engage her on the

FIGURE 12.1 Ginger Baker attacks filmmaker Jay Bulger in *Beware of Mr. Baker*

subject that she's about to delve into (which her father calls an "interrogation"). "I honestly need pills," says one of her siblings. "I'm sweating!" says another. Even though we've only been given a vague idea of what this is about, it must be juicy for it to inspire this kind of heartburn!

Others simply take an impactful piece of footage and run with it, such as when Rock n' Roll Hall of Fame drummer Ginger Baker physically attacks director Jay Bulger (see Figure 12.1) in the first scene of *Beware of Mr. Baker*. Or still others present a scene out of context and challenge us to make sense of it, as in Frederick Wiseman's classic *Titicut Follies*, when we are confronted with an awkward and surreal performance of "Strike Up The Band" by the members of the State Prison for the Criminally Insane in Bridgewater, Massachusetts. The fact that neither the location nor the participants have been identified only serves to increase our curiosity.

A good opening scene is one with attention-grabbing content, but also one that has dramatic resonance that transcends its origins.

▶ The opening of Heidi Ewing and Rachel Grady's *Detropia* begins with a conductor, as seen from the back, vigorously motioning to an orchestra at a moment of great drama in the music. While the music continues, the picture cuts to an African American man walking down a blighted city street at night, headphones on, walking away from the camera while he holds his hands up as if directing an orchestra himself. The linkages make for a striking juxtaposition, and also perfectly reflect the theme of the film: Detroit as a city of contrasts.

▶ The Maysles Brothers' *Grey Gardens* opens with mother and daughter exclaiming that a cat has gotten out, and then remarking on a raccoon that has recently damaged the ceiling. It allows the filmmakers to show a little of the ghastly state of their home, and the choice of dialogue at the end is perfect:

"We'll be raided again by the village of East Hampton—they can get you in East Hampton for wearing red shoes on a Thursday!" This sets up the theme of the film: two eccentric and reclusive women living as outcasts from their high-society town.

▶ Ross McElwee's **Sherman's March** also encapsulates the entire dynamic of the film within a single scene: we hear an authoritative narrator's voice start a historical discussion about Sherman's March to the Sea over shots of a map, only to have him abruptly stop and ask to do another take. It's not going to be a movie about Sherman's March, we quickly learn. Instead, it's going to be a movie about the making of a movie called *Sherman's March*.

▶ Morgan Spurlock's **Super Size Me** begins with a camp full of kids enthusiastically singing a song that goes, "Pizza Hut, Pizza Hut, Kentucky Fried Chicken and a Pizza Hut!" It is funny and a little weird, but the second-to-last shot is a giveaway for what's about to come next: the two kids in the shot are visibly obese, and one looks like he's so sluggish that he can't even finish the song.

▶ THE BEGINNING

Establishing the Problem

Stretching out beyond the first scene, most editors agree that building the opening 5–15 minutes of a documentary feature is one of the most difficult tasks of the entire endeavor. This is because of the old chicken and egg problem: we need to know the precise nature of the *resolution* in order to properly construct the beginning. Editor Kim Roberts learned this the hard way on one of the first films of her career:

> When I edited *Daughter from Danang*, we cut 32 different openings before we settled on the one we wanted! You think you know what the beginning should be because the director wrote the grant applications and shot it, but you don't really know until you're well into your second or third rough cut. And that's when you really know what that opening needs to be. Because what that opening does can be so different, depending on the film. It's not just about setting up the stakes and the issues, it's also setting tone, it's also figuring out a way to break whatever expectations the audience has about what the film is going to be. So I try to wait to build the opening until we're well into the cut.

When considering what kind of opening to construct, one must consider the distribution strategy and the ultimate exhibition environment. If this is for television, convention dictates that you need to create a strong "teaser," telescoping the entire drama of the film into a 2- to 3-minute montage so that your audience doesn't drift away to another channel. If it's a feature, one used to assume this was unnecessary, but with everything heading toward streaming the presumed attention span of a general audience has dropped.

So you face a major choice in the opening: *do* you create a capsule summary of the whole film at the outset? Every film is different, so it's instructive to look at films that concede the need to do this, but manage to pull it off artfully. Look at the opening sequence of Amir Bar-Lev's masterful *Happy Valley:* it opens with verité footage of patrons slowly filling the rolling fields of State College, Pennsylvania, as they arrive for a football game. As the crowds grow and the game begins, the shots segue into slow motion as we hear Joe Paterno wax poetic about the game. "College football," he concludes, "is something special, it really is. Hopefully we'll never lose sight of that, or screw it up." Paterno is identified onscreen with only his name (no further identification), and nothing explicit is said about the scandal that would ultimately bring him down. That drama is saved for the *second* scene of the film, an elegant montage of slow-motion newscasters onsite at a Penn State football game as we hear them summarize the outcome, which effectively acts as a teaser: "the [Jerry Sandusky child sex abuse] scandals led to the removal of Penn State's president, and head football coach Joe Paterno."

Regardless of whether or not you use a teaser, there should be a clearly defined problem/goal for the protagonist(s) within the first 15 minutes, if not much sooner. In *Murderball*, the "problem" is whether the United States can avenge its first-ever loss to Canada in the world championships of wheelchair rugby. In *God Grew Tired of Us*, the problem is about how the Lost Boys of Sudan, who endured an arduous 5-year journey migrating through Africa to escape civil war, will fare with the task of assimilating into the culture of the United States. In *Capturing the Friedmans*, we are provoked with the question of whether Arnold and Jesse Friedman are really guilty of child molestation.

Also in this first section, you need to set up the world where the film is going to take place, and take us there "both in the physical and the psychological space," as Mary Lampson puts it. "I think the geography of a place is a very important element in the beginning of a documentary," she says. Thus, we are not only being given raw questions but also a feel for *where we are.* "So it's the people moving into their college dorms in *The Hunting Ground*," says Kim Roberts. Or in the case of *Harlan County U.S.A.*, it's the insides of the coal mines and the hardscrabble living quarters where the miners and their families live.

Humanizing the Main Character

In order for the problem to be compelling, we also have to care about the person who *has* the problem. Thus, another crucial element of the beginning of the film is the introduction of your main character(s) to your audience. We are getting to know what they look like, sound like, and act like, and we are ideally being given a reason to empathize with them. As Kim Roberts says:

> People are getting to know a character, so you're figuring out the most humanizing way to do that. For *Food, Inc.*, one thing we wanted to avoid was the "talking head expert" thing. *Who is this person lecturing me about what I want to eat?* So we

FIGURE 12.2 Eric Schlosser eats a hamburger in *Food, Inc.*

started by trying to humanize Eric Schlosser by having him go and eat a hamburger and talk about how much he loved hamburgers, which was something we came to in the edit after everything else had been shot. We arranged another shoot so we could show that he is like us—he is somebody who came to this because he was curious about this thing that he loved.

Notice how in the above example, the director–editor team took a "devil's advocate" point of view when evaluating their own lead character. Instead of blindly assuming that their audience would love Schlosser as much as they did, they assumed a *skeptical* audience and acted accordingly. Taking a somewhat jaded viewpoint can be helpful, as it causes you to get outside the bubble of your own experience and imagine an audience that needs to be won over.

Establishing the Storyteller and Mode of Address

The beginning of a film also does something else that is crucial: it establishes the point of view of the film. Whose eyes is this film being seen through? Whose story is being told, and by whom?

Some films have a single omniscient narrator, which gives a clear and blunt answer to this question. With omniscient narration, it is the editorial voice of the film itself that speaks. In other films, the narrator may be one of the subjects of the film and the first person singular will be used, as when guitarist Andy Summers is established as the narrator of his own experience at the beginning of *Can't Stand Losing You: Surviving the Police*. The voice-over is given context via shots of him scribbling in his notebook, and we are meant to understand the entire rest of the film as originating from the diaries that he kept over the course of his career, and which resulted in the book on which the documentary is based.[1] Sometimes there is more than one narrator and a nested point of view, as when filmmaker Steve James narrates small sections of his film *Life Itself* even as Roger Ebert, the subject of the documentary, becomes the narrator for other sections.

The beginning also establishes *how* the story is going to be told. A consistent mode of address enables the audience to feel like they know what to expect from the rest of the film. As Fiona Otway relates about cutting *The Pearl*:

> We worked so hard on the opening scenes for that film it was a really tricky opening for us. One of the things we had to figure out was the issue of how much the film was going to use verité as its primary device versus how much it was going to lean on voice-over. In our early drafts of the film, the opening scene was all verité and there was no voice-over until about 20 minutes in the film. When the voice-over appeared in the film, it was like "whoa, where did this come from, I wasn't ready for this!" Eventually, through many stages of revision, we went back to the opening scene and brought voice-over into it. This felt like a compromise to us in some ways. But we knew we needed to do it in order to establish a language for the rest of the film, which was going to consistently employ voice-over as a device.

Thus, the beginning of a film also establishes a template for what types of footage will be employed, and what relationship that material has with the viewer. You want to set expectations in a way that the rest of the film can deliver.

Extra-Filmic Considerations

A documentary never exists in a vacuum. From the poster graphic to the trailer to the capsule summary seen on the film's website, there is a lot of information about the subject matter of your film that an audience knows before they enter the theater or press play on their laptop.

You should not ignore this fact when cutting your film. It can solve basic issues for you, absolving you from the obligation to overhype your material and from needing to lay out information that the audience may already be familiar with.

Consider the marketing for the film *The Waiting Room*. The tagline, as seen in the film's poster (Figure 12.3), is "24 Hours. 241 Patients. One stretched ER." We are thus invited to understand the film as an account of a single 24-hour period in the life of one emergency room unit, which relieves the pressure of the film to state this explicitly.[2]

In *Lost in La Mancha*, we struggled with the issue of how much we needed to tell the audience in the opening minutes about what had happened to Terry Gilliam's original production of *The Man Who Killed Don Quixote*. How can we convince them to stay in their seats for the juicy part of the film when the production goes horribly wrong? Should we flash-forward to Johnny Depp's entrance so they'll stick around to see him? How do we explain the basics of the film?

At a certain point in the editing process we came to the conclusion that an audience coming to watch the film would have likely read a blurb about it that would give them at least the following information: this was a documentary that showed the demise of a big-budget Terry Gilliam film starring Johnny Depp. Thus, our opening sequence did *not* have the explicit burden of giving such information.

FIGURE 12.3 Promotional poster for *The Waiting Room*

▶ THE MIDDLE

Moving beyond the beginning of the film, one of the principal challenges of building a structure for a documentary is deciding which storyline to feature, and how to use it in a way that will successfully anchor the rest of the film.

Anchor with Narrative

In some cases there is enough compelling material to build the film around a single drama. *The Queen of Versailles* has enough footage with Jackie and David Siegel to build the entire film around their struggle to build one of the largest single-family residences in the world amidst a financial crisis that threatens their extreme wealth. And *Burden of Dreams* is exclusively about Werner Herzog trying to make his film *Fitzcaraldo*. But take heart in the fact that it is common for a film to have only a limited amount of material from its primary storyline.

Filmmaker James Longley solved this in a unique and compelling way in his Oscar-nominated *Iraq in Fragments* by splitting his film up into three completely separate stories told in succession—"Part One: Mohammed of Baghdad," "Part Two: Sadr's South," and "Part Three: Kurdish Spring." But a more common strategy is to *anchor with narrative* by weaving the "A" story throughout the entire film while cutting to secondary stories along the way. With this strategy, you are building one core story and embroidering around it. In so doing, you are also often showing the linkages between the "A" story and the other stories, and between the micro and the macro picture of the issue at hand.

In *The Cove*, the 2010 Academy Award-winning documentary edited by Geoff Richman, well under a third of the total running time is actually spent on verité of the planning and execution of the mission to expose the dolphin slaughter in Japan.[3] The rest of the film is devoted to giving the history of the whaling industry, the backstory of its main character, and numerous other segments devoted to secondary characters and related topics. But in a well-structured film like this one, this lack of constant forward motion is not a drawback since every bit of the extra material strengthens the emotional impact of the spine.

Take *The Hunting Ground*, which uses the redemptive story of Annie Clark and Andrea Pino in their transformation from sexual assault victims to highly effective activists as its "A" plot line while weaving multiple other stories into the narrative. The film begins with the disturbing accounts of their assaults, ends on their triumphs, and features them throughout the film, but their scenes make up only 33 minutes of the 104-minute film (see Figure 12.4).[4]

The triumph of the editing is in the fact that the film feels stronger (not weaker) because of the multiple other characters whose stories populate the film. It also helps that there is strong emphasis on the recurring imagery of their self-made map of the United States featuring known campus sexual assault survivors represented by brightly colored sticker dots. This image appears in the film several times, each time with more dots attached to it, and represents their growing understanding of the pervasiveness of the problem and also their inclusion in a wider network of survivors.

FIGURE 12.4 Structural diagram of *The Hunting Ground*

FIGURE 12.5 Structural diagram of *The World According to Sesame Street*

The same "anchor with the 'A' story" strategy is employed in *The World According to Sesame Street*, coedited by Kate Amend, Johanna Demetsakas and Alicia Dwyer, in which the Sesame Workshop's project to mount a new show in Bangladesh serves as the "A" story. Collaborations in Kosovo and South Africa serve as secondary stories, with small segments shot at the New York headquarters inserted in between (see Figure 12.5). Each country features its own story, but also has themes in common with the others.

This approach made even more sense because the Bangladesh story was the one that took place over the longest period of time. "It played out over a period of a year and a half or so, with breaks in the shooting from time to time, so there were moments when we could naturally go away to another story and then would pick up the Bangladesh thread two months later," says Amend.

This spreading out of the "A" story is also used with the storyline of Daniel McGowan in *If a Tree Falls: A Story of the Earth Liberation Front*, directed and coedited by Marshall Curry. McGowan was but one of over a dozen core members, but it is his story that grounds the film and shows the personal consequences of the actions of the group.

To summarize, the "anchor with narrative" strategy is as follows:

▶ After the opening, **lead with the "A" story** to indicate its primacy and to provide a strong narrative and emotional hook.

▶ **Close with the "A" story,** giving further symmetry to the structure to the film.

▶ **Intersperse the other remaining "A" story material throughout the duration,** determining through trial and error how long the audience will tolerate being away from it in any given stretch without feeling like the film is losing its way.

Eat Your Vegetables

Almost inevitably, there are pieces of historical information and/or bits of backstory that are vital to get across to the audience but which are somewhat less gripping than the main narrative at hand. Somewhere along the way, you've got to insert the three minutes of archival stills that will explain the background of this or that character or give a condensed history of an issue. For lack of a better analogy, let's call these the broccoli and the spinach of the documentary meal: good for you, but not immediately appetizing since on first inspection they only provide nutrition (context and background), not juicy bits of meat and fat (emotional drama and narrative development).

The key to presenting these sections is to tuck them into the narrative in places where your audience won't mind them. Unlike a history textbook that starts at the beginning and moves methodically forward, a documentary almost never moves linearly throughout its full running time. Instead, we want to get things moving right away with scenes that immediately march the narrative forward, and then wait for a later moment to drop the history segments in. The idea is to reassure your audience by showing them right away what the main story is. Once they are invested in this, they will be only too happy to take a pause so they can learn more about *why* elements in the present are happening as they are. In this logic, these "vegetables" will deepen and strengthen the story that's already barreling forward, rather than acting as an impediment to its progress.

Examples are numerous. *Cartel Land* waits until over 14 minutes into the film to give us a history of the violence done by the drug cartels that dominate its narrative. *The Armor of Light* waits until 51 minutes into its 88-minute running time to give us the backstory for its protagonist, Rob Schenck. And in *The Cove*, the backstory of protagonist Ric O'Barry is divided into numerous small sequences that are woven throughout the entirety of the film's running time.

Delaying Gratification

There is something irresistible about a good story. We read thrillers, binge-watch TV series, and click on news stories because it's pleasurable to be teased with a question and then find an answer. Good documentaries create this narrative tension not only in big, obvious ways (via the narrative arc) but also in small ways in every single scene, and often even within individual shots. We *always* want to be on the lookout for how to generate narrative pleasure. Here are some ways to accomplish this:

Complicate the resolution

If there's one thing that can kill a film, it's having a resolution that comes too easily. If a character reaches their goal without really working for it, or if an issue is resolved without any conflict, an audience feels let down. So take every chance you get to build obstacles and roadblocks for the resolution of your stories.

In *Precious Knowledge*, we set up a problem–solution structure by showing the pitiful graduation rates among Latino teenagers in the United States and then introduced our audience to three Latino characters, each of whom has their own reason for being at risk of dropping out at Tucson High School. A potential solution to the problem is a new program focusing on a culturally relevant curriculum for Latino youth. But for the program to seem credible, we couldn't just depict it as being an instant success. If it "worked" right away, then our audience might question its validity or fail to see the problem as being sufficiently severe. Thus, we set out to make each character's "conversion" as interesting and thorny as possible.

We had a particular issue with our character Pricila, a young woman whose raw footage initially seemed to lack any drama in this department because she was such a fan of the program. But as we searched, we eventually found what we needed: a section in which she dwells on her initial skepticism.[5] "At first I didn't really accept it," says Pricila. "All the posters up on the wall, I didn't know what most of them meant." Now we needed to illustrate her moment of conversion, but we didn't have footage from her first days in the program. After much searching, I found a verité scene in which Pricila wears a characteristically serious expression on her face (see Figure 12.6), and then breaks into a reluctant smile after an amusing comment from one of her teachers; I then found another anecdote from her interview in which she praised the sense of humor of that same teacher. Matching these two clips together with a third element—her teacher characterizing her as a "tough kid"—led to the result we needed: a carefully crafted "conversion" moment in which we see a "tough kid" finally open up and begin to enjoy her education. Without this moment of difficulty, the success of the program would not have seemed as interesting or as important.

Harness the Power of the Reveal

Every shot is composed to focus our attention on its subject. But before that focus is made clear, you can use the *development* of a shot (a pan or a reveal of some kind) to inspire curiosity. By giving the audience visual information that is intriguing but *partial*, we can mildly frustrate them and inspire curiosity. This can be a very small reveal that takes only a second or two to play out, or a more protracted one that develops over a longer period of time.

A simple example of this takes place during the first minute of *The Waiting Room*. The film opens with a wide shot of passengers on a city bus as we see the world pass by outside. It then cuts to an exterior shot of the bus crossing the frame. When the bus leaves the frame, it reveals a bright "EMERGENCY" sign in front of a hospital (see Figure 12.7).

FIGURE 12.6 "Tough kid" Pricila in *Precious Knowledge*

FIGURE 12.7 Bus exits frame and reveals "Emergency" sign in *The Waiting Room*

The moment passes without notice, but this second shot is made significantly better because of the reveal. Instead of just cutting straight to the sign, we have been made to *wait* a couple of seconds, and this tiny problem–solution moment makes the viewing more interesting. It also has the added benefit of linking the two bus shots.

For another example, consider the shot of pieces of meat hanging in a train vestibule near the beginning of *The Iron Ministry*.[6] When this shot hits the screen, we have no idea what we're looking at because the shot is such an extreme close-up and is so abstract. It looks like folds of deep red flesh, but we have no idea what it really is or where it's situated. As the shot continues, it widens out and tilts down, revealing 30 seconds later that a small-time food vendor is using this tiny area between two train compartments as a place to hang his raw wares.

Anchor Your Narrative Beats with Verité or Archival, then Follow with Interview

When a new development occurs, don't just tell it to us right away via talking head interview. Instead, begin with a piece of verité or archival footage, giving your audience the chance to apply their curiosity to it. After letting them observe what's happening for themselves, then follow up with interview bites that will explain it further.

Geoff Richman explains the technique like this:

> If you're just feeding information, the audience will take it passively and process it intellectually. Whereas if you can somehow get them to say, "What do you mean by that?" or make them confused by something for just the right amount of time, then they want to know a certain piece of information that you can provide them.

FIGURE 12.8 *Into the Arms of Strangers*

Into the Arms of Strangers: Stories of the Kindertransport has multiple moments like this. At 17:00 a new scene begins abruptly with the violent sound of glass breaking and a series of four archival stills showing vandalized windows and storefronts. We are intrigued but unsure exactly what is going on. Following this, we see the image of someone on a bicycle (see Figure 12.8) and hear the sound of a loose fender rattling against a wheel. Still we don't know the relationship between the windows and the bicycle. Then an interviewee explains, "I took my bicycle and went to school as always, [and] there was no Jewish business that I passed that wasn't broken into." By the end of the sentence the question has been answered and the story is clear. Kate Amend, who edited the film, says, "I always think of it as *show, then tell.* Signal it visually first and then bring in the dialogue that refers to it or explains what the story is."

Another subtle example of this technique takes place at 10:45 in *The Waiting Room.* We've just been introduced to a young African American girl with a fever and a swollen throat who is brought into the ER by her father. After a pause of several minutes to cut away to another story, we return to her room and see the girl with her father again. But this time there is also a woman present; the woman disputes the father's claims to the doctor about the girl having a cough. "No, she doesn't have a cough," the woman explains in an irritated tone of voice. Now we're curious: who is this woman, and what's she doing here? Is this the girl's mother?

At precisely the moment when our curiosity might turn to confusion, interview audio from the father reasserts itself as he explains, "I have visitation for my children, and I was supposed to show up yesterday for them. I didn't even have money to get out there to come see 'em." Now we have our suspicions confirmed, and the situation becomes both more clear and more complex as we learn that the parents are divorced.

In the above examples, the film has invited curiosity by posing challenges to the audience via the presentation of new information that is deliberately partial. This then triggers a ping of curiosity in the audience, which can in turn be quickly fulfilled. As Aaron Wickenden puts it, "What is the audience curious about? What kinds of questions are we generating in the audience's mind? That should propel you to the next piece of information that you give."

Use Visual Metaphors and Visual Progression

Narrative arcs can be built with big, earth-shattering developments, but they can also be built with small, subtle shifts. One often-overlooked way to create a satisfying sense of progression is to build multiple small developments in the visual metaphors being offered by the film.

Happy Valley uses recurring shots of a sprawling field of State College grass to act as a bellwether for the level of intensity the fans feel for their Penn State football team. The film begins with shots of these rolling, green hills, populated by thousands of tailgaters settling in for a football game (see Figure 12.9).

The hustle and bustle of this scene on the grass is one we get used to as the film goes on. But when we return to this same site halfway through the film, once the Sandusky child sexual abuse scandal has rocked the football program and caused it to be sanctioned by the NCAA, this time the fields are empty (see Figure 12.10). There is no hustle and bustle, and things feel eerily quiet. Without uttering any words, the film has managed to make a statement that is powerful precisely because it is so simple.

In reality, Penn State continued to play its regular season schedule even though it was banned from bowl games, and the fields were likely still full of fans. But the *feeling* in the film is that football as we know it has ceased to exist. Near the end of the film, after

FIGURE 12.9 The Penn State tailgate in good times in *Happy Valley*

FIGURE 12.10 Penn State in mourning in *Happy Valley*

FIGURE 12.11 The Penn State tailgate shows signs of rebirth in *Happy Valley*

the scandal has faded into memory a bit and the school is trying to construct a powerful new myth to replace the old one that had been shattered, another tailgate is seen (see Figure 12.11). This time it is also populated, though perhaps less so than in the good old days, as if the fans are making their first tentative steps toward resuming the old traditions.

Another example comes from *The Iron Ministry*. In a memorable scene about a third of the way through the film a train employee walks the aisles, selling snacks and bottled water from a cart. He gets six different requests for instant noodles, and by the end of the scene it becomes a bit of a running joke as he has to keep telling them that he's run out. Later, one of the final shots of the film shows a man silently crouched in the vestibule between train cars eating noodles out of an instant container, as if he came with his own supplies or has managed to persuade the vendor to part with an emergency stash. It's a very small nugget of narrative completion, but it's a satisfying one for all the perceptive viewers who find it.[7]

Just as you want to delay gratification and limit perspective in the narrative, so, too, should you provide a clear, logical, and restrained approach to the flow and progression of your visual ideas. Imagine the opening of a film: within the first five minutes, it blasts from talking head interview to a grainy archival still, to stylized reenactment, to handheld verité, to animated graphic, to title cards, and then back to more interview material. At this point the film has no more visual surprises up its sleeve, and nothing left to reveal from a stylistic point of view. The audience may be *stimulated* by all of the various images, but there's a strong case to be made that they've also been exhausted by them.

Instead, your cut should create a *flow* of visual ideas that introduces each one patiently and with a logic that ties into the film's unfolding tone and narrative. Each type of footage can be associated with a new development in the audience's understanding, and revealed at an opportune moment.

One of the opening scenes from *The Cove* is a fascinating example of how this logic can be developed in the course of editing. The film begins with shots of a lighthouse on an ocean bay at night, followed by an emergency vehicle passing a car that sits idling on the road. Ominous music is cued, and we cut inside the car to see spooky night-vision shots of four men loaded up with gear like a Special Operations team. The following voice-over is heard: "I do want to say that we tried to do this story legally. I thought of all the possibilities of what could happen, and it kept me up at night." Suspense successfully created, the opening credits of the film roll and we are then delivered into the first post-credit scene of the film. *The Cove* editor Geoff Richman explains how it plays out:

> We're In a car seeing Ric in the driver's seat and in order for the scene to work, we had to preserve the tone of mystery we just created. So Louie [the director] is talking in voice-over, narrating Ric's story over verité shots of Ric driving. Anytime Louie was talking it came from the sit-down interview but we held back from *showing* it because just cutting to him in the formal interview would break that tone immediately. So instead, we're *using it as voice-over*, but at some point you have to understand who's talking. To solve this, we found a couple shots in the car where Louie had swung the camera in his own direction so you see him shooting himself in the passenger seat. So you conclude, "Oh, this is the guy who's talking because you know that he's with Ric" but you don't have to break the mood by going to him on camera in a boring office somewhere. The mood is preserved.

Sometimes the visual logic of a scene can be created just by concealing and revealing geographical information in a deliberate way. At the beginning of *Tell Me Do You Miss Me*, a documentary I edited for director Matthew Buzzell about the indie rock

band Luna's final tour, we began with the final song from the band's farewell performance at the Bowery Ballroom in New York City. But we decided to hold back on
showing the big wide shot of the band onstage amidst a sea of devoted fans. Instead
of revealing the band onstage right away, the first two minutes of the song are given
to crosscutting between three separate scenes of each of the band members finishing
up their final preparations at home and making their way through the snowy city to
the venue. When they do reach the venue, we enter *with* the band members and head
backstage. The Bowery Ballroom is only revealed from their point of view as they come
out onstage, the audience a black void amidst the spotlights. Even now, we do not see
a wide shot of the band onstage. As we finally cut to sync sound, we see each of the
members of the band playing in single medium and close-up shots (one shot for each
member), and then finally, on a big power chord, do a shock zoom out to the payoff,
a satisfying wide shot of the band onstage in all their glory, with the audience rocking
out. By building a progression to the way the geography is revealed, we created a sense
of flow and anticipation that would not have been possible if the various elements had
been used willy-nilly. You might say we were using the visual logic of *Stop Making Sense*,
the impeccable Talking Heads concert doc by Jonathan Demme that waits until the
penultimate song to finally show full shots of the auditorium.

A final example of this strategic approach to the revealing of visual information comes
in the form of a description of the opening to *Finding Vivian Maier*, the 2013 film
about an enigmatic photographer whose life story is slowly uncovered by director John
Maloof. Editor Aaron Wickenden explains:

> One of the things we asked ourselves as we were putting the film together was, "At
> what point should the audience see what Vivian looked like?" Because she was so
> private, and because the director's journey of discovery about her was so fraught
> with anticipation, we had to consider this really carefully. In the end, we don't actu-
> ally show you a picture of Vivian until over 16 minutes into the movie. Delaying that
> information was both true to John's experience as he was doing the investigation,
> and also enhanced the narrative drive.

▶ ENDINGS

Endings are difficult. The perfect one will be conclusive but not overbearing, appropriate but not obvious. Consider the fact that *simply by its placement, a scene at the end
of a film will take on special significance.* Instead of being just another clip, it suddenly
is elevated to the status of a "wrap-up" comment, so trying to drive your point home
too strongly in the ending may actually backfire, leaving the audience feeling like you're
trying too hard. It's also important to note that the last scene of a film is not the same
thing as its conclusion. The conclusion usually comes before this, as the film reaches its
climax and answers the questions that were asked at the outset. The last scene itself is
often something of a coda, a final note that can give us one more thing to think about,

or add a little grace note, and it needs to feel consistent with the tone and character of the rest of the film.

This special spot needs to be treated carefully. If the long soliloquy by the young boy on the train in *The Iron Ministry* ("those who have explosives with them please hurry aboard and ignite them . . . to contribute to our nation's population control policy . . . ") was used as one of the final scenes of the film, his humorous but apocalyptic speech might play as an editorial comment on the insanity of modern life in China.[8] Given that it's used early in the film, it carries no such significance.

Sometimes you can imply a specific note of subtext in the ending, like in the last scene from *Startup.com*. The conclusion has already come a few minutes prior, when we learned what has happened to Kaleil Tuzman and Tom Herman's company govWorks, as well as how the relationship between the two men has resolved. The last scene is simple: it shows Kaleil's new girlfriend picking up a ball and throwing it to a dog. On its own, it means almost nothing. However, given that it's the last scene, it functions as a concluding statement that Kaleil has learned to achieve a better work–life balance, because we saw his previous girlfriend begging for more time in his hectic schedule and explaining that his refusal to give her a dog was a sign that he was unwilling to commit to their relationship.

"Bookend" endings are also attractive because, by their very nature, they provide symmetry and closure. *The Bad Kids* starts with scenes of principal Vonda Viland welcoming a new crop of students to her school, then takes the audience through a school year's worth of drama with the three main characters. The ending concludes with the school bell ringing one last time and Vonda heading out to the curb to greet the next year's crop; it gains its significance entirely because of its status as the commencement of a new cycle.

Last Train Home also has a "bookend" ending, showing the start of a cycle that we already know well. After having twice witnessed two of the film's protagonists making the arduous journey across China to go home for the New Year's holiday, we again see masses of people boarding trains, on their way to see their families. By including only large crowd shots (and none with the protagonists) this last scene not only feels appropriate because it signals the close of another year, but it also makes a subtle comment that the heartache experienced by the film's subjects is also experienced by many, many other families across China.

Or an ending can give one final note of editorial commentary, useful in a film that has a more activist stance. In Lisa Molomot's *The Hill*, we have seen subtle institutional racism at work in the decision by the City of New Haven to knock down three city blocks of housing in an African American neighborhood, but the film has remained understated in the way it makes its point. The last line however, from civil rights attorney John Williams, finally puts the film's editorial stance front and center. "How can people be so blind as not to see what they're doing?" he asks incredulously, after we have witnessed the damage done to a community that did not have the same political clout to affect policy as other more affluent neighborhoods did.

Endings can often contain even more explicit calls to action. *An Inconvenient Truth* was perhaps the model for this strategy, with its direct question to the audience via title card at the end—"Are you ready to change the way you live?"—followed by a link to a website and multiple suggestions of actions to take. But such calls to action have been repeated time and time again by films like *The Cove, Honor Diaries,* and others.

Whatever your ending, perhaps the most important thing is that it must truly feel of a piece with the rest of your film. For a great example of this, look no further than *American Movie,* Chris Smith's smash 1999 documentary about amateur filmmaker Mark Borchardt's attempt to make his gonzo masterpiece *Coven. American Movie* is a film constantly toying with the idea of miscellanea and stupidity doubling as profundity, as it takes its marginal character and makes him into a hero of sorts: a champion of artistic freedom despite his manifest alcoholism and self-destructiveness. In the penultimate scene of the film this duality is played out in perfect form. Mark sits with his uncle Bill, an elderly gentleman with a case of dementia, who acts as Mark's benefactor as well as one of his primary critics. Mark speechifies once again, this time urging his uncle to invest $40,000 in his next project. Uncle Bill resists, and ends with a bit of rambling dialogue worthy of Beckett: "Hello, come again, come again? Stay, stay awhile. Stick around awhile, stick around as long as you can. Heaven help you, God help you, Jesus help you, everybody else help you, everybody make happy. Make everybody happy, be a comedian . . . " These are the last words in the film, and they are simultaneously meaningless, strangely touching, and absolutely appropriate given what's happened in the previous 100 minutes.

▶ RESHOOTS

Unlike in narrative films, it is not uncommon in documentary filmmaking to return to production to do a significant amount of new shooting relatively late in the editorial process. Often, the sharp focus of the story does not become clear until well into the cutting process, and it is at this point that some targeted shooting can fill in gaps, provide needed interview material, or in some cases even change the thrust of the film entirely. Witness Kim Roberts' experience on *The Hunting Ground*:

> When I started on that project, the film had a different main character. And the problem was that this character was very flat, and a lot of the things that she was struggling with were really more personal to her life, like financial issues and problems with her mother, and not really related to sexual assault. And so one of the big changes that we did was change the focus to Annie and Andrea and turn them into the main characters, because they had such a strong arc and they also had

different emotions that they were bringing to it, like, "We're going to take on this university even though we're young, we're going to meet with these other women." There was humor and excitement! But of course the interviews that they had done years ago weren't quite enough and so we went back and we reinterviewed them on green screen wearing the same outfits, and then we took a wide shot from the previous interview and created a background out of it, putting it behind them in the green screen so that it would match.[9]

If you look at Figures 12.12 and 12.13, you'll see that the two interviews look remarkably similar. Only upon close inspection does one notice slight differences in the styling of Pino's hair and the lighting on her face.

In other cases, reshoots will simply help build the material for a certain section of the film that is lacking or strengthen a few key concepts by asking the interviewees very targeted questions. On *Food, Inc.*, there were several interviews conducted once editing was well underway. As Roberts notes:

On *Food, Inc.*, we interviewed Eric Schlosser and Michael Pollan four or five times. We had no narrator—those guys were our embedded narrators. So as we discovered

FIGURE 12.12 Original interview of Andrea Pino in *The Hunting Ground*

FIGURE 12.13 Reshoot interview using green screen in *The Hunting Ground*

new connections in the editing we were able to go back and do new interviews with them. One of those interviews was in the director's kitchen, so it was easy to get back to. Then the other was in Michael Pollan's house, and if you look carefully you can actually see the greenery behind Michael Pollan changing.

Thus, one thing to consider when refining your rough cut is, "What could we shoot to improve this section?" Logistical and budget considerations will of course apply, but it's important to be open to solutions that go beyond the confines of what the present material contains.

▶ CREATING MEANING THROUGH ASSOCIATION AND JUXTAPOSITION

At the outset of this book, I noted that the meaning of a particular piece of footage comes not only from its intrinsic attributes but also from its context, and that being able to harness the power of this essential truth is one of the keys to creating a great documentary. An audience is always looking to *interpret* what's in front of them, and you can greatly influence that interpretation by carefully sculpting the narrative information and emotional content of the scene/moment/shot that leads into it. "Priming your scenes properly is the goal," says Geoff Richman. "It's not necessarily just the *information* that leads you there, it's the feeling or the question that makes you look for answers in the next scene or makes you feel a new way."

Consider a crucial sequence in *The Bad Kids* in which Black Rock High School principal Vonda Viland comes to a crisis of faith.[10] She supports her students in profound ways that go well beyond the classroom and is accustomed to seeing them make great strides. But 17-year-old Joey has problems that are so deep that she's unable to solve them. She has become emotionally invested in his case, so when he gives her the cold shoulder in a one-on-one meeting and then leaves the school angrily, perhaps never to return, she is shaken. This moment is positioned at 83 minutes, and represents the film's climax. Yet Vonda is a stoic, and deals with these emotions in a very private way that often eluded the camera's gaze, so we had no scenes of emotional catharsis from her with respect to Joey. In order to make the film work, we *had* to find a way to get across the private pain that Vonda was feeling over her break with Joey while also showing that Vonda is a professional who well understands the boundaries of her role.

We did have some assets that could be put into play. First of all, the directors had shot a couple of scenes of Vonda going for walks in the desert. She takes these workouts seriously and often sets a vigorous pace, so the shots of her chugging up the hills had a certain intensity to them. Even better, they were shot from behind, so the audience is left to fill in more of the blanks about their emotional content since we can't see her face. We also had scenes of Vonda disciplining students that reflected some of the frustration she sometimes felt on the job.

We started by making sure the scene of Joey leaving the school would have as much emotional charge as possible. Joey marches out, and we included shots of Vonda peering out after him from inside the school with sadness in her eyes, then cued the score. After playing this moment out for as long as possible, we cut to Vonda marching up the hill. With her vigorous pace complemented by a couple of aggressive jump cuts, she seems like she's wrestling with something important. When she gets to the top of the hill and overlooks the rugged terrain of the Mojave Desert, the camera rises to show the back of her head. The force of emotion from the previous scene, greatly enhanced by the music, gives us a full head of steam: she seems filled with emotion, yet still unwilling to share it.

Next we went back to the selects reel called "Discipline" that we had created, found two scenes in which she was curt and even a little angry, and cut them to accentuate her angst. Then we landed on a longer scene in which she is seen expelling a student. Expelling students was her least favorite part of the job—both because it represented the failure of the school to overcome behavior problems and also because it reminded her of her own past as a troubled youth—and in this scene she is visibly upset and on the verge of tears. Putting these three discipline scenes directly after the walking scene, with music still pushing the emotion at full throttle, gave us a great emotional payoff.

To summarize, the sequence starts with Vonda's stoic look of sadness as Joey angrily leaves, then cuts to the walking footage in which we interpret her physicality as anger and upset (but still do not see her face). We then see the first two discipline scenes in which this upset takes a specific form as she tells her charges to shape up their behavior, then we cut to the final discipline scene in which the tears finally start to roll. The sequence ends on an extended shot of an extreme close-up of Vonda's left eye as she sits at her desk (see Figure 12.14), taken from material the directors had shot in which they asked her to think silently about the joys and difficulties of her job. These five scenes extend Vonda's upset over Joey to show the full arc of her emotions. It is a highly constructed sequence using scenes that were shot months apart from each other, and yet Vonda agreed when the film was done that it was accurate in how it depicted her feelings.

FIGURE 12.14 Principal Vonda Viland in *The Bad Kids*

The lesson here is that you can transfer the emotions of one scene into another, and that you can use emotionally ambiguous material and lead an audience to a specific interpretation about it if you are careful with your editing.

* * *

Let's look at two more examples of editing by association, both from *God Grew Tired of Us*, the winner of the Sundance Grand Jury Prize in 2006 and edited by Geoff Richman. The film explores the difficulty of assimilation for the "Lost Boys of Sudan," a group of male refugees who emigrated to a handful of U.S. cities following their harrowing journey out of war-torn Africa. It explores the lighter side of their situation when they first arrive but, as the drama unfolds, we see the strain of life for the orphan boys in these unfamiliar places, and the challenges of dealing with the trauma of war. At one point we learn that one of the boys has gone missing in Syracuse, New York.[11] He did not return from his job as usual, and his fellow refugees call the police to report him missing. We learn through Nicole Kidman's narration that when he is found two days later, it is on a bus where he has been rambling incoherently to strangers.

It's important for the film to provide context and meaning for this event, especially because there was no footage of him being found. So in the scene that directly follows, a *different* character named Daniel describes in lucid detail the difficulty of moving on from the trauma *he* experienced on *his* long journey out of Sudan. He recounts the horror of watching his father being killed in front of him, and describes how difficult it is to get such memories out of his head. Here, the filmmakers have gracefully made a link between the two situations, showing the consequences of such trauma even though the boy found on the bus is not the same one telling the story. While there is no direct causal link between Daniel's story and the missing boy's story, we cannot help but draw the conclusion that witnessing those kinds of horrors could lead to mental illness.

In another scene from the same film, a helpful bit of narration primes the audience to interpret the scene that follows in a particular way.[12] It begins with a shot of eight of the refugees walking through an outdoor parking lot together in the daytime, over which Nicole Kidman's narration is heard: "Merchants in Daniel and Panther's neighborhood have filed complaints with the local police in Pittsburgh. They feel intimidated by the boys entering their stores in large numbers, so a meeting was called to advise the boys not to travel in groups." On this last sentence, the film cuts to a shot of just two of them walking together, approaching a convenience store. Daniel and two other refugees are then seen at a local municipal swimming pool in a scene that consists of the following shots:

1. They stand by their towels, tying the strings on their swimming trunks, and get ready to enter the pool.

2. Daniel splashes water on his face in the pool.

3. A middle-aged woman talks to two of the refugees, asking brightly, "Do you find everything really new and different here? Do you have a lot of freedom here that you didn't have?"

4. Rack focus shot from two middle-aged white women talking with each other, to Daniel looking around tentatively at his surroundings.

5. Dialogue of Daniel talking to a group of a dozen young white girls, who ask him to spell out the word "Sudan" because they don't know what he's talking about. "What does that mean?" they ask. "It's the country where I come from," he responds with a smile. "Oh!" they respond in unison. "It's a country of black people," continues Daniel. "There are not white people there."

6. Another rack focus shot from the two middle-aged white women, who are now looking (suspiciously?) in Daniel's direction from across the pool, to Daniel looking around in the foreground at his surroundings.

7. Shot of Daniel near a ladder at the edge of the pool, looking around at his surroundings.

Consider the power of the two brief lines of narration in this sequence ("merchants . . . feel intimidated"). Without them, we might not interpret the shot of the eight refugees the same way, nor any of the other shots that follow. Daniel is a gregarious, articulate, delightful young man, but when we see him surveying his surroundings we can start to feel the tension that accompanies many of his interactions and the subtle racism that he deals with daily. We are much more highly attuned to the behavior of the women, and we see the possible suspicion in their eyes. Taken together, the narration (which has little overt emotional charge of its own) mixed with the verité scenes shows how racism is infecting every interaction that Daniel has, and we can start to feel its damage.

FIGURE 12.15 Daniel at the swimming pool in *God Grew Tired of Us*

Ethical Implications

The ethical implications of this kind of editing are significant, of course. Where is the line between subtle embellishment and outright manipulation? How far is too far when rearranging elements within a narrative? Most documentarians will tell you that the ultimate answer comes when presenting the final film to the subjects. Will they feel respected by the filmmaker's portrayal of them, or will they feel used? In the "Cutting a Verité Dialogue Scene" video tutorial on this book's companion website you will find a three-scene sequence from *Small Farm Rising* in which farmers Ian Ater and Lucas Christenson strategize about how to deal with an unnamed buyer who is squeezing them on the pricing of their produce. To build the sequence we combined two unrelated phone conversations into one, changed the chronology of events, and altered the wording of offscreen lines. When showing Ater and Christenson the result, they told us that it rang true to them, and accurately represented the financial challenges of being small-scale farmers. They didn't remember the particulars of the day in question, and didn't notice that the scene was heavily manipulated to simplify the drama.

Another way to frame the question is, "does this series of small lies tell a larger truth?" Or are the fundamental meanings of the subjects' actions being so altered that the subjects no longer recognize themselves? Some documentarians will show rough cuts to some of their subjects if they are concerned about these issues so that the subjects can have a chance to offer comments ahead of final editorial decisions. This can be a great way to bring the subjects into the authorship process, though it can cause complications since the subject has little perspective on the complex set of considerations that went into constructing the edit. (A subplot may have to be removed for time reasons, for instance, but this is of little consolation to someone whose life story has been removed from the film.) It also has the potential to cloud the editorial judgment of the director who is, for better or worse, the ultimate author of the work. Needless to say, this is a complex ethical issue that needs serious consideration ahead of locking picture.[13]

▶ ALTERNATIVE APPROACHES TO NARRATIVE

Up until now we've been going forward with the implicit assumption that a documentary's health is defined by the strength of its narrative drive. But what if we open ourselves to other opportunities? Might there be structural forms that could focus our audience's attention on other associations between the scenes and still build an equally satisfying work?

Frederick Wiseman's films are a fascinating example. They are patient explorations of institutional environments (*Hospital, Juvenile Court, High School*) and specific locales (*At Berkeley, Aspen, Boxing Gym, Zoo*), and tend to have many more characters than a typical documentary. Rather than following one or two protagonists through a large number of social situations, they feature many protagonists through a very limited set of locations and social situations. Thus, they are "associational rather than expository; poetic rather than assertive or narrative,"[14] as Bill Nichols puts it, and their structure puts the focus on the constraints, customs, and assumptions of the institution rather than on the individual.

Instead of traditional narrative, his best films focus the audience's attention in a new way and create the possibility for rich observation, analysis, and critique. *High School* is about conformity and rules; *Near Death* (shot in a hospital ward) is about the futility of modern medicine in the face of end-stage disease; *Zoo* is about the creation of a carefully stage-managed experience at the possible expense of the animals' best interests; *Boxing Gym* is about the unexpectedly graceful and balletic movements of small-time boxing amateurs at an Austin, Texas, gym. The key point to be made here is that *the constraint offered by the shooting method provides the blueprint for an alternate type of structure.*

In Wiseman's films, the everyday routines of the institution are often used as periodic breathers in between sets of full-length scenes. Thus, in *Near Death* visuals of the janitors cleaning the halls and sounds of the droning medical monitoring equipment punctuate scenes of doctors trying to keep their patients alive, and in *Zoo* (Figure 12.16) shots of compliant patrons pointing cameras at the animals punctuate shots of the staff brushing the animals' teeth or throwing their remains in the incinerator after they have fallen ill. The mundane nature of the everyday serves to reinforce the sense of an institution that chugs on with its mission, regardless of the players that happen to populate it on any given day.

And though it can be difficult to spot, there *is* narrative development at play in most of Wiseman's films. In *Titicut Follies*, two scenes show the horrifying trajectory of a

FIGURE 12.16 *Zoo* **(Frederick Wiseman, 1993)**

mental patient who gives a lucid critique of his own treatment to his doctor, only to be told later in the film that his protestations are just part of a worsening in his delusional state; *Zoo* contains a mini-narrative about the birth of a rhinoceros calf; and in *At Berkeley* we see administrators prepare for the possible occurrence of student protests and then witness the protests actually occur.

Another documentary filmmaker who has long eschewed traditional narrative is Godfrey Reggio. Beginning with his landmark film *Koyaanisqatsi* in 1982, continuing in 1988 with *Powaqqatsi* (Figure 12.17), and concluding in 2002 with *Naqoyqatsi*, his "*qatsi*" trilogy made heavy use of time-lapse photography to give a novel perspective on contemporary life and challenged the audience to draw conclusions about its possible problems and contradictions. Cinematic and sweeping yet undeniably experimental, the films' relatively wide release in theatrical venues was unusual, and was made possible in part by the stewardship of their executive producers (Francis Ford Coppola, George Lucas, and Stephen Soderbergh, respectively). The films have no dialogue, no titles aside from the opening and closing, and a single continuous music soundtrack dominates, with few sound effects. Despite the lack of a traditional narrative, the films are not "random" by any means; they are given a distinct identity by the specificity of their approach, which focuses attention on the juxtaposition between the images following a single title card with the name of the film in the opening. This name provides an implicit challenge to the audience ("what does *Koyaanisqatsi* mean?"), which is then explored via the juxtaposition of the images that follow, and answered more definitively at the end, when the title reappears supplemented by a dictionary definition ("Life out of balance"). The films are most successful when the juxtapositions occupy the sweet spot between being arbitrary and obvious, and we feel a definite directorial point of view without it becoming hectoring or didactic. Interestingly, I would argue that the third film in the trilogy is the least successful of the three because of its heavy use of visual effects. When we are seeing images of things that we understand as real, then

FIGURE 12.17 A scene from *Powaqqatsi*

the time-lapse photography and the editing juxtapositions create an effect of seeing the "real world" in a brand new way, but when the images themselves are synthetic it nullifies much of the power of the conceit.

Other documentaries offer narrative gratification but instead of attaching it to a single character they offer multiple overlapping storylines. *The Waiting Room*, for instance, successfully weaves five main storylines into a multilayered whole and breaks some conventions—the "A" story is wrapped out well before the ending, for instance—even as it conforms to others (see Figure 12.18). The film profiles the life of an ER unit in a public hospital in Oakland, California, and oscillates between scenes with individual patients and those that take place in the waiting room itself.

With this structure, there is a sense of overlapping dramas that progress over the course of the night. Interspersing them like this gives room for their cases to evolve as the film progresses, and to crate a "mosaic" effect that feels immersive and intimate even though the level of narrative payoff is perhaps less than if there had been only one or two main storylines.

Many topic-oriented documentaries will also do without a central character that moves through time, and will instead be anchored by two or three interviewees who appear consistently throughout the film and push it forward. To provide structure these films may use title cards to overtly break up the film into distinct but connected topic segments.

Food, Inc. is divided into 10 such sections: "Fast Food to All Food," "A Cornucopia of Choice," "Unintended Consequences," "The Dollar Menu," "In the Grass," "Hidden Costs," "From Seed to the Supermarket," "The Veil," "Shocks to the System," and "Power to the System." While each section covers a different topic, they also work together to create a feeling of forward momentum, with the last two sections offering solutions to the problems posed elsewhere in the film. It's interesting to note that while all sections *begin* with the stated topic, many veer off into other issues by the time they close, and yet the film still works brilliantly because every individual topic also relates to the broader themes of the documentary. The visual design of the film also brings a strong

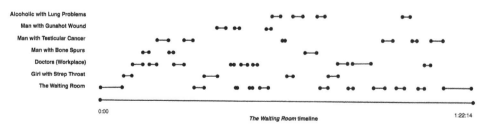

FIGURE 12.18 Structural diagram of *The Waiting Room*

sense of unity to the affair. As is often the case with "section" films, the very existence of the sections brings a feeling of structure to a film that might otherwise feel a little unmoored.

This section only scratches the surface of nontraditional documentaries, which deserve a book-length discussion of the varied strategies they use to structure their material. In the above examples we see that even documentaries that follow a less traditional path usually find alternate structural forms that give them shape, focus, and coherence.

▶ NOTES

1 The audience is meant to forgive the conceit of showing Summers writing in his journal as if he's actually jotting down the notes that resulted in this film. In reality the film was based on his autobiography, which predated the making of the film by five years.

2 The fact that the film was shot over a two-month period and was edited to its trim 82-minute length from 175 hours of raw footage is another story. Adam Grossberg, "Spending Time With the Waiting Room, a Documentary on Oakland's Highland Hospital." *Oakland North*. oaklandnorth.net. March 27, 2012. Web.

3 25:12 of the 1:31:20 running time is spent on these activities (1:14–1:48, 29:15–30:30, 31:04–31:31, 32:12–34:40, 36:50–42:11, 49:15–51:37, 52:56–58:20, 01:01:04–01:02:05, and 01:12:48–01:17:08).

4 32 minutes and 49 seconds out of the 103-minute-and-53-second film, to be exact.

5 This segment begins at 12:45 in *Precious Knowledge*.

6 This shot begins at 6:34 in *The Iron Ministry*.

7 The food vendor scene starts at 36:01, and the scene with the man eating noodles is at 1:17:15.

8 This scene with the boy can be found at 17:57 in *The Iron Ministry*.

9 A clip from the first interview can be found at 5:15; a clip from the second interview with the green screen can be found at 31:33.

10 This sequence runs between 1:27:40 and 1:30:35 in the full-length version of *The Bad Kids*. (The version which ran on *Independent Lens* is shorter.)

11 This scene occurs at 1:03:00 in *God Grew Tired of Us*.

12 This scene runs between 50:34 and 51:39 in *God Grew Tired of Us*.

13 The Center for Media and Social Impact's white paper "Honest Truths: Documentary Filmmakers on Ethical Challenges in Their Work" is a must-read on the subject. For

a longer and more theoretical discussion, Bill Nichols' important book, *Introduction to Documentary* (Bloomington: University of Indiana Press, 2010), contains several sophisticated sections of the ethical issues raised in the practice of documentary filmmaking.

14 Bill Nichols. "Fred Wiseman's Documentaries: Theory and Structure." *Film Quarterly*, Vol. 31, No. 3, Spring, 1978.

13

Working with Details

▶ MUSIC

Music's ability to underscore emotional, thematic, and narrative information for the audience is uniquely powerful. Many of Errol Morris' films would simply not function as they do without the scores of Phillip Glass, and the engine of most great montages is, of course, a great piece of music. Yet there are films that overplay their hand with music, taking the audience to an emotional place that hasn't been earned with the footage, or simply use it so ubiquitously that it loses its power from overuse.[1] There are many great documentaries that function with little or no music at all. So figuring out the musical logic of a documentary is a fundamental aspect of any edit.

One determining factor, of course, is the intended audience and exhibition environment. Nonfiction shows on cable networks (History Channel, HGTV, etc.) almost universally blanket their shows with wall-to-wall music, an acknowledgment that the "content" is fundamentally a piece of entertainment rather than a work of art, and that it is being watched more casually than a film would be (thus the need to intensify every moment, lest the audience drift away). Which kind of work is yours? It's always worth asking yourself, "How does this scene play without music? Is music really necessary here?"

Another thing to consider is whether you have done everything you can to build images that will respond well to a music track. Sequences featuring images of talking head interviews will be more limited in their ability to be helped by music than sequences featuring images that allow the audience to actually place themselves within the event being discussed. As composer Ted Reichman states:

> If there is a dissonance between the story being told by the film and what you are actually seeing on screen, it can be very hard to score. It's challenging because you're being asked to score the emotion of what they're talking about—let's say it's a murder—but the only thing happening on the screen is a talking head of the person telling the story. There's a limit to what you can do with music in that situation.

It's interesting to note that successful film scores with lots of talking head material sometimes do not attempt to *directly* score the specific emotions of each scene, but rather create a "third element" that exists independently. Take Philip Glass' justly celebrated score for *The Fog of War*. Here, the music provides a sort of "invisible scenery," as Reichman puts it, a backdrop that gives an overall texture and tone for the film without promising to underscore specific emotions related to each separate scene. To do otherwise would risk overplaying the hand of the score.

To arrive at a strong musical score for a documentary, it is essential to *start early*. Most documentary editors consider the building of a temp music library to be an essential part of setting up any edit, just as one also has to build the select reels. When directors can specify suggestions for temp music or (even better) deliver a set of music files along with the raw footage, this is a way of offering crucial editorial guidance on what kind of tone they are going for. On *The Bad Kids*, for instance, directors Keith Fulton and Lou Pepe provided me with a folder containing about 80 music tracks from a half dozen different artists, and I gravitated instantly to the hazy electronic soundscapes from composer Blair French for the film *Detropia*. Those temp tracks became the main method we communicated our intentions to our Polish composer Jacaszek. Another way to build a temp music library is to get it from the composers themselves; many composers will provide a back catalog of tracks to use as temp score in the early stages of the rough cut if they are brought on early.

If the director isn't sure yet about music, it will likely be up to the editor to scout for it. Scour your own music library for tracks (instrumental ones are best), and start piling up possible sources. You never know how a piece of music is going to interact with an image until you put it in the timeline and play it through, so think broadly and avoid limiting yourself to the obvious.

There are more and more sources these days for finding music that can be licensed for films. The tracks available on websites like Audiosocket, Musicbed, SmartSound, and Free Music Archive are often quite good, and these sites have powerful search engines to quickly scan through large catalogs of music. (SongFreedom even offers a search field to find music that sounds similar to artists or tracks that you already know.) Many musicians have signed up with intermediaries like Marmoset to represent them, which greatly simplifies the licensing process for their music and can lead to some interesting discoveries through the Marmoset website. The Filmstro and SonicFire Pro apps attempt to simulate the experience of working with a composer by letting you find a piece of music with search terms and then customize it to the contours of your particular film with sliders for attributes like "momentum," "depth," and "power."

But expecting an algorithm to score your film for you is unrealistic. Hiring a composer gives you the ability to come up with a coherent strategy for the music of the film as a whole, something that is difficult with off-the-shelf tracks. Most vitally, composers can throw out ideas that relate to the film on a more complex level than just raw "drama," and they can take direction and experiment with ideas on a level that is simply not possible otherwise. For instance, when Reichman scored an unreleased documentary I edited, he deliberately avoided anything too melodic because there was so much music already in the subject matter of the film, and when he scored Lisa Molomot's film *School's Out: Lessons from a Forest Kindergarten* he chose a finger piano as the main instrument to reinforce the theme of the simple pleasures of childhood.

To successfully communicate with a composer, one needs to develop a shared language. Many directors and editors are intimidated by the prospect of trying to speak the language of musicians, but most composers will tell you that knowledge of specific terminology isn't necessary. Once some actual references exist (either temp music tracks or the first draft of a cue from a composer) then a director and editor can comment on it with their own set of terms. As long as the composer arrives at an accurate understanding of what the director means by those words, then the choice of words itself is not especially important. As Reichman says:

> It is less important for a composer to hear musical terminology than it is to hear dramatic terminology—even just adjectives. It can be a synthesis of dramatic and musical terms, and it is unique for each project. It can be anything, as long as you arrive at a shared meaning. As long as the director is consistent with their terms, I can decode from them what they really mean.

Let's look at a couple of examples of great uses of music in documentaries.

In *My Kid Could Paint That*, we are under three minutes into the film and have already been introduced to the fact that Marla Olmstead, age four, has become an international celebrity due to her uncommonly precocious abstract paintings. Is she a prodigy? What's it all about? As we arrive at the next scene, we're about to find out.

A jazzy, marimba-driven cue with a driving percussion track and slick production values greets us as we enter into a gallery that is teeming with excited visitors.[2] The music says, "urban/sophisticated." It is unpretentious, but exudes cool. "Today is the opening of Marla's show here at the gallery," says gallery owner Anthony Brunelli, "and it's just complete and utter bedlam with all the news crews that are here." Indeed, the gallery is packed, with camera crews in every direction, and the music invites us to share in the glory of being a part of such a hot event. "If you picked a name out of a hat from a TV program, they called," says Brunelli. "Conan O'Brian, Oprah just called, *60 Minutes* is here—it's probably the most popular story in the world right now."

Suddenly, there is a shift in the music. Gone is the propulsive percussion, replaced with long, reverberant notes of a synthesizer that takes the place of the more organic marimba. The background noise of the gallery is also almost gone, and we are left in suspended animation, suddenly reconsidering how we feel about the situation. The shots of Marla's parents celebrating amidst an adoring crowd go on, but now they take on a much different cast. "I will admit, though," says Brunelli with a touch of apprehension in his voice, the pauses between his sentences lasting much longer now, "[I told] the parents the first time that I saw her work, 'you're in for a wild ride, I hope you're prepared for this.'"

The music cues have accomplished something quite extraordinary: they have suggested a new way to feel about the images. Even before the voice-over makes explicit the idea that there may be a strong downside lurking amidst the cheer, we somehow know it intuitively. The music and sound cues have done this all on their own.

Another great example comes from *Food, Inc.*, widely regarded as one of the most successful advocacy documentaries ever made. It winds its way through a host of different issues related to industrial food production in a way that is engaging, coherent, and lively, and a large part of its success is due to the terrific score by Mark Adler. One section in particular is worth noting.

At 10 minutes into the film, we are introduced to Vince Edwards, a Tyson chicken farmer with a strong southern accent, as he drives through idyllic rolling fields of Kentucky bluegrass in his pickup truck. A relaxed, gently picked acoustic guitar melody is heard, backed by another acoustic guitar strumming the rhythm, the occasional plucking of an acoustic bass and the gentle thud of a bass drum. The associations from these acoustic instruments (the lead guitar sounds almost like a banjo) are unmistakable: country, earth, nature, home. The film is leading us into an idealized view of farming as Vince talks about the way that Tyson's arrival in McLean County has helped the local economy. ("Smells like money to me," he says with a broad smile as he rolls down his window and takes a breath of air.)

Yet as the sweet persuasions of the music fade out and we learn that Vince has changed his mind about opening up his operation to further filming after multiple visits from Tyson representatives, we start to wonder whether there might be a downside to all this development. Multiple other chicken farmers decline requests to be interviewed, and finally a Perdue grower named Carole Morison agrees. She shows us the intense overcrowding of the hens and the way that the massive size of the specially bred birds makes them too big to stand on their own feet for more than a few seconds at a time; she speaks resentfully about the awesome power the conglomerates hold over the growers.

At the end of the segment the same acoustic guitar melody is repeated. It's notably slower this time, and without the backing of the second guitar or percussion it sounds strangely mournful. It's accompanied by a subtle synth sound that further colors it as "sad." As we see Morison wandering the pen picking up dead birds to dispose of, the music has done its job of giving us an unmistakably bleak view of the industry that just a few minutes ago we were celebrating. Later in the film the acoustic instrumentation returns, this time in the form of a banjo, but it's lost its homey feel. Instead of playing a loose, relaxed melody it's repeating just a few notes over and over again in a monotonous staccato as we see more evidence of factory farming's destructive consequences.[3]

Again, music has guided us to an interpretation of the images in a subtle way that is all the more powerful for its lack of words. And it need not be overtly rhetorical. Witness the exquisite artistry of Fred Frith's supple score for *Rivers and Tides: Andy Goldsworthy Working With Time*, Wiley Webb's generous tonal washes in J. Christian Jensen's *White Earth*, or James Longley's mesmerizing soundscapes for his own film *Iraq in Fragments*, and you will find examples of music being used in ways that increase a film's complexity rather than decreasing it.

▶ ARCHIVAL MATERIAL AND STOCK SHOTS

The career of documentarian Ken Burns is living proof of the power of archival material. Used properly, simple assets like photographs and old films can be highly dramatic. A photo has a link with the past that is more pure than reenactment or interview footage, and an audience can feel the difference. The very texture of archival footage—grainy, usually black-and-white, distressed and scratched—has properties that we associate with something "authentic" and "real."[4] Used in the right way, it has huge advantages over other footage that could illustrate the same concept.

When working with archival stills, the slow zoom-in is a tried and true method of adding some subtle visual drama to the image. (Apple has even designated it the "Ken Burns Effect" in its iMovie software.) To get the most out of this material:

▶ Make sure the beginning and ending frames are both strong compositions.

▶ Zoom in to the eyes of the subject, rather than into the center of the image.

▶ Create reveals by starting on an abstract part of the image and then reveal the full nature and context of the shot.

Think for a moment about the raw power of the archival material in Alain Resnais' vital 1956 documentary short *Night and Fog*. A poetic meditation on the meaning of the Holocaust, the film is divided into black-and-white sections and color sections. The color sections feature present-day dolly shots of the overgrown fields surrounding the ovens at Auschwitz and are accompanied by narrated reflections spoken in the past tense ("[the inmate's] world was this closed, self-contained universe, hemmed in by observation posts from which soldiers kept watch"). The black-and-white sections feature archival images taken from the horrific period during and just after the Nazi reign and are narrated in the *present* tense ("everything is but a pretext for taunts, punishment"), putting us in the moment as if we are actually there. Fascinatingly, the film never explicitly claims that all of the black-and-white footage is actually archival in nature, and in fact it is not. Several of the black-and-white images, including the one shown in Figure 13.1, were shot expressly for the film in 1955. This strategy of bringing the reverence we carry for archival footage and transferring it to other images shows the intense power that archival can carry.[5]

An analogous strategy is used in *If a Tree Falls* in a gut-wrenching segment showing the slaughter of horses. At 29:45, we see an exterior shot of the Caval West Meat Packing Plant and hear the following narration over footage of dead horses strung up on meat hooks and an employee standing in pools of blood: "the horses were being sent to slaughterhouses, including the Caval West plant in nearby Redmond, Oregon. There were so many horses being processed at the plant that horse blood would sometimes overwhelm the town's water treatment facility and shut it down." Yet, crucially, the images of the dead horses are clearly identified via onscreen titles as *not* from Caval West, but rather from a plant in Quebec, almost 3,000 miles away. Director/editor Marshall Curry explains:

> To understand why the Earth Liberation Front would attack a horse slaughterhouse—the sense of outrage and urgency that they felt—it was important for the audience to see the blood and to share that visceral horror. But there was no footage of Caval West—not many slaughterhouses allow cameras inside—so we had to use footage from a different plant that was doing the same work.

FIGURE 13.1 Expressionistic lighting on the entrance to Auschwitz in *Night and Fog*

Thus, the power of the archival footage was strong enough to warrant its usage even though the audience had to be reminded that it was, in a sense, a stand-in for the real thing.

Sometimes it's the very disconnect between the event depicted in the archival document and the one that it's juxtaposed with that is the source of its power. *Daughter from Danang* is an extraordinary 2002 film showing the heartbreaking reunion of a 25-year-old woman named Heidi with the Vietnamese mother she was separated from as a child when she was adopted by an American family as a part of Operation Babylift. The film has multiple sequences in which Heidi narrates her personal experience, and these anecdotes are illustrated visually by cuts to archival footage of *other* children involved in the same program. As she recalls her confusion about what was happening when she was separated from her family and sent to live in America with strangers, we see footage of other confused-looking children onscreen. We ride on an airplane filled with crying children, and even though none of them are Heidi herself, they effortlessly illustrate her experience as well as the broader historical reality.

This reveals a fundamental truth about documentary, which is that the historical provenance of a piece of footage does not need to be perfectly aligned with the particular story in order to have emotional resonance and legitimate rhetorical value. For instance, at four minutes into the opening of *The Invisible War* the film's lead character Kori Cioca discusses her experience of being a little girl and dreaming of entering the military as we see a slow-motion shot of an unrelated girl on a July 4 parade float holding a flag (see Figure 13.2). This cutaway is essentially a stock shot—a piece of footage that could have come from anywhere—but it illustrates the emotion by giving us a face to place with the words, and expands its meaning out to a broader context since the girl is *not* Kori. Suddenly Kori's experience is "every girl's" experience, and the sexual assault that Kori later suffers is a stand-in for that of a huge cross section of women in the military.

FIGURE 13.2 A girl holds an American flag in *The Invisible War*

▶ REENACTMENTS

Reenactments have been a part of documentary filmmaking for as long as the form has been in existence, right back to Robert Flaherty's 1922 film *Nanook of the North*. When Flaherty assembled "Nanook" (not his real name) and his compatriots for a scene that would show the excitement of an "authentic" Eskimo walrus hunt, Flaherty insisted on carrying it out with the old-fashioned implements of spears rather than firearms to make it more romantic—a choice that carried with it considerable personal risk for the subjects. To make matters even more ethically dubious, the viewer is not given any sort of indication that this moment was staged for the camera.[6]

What *are* the ethics of staging reenactment footage in a genre that is ostensibly built around documents that have a direct connection to historical reality, and how should its use be highlighted within the film to inform the viewer of its origins?

While most documentarians would insist that they want to avoid tricking their audiences, they're also trying to craft a coherent artistic statement that would make flashing a big "REENACTMENT" title card on the screen a poor artistic choice. Thus, it's common to use more subtle cues to mark reenactment footage as such.

In most documentaries, it is the very stylization of the footage itself that indicates the film has transitioned into reenactment territory. In the 2008 film *Man on Wire*, for instance, the clean, artfully lit nature of the reenactments contrast obviously with the grainier, lower-resolution quality of the archival images. In *The Thin Blue Line*, the low-key lighting and minimalist staging lend the reenactment footage an assertively anti-realistic feel. In *The Jinx*, we are expected to be able to distinguish reenactments from archival documents because the archival material is presented in a different aspect ratio with a bit of vignetting at the corners.

But in other films, the line separating archival from reenactment becomes very thin indeed. Take Kelly Duane de la Vega and Katie Galloway's brilliant *Better This World*, about an FBI informant's role in the prosecution of two college-age men for terrorism charges related to their protests at the 2004 Republican National Convention. In order to put the audience inside the point of view of its protagonists, they make heavy use of archival surveillance footage from the many cameras placed around the city of Philadelphia, and then combine this with original footage that is animated into something that *feels like* surveillance footage because of its herky-jerky, back-and-forth movement. At some points it is difficult to distinguish between the two, but the effect is undeniably effective at putting the audience into the mind-set of its protagonists, who are being pursued like hardened terrorists before they have even considered the use of violence.

Another fascinating case is the selective and exceedingly effective use of reenactment footage in the 2000 documentary *Into the Arms of Strangers: Stories of the Kindertransport*, edited by Kate Amend. Made up overwhelmingly of archival footage and talking

FIGURE 13.3 Reenactment footage made to look like surveillance footage in *Better This World*

head interviews, the film succeeds at every turn in using its assets to reflect the point of view of the protagonists, who were all young children at the time of the depicted events. "We had this incredible archival material from researcher Corinne Collett," explains Amend. "The director asked her not to just find standard WWII footage, but to look for anything that looked like it was from a child's perspective or any shot that had children in it."

From here Amend worked to fill in the minor gaps with reenactment footage, some of which was shot by her assistant, Alicia Dwyer, with an amateur video camera.

> The packing sequence we actually made up at my house—Alicia and I found an old suitcase and teddy bear in my garage and mocked it up. And we filmed her brother riding a bicycle for the bicycle sequence, and filmed her feet running on cobblestones. We just got the feel of it down and then it was redone professionally, but we started trying things out right there in the editing room.

The effect is seamless. The bicycle footage, for instance, is used for under three seconds but it provides a kinetic burst of energy for the aforementioned moment when a subject describes riding his bike down the street and finding Jewish shops broken into; this helps the audience remain "in the moment" as the conditions in Germany of the early 1940s deteriorate.

Indeed, the point of using reenactment footage is often to facilitate crossing this line from "objective" reporting into subjective experience. Documentarians are always looking for ways to create a *feeling* of a moment, and to put their audiences directly inside of the shoes of their subjects; reenactments are one tool for allowing this to happen. In the best-case scenario, it actually doesn't matter if we know that what we're seeing was created by the filmmaker, because it nonetheless brings us inside the emotional experience of the event. One could even argue that the distancing effect that reenactments perform is a plus, because it asks audience members to use their imagination and draw on their own experiences, rather than being confined to the specifics of the situation in front of them. This willful suspension of disbelief is often made easier if the footage used remains somewhat abstract to avoid calling attention to the disparity between the real people and the actors playing them in the reenactment. Thus, it's usually a good idea to avoid using any close-ups of faces and to keep the attention on the *details* of the characters' actions without showing too much geography. "Keep it as nonspecific as possible," suggests Amend.

A highly successful use of reenactment footage can be seen in the Las Vegas hotel room scene in Part 5 of the ESPN documentary *O.J.: Made in America*, edited by Bret Granato, Maya Mumma, and Ben Sozanski. Near the end of this concluding episode, O.J. concocts a scheme to recover a trove of memorabilia items that were stolen from him by setting up a meeting with a dealer in a Las Vegas hotel room.[7] The scene plays out with a combination of crime scene photos and lots of reenactment shots taken of hotel room #1203 at the Palace Station hotel. If you look carefully at the progression of these shots, they start wide (showing us the whole room) as the scene is being set for us by O.J.'s former associates. The associates narrate details of the ill-conceived plan, and then the shots become tighter when it moves into the blow-by-blow description of the event. The images themselves are almost comically mundane—the corner of a night table, a desk lamp with its lampshade askew (Figure 13.4), a pan from the shower tile down to a shower drain—but with the skillful cutting of the voices telling the tale of O.J. and his associates entering the room with a gun, they bring the scene to life as if we are there. The cutting matches the pacing of the narration, and soon it feels as if we are looking left, looking right, and seeing the whole thing play out even though the images show nobody in the hotel room at all. Our imagination fills in the rest.

Another section plays even more subjectively. "Room 1203, I don't think I'll ever forget that room number," says Michael McClinton, O.J.'s friend who was part of the raid. "Simpson asked me to look menacing," he continues. "So I had my gun out, and he was getting angrier and angrier." As these words "angrier and angrier" are said, the

FIGURE 13.4 Mundane details of a Las Vegas hotel room made dramatic in *O.J.: Made in America*

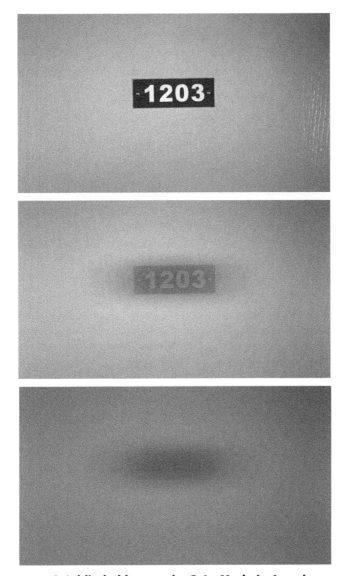

FIGURES 13.5–13.7 O.J. blinded by rage in *O.J.: Made in America*

close-up shot of the room number (a cheap tile reading "1203" on a plain white door) is digitally defocused until it becomes a complete blur.[8] By doing this, the film is asking us to associate this image with O.J.'s own state of mind, as if he is becoming blinded by his own rage.

One more example is worth mentioning. Consider the brief shot in *20 Feet from Stardom* when the outrageously talented backup singer Darlene Love relates the despair she felt when she lost her bid for stardom and was cleaning houses for a living.[9] The theme of the film, of course, is the angst that singers with such great talents feel by being relegated to lives of such modesty, and thus the filmmakers make a very specific choice of the *kind* of bathroom to stage the reenactment in. They choose a large, opulent bathroom, which could belong to one of the very stars she helped make famous, and we feel that angst to a greater degree than we would if we saw her cleaning more ordinary quarters.

▶ GRAPHICS AND ANIMATIONS

From the simple maps of northern Canada in the introduction to *Nanook of the North* to the provocative animated segments of the WWII-era *Why We Fight* series and into the present day, documentary filmmakers have long utilized graphics and animations to help tell their stories. Today, with sophisticated off-the-shelf software like Adobe After Effects becoming cheaper and more ubiquitous, computer-aided imagery is within the grasp of more and more filmmakers.

What do animated segments offer for a documentary? On the most fundamental level, they allow a complex idea to be condensed into a simple one and represented in a way that distills its meaning down to its essence. But they really do much more, because they provide tonal and thematic embellishment to the spoken words that anchor the segment, giving additional emotional information without saying a word.

Witness four animated segments in the opening to Morgan Spurlock's *Super Size Me*, edited by Julie Lombardi and Stela Georgieva working with lead animator Svilen Dimitrov. Taken together, they show a wide range of the types of graphics often used in documentary.

Super Size Me *Animation 1: Map*

In the first segment,[10] Spurlock's 15-second narration is simple and straightforward:

> Since 1980, the total number of overweight and obese Americans has doubled, with twice as many overweight children, and three times as many overweight adolescents. The fattest state in America? Mississippi, where one in four people are obese.

Until now, the film has simply used shots of obese people in public situations (shown from behind or with their faces blurred) to give a visual corollary to its message, but those shots can only be used so many times before their novelty wears off, and they can't give the visceral sense of progression that an animated graphic can. A simple map of the United States is shown, with a color-coded key at the bottom showing white and two deepening shades of blue as corresponding to worsening percentages of obesity in each state (see Figure 13.8). As the narration proceeds, we see the map turn from almost all white to baby blue to dark navy blue as the years tick by, eventually turning to canary

FIGURE 13.8 Obesity map in *Super Size Me*

yellow and then an alarming bright red as new percentages of obesity are introduced in the key at the bottom.

The graphic gives the startling impression that obesity is literally taking over the United States, and when the yellow and red categories are introduced the subtle impression is that the statisticians at the Centers for Disease Control never even anticipated that the percentages could ever go any higher than 19% (navy blue), and had to create new categories for the out-of-control numbers that started to present themselves in the late 1990s. The animated map graphic is on the screen for less than 15 seconds, but it gives a visceral impression that could not have been accomplished with words and B-roll images alone. (It's worth noting that if you look carefully, the clean white category actually corresponds to "no data" rather than to the smallest level of obesity, thus turning neutral data into "weaponized" data used in service of the film's argument.)

Super Size Me *Animation 2: Photos*

Immediately following the animated map segment, Spurlock continues:

> I'm from West Virginia, the third fattest state in America. When I grew up, my mother cooked dinner every single day. Almost all my memories of her are in the kitchen, and we never ate out—only on those few, special occasions.

Over these words we see a second animation: a postcard of West Virginia appears on a faux wood background (as if it's sitting on a table somewhere), and five candid photos of Spurlock's mother and family drop one by one on the table as the overall shot zooms out slowly. The motion of the photos is obviously computer generated, but by simulating actual physical motion the animation gives a homey, human context to them, as if someone is laying down treasured snapshots to show to a friend (see Figure 13.9).

FIGURE 13.9 Photos of Morgan Spurlock's mother in *Super Size Me*

This segment also takes 15 seconds, and the animation adds a vital unspoken element that helps to humanize Spurlock and his mom as relatable characters.

Super Size Me *Animation 3: Animated Drawing*

After talking about the rising number of people who eat out instead of cooking for themselves, the film introduces the audience to a landmark lawsuit:

> [The lawsuit was] filed in New York on behalf of two teenage girls, one who was 14 years old, four foot ten, and 170 pounds. The other was 19 years old, five foot six, and 270 pounds. The unthinkable had suddenly become reality: people were suing the golden arches for selling them food that most of us know isn't good for you to begin with.

These numbers are somewhat alarming, but without some kind of visual they remain abstract so the film portrays the two girls as stick figure drawings on a blue background. As the narration is read, we see their figures grow in size dramatically, and a terrifically expressive sound effect of a balloon being stretched is added. The audience is given the additional information of their *starting weight* in the animation so that we can see the *growth* in their size, adding another dimension to the data and giving an unspoken corollary to the map graphic.

Super Size Me *Animation 4: Animated Archival Documents*

Finally in this segment we have animations showing specific passages from the text of the lawsuit. As Spurlock starts to narrate, three pages of the double-spaced text of the lawsuit fly onto the screen. "Lawyers for McDonald's call the suits frivolous," he says,

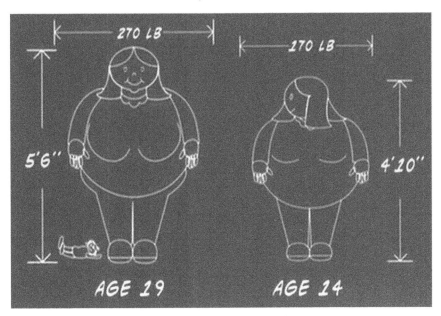

FIGURE 13.10 An animated drawing in *Super Size Me*

"stating that the dangers of its food are universally known," while a specific paragraph is circled with a big red marker and the words "the dangers of its fare were well-known" are highlighted in yellow in the text. Spurlock continues: "[McDonald's claims] that these kids can't show that their weight problems and health woes were caused solely by their McDiets." Meanwhile the original page quickly drops from the screen to reveal a second passage circled in red and highlighted in yellow. "The judge states, however," Spurlock concludes, "that if lawyers for the teams can show that McDonald's intends for people to eat its food for every meal of every day, and that doing so would be unreasonably dangerous, they may be able to state a claim." The same visual pattern is repeated, and this time a zoom is added so that the phrases "every meal of every day" and "unreasonably dangerous" are prominently displayed onscreen in bright yellow. Those two phrases are precisely the experiment Spurlock proceeds to carry out over the course of the film's duration, eating McDonald's for breakfast, lunch, and dinner to see if it's "unreasonably dangerous."

When considering the commissioning of animated segments, think about which parts of the film are well suited to them. Are there concepts or statistics that could be simplified and visualized with animation? What is the ultimate function of the segment? Finally, what style would be specifically suited to the theme and tone of your film?

Look at Ava DuVernay's Academy Award–nominated *13th* and you will find animated segments so completely integrated into the visual style of the film that the transitions

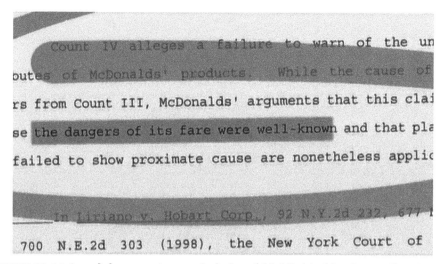

FIGURE 13.11 Legal documents are circled and highlighted in *Super Size Me*

between photo montages and animated graphics sometimes happen without one even noticing. Both are in black-and-white, and the titles have a particular texture that feels more photochemical than digital. The titles are used in two ways consistently throughout the film: first, to show the statistics of the rapid growth in the U.S. prison population, and second, to flash the lyrics onscreen of many of the songs that depict aspects of the African American experience in the modern era. By choosing these specific functions and so tightly integrating the graphics into the overall visual design for the film (the interviews are conducted against desaturated backgrounds with harsh textures that feel like the same ones found in the titles), the titles become a crucial part of the editorial stance of the film. Indeed, the very first graphic shown on the screen is of a faded/distressed white outline of the United States overtaken by black bars, like those of a prison cell.

Animation can also be used to bring archival stills to life, such as the storyboard drawings in *Lost in La Mancha*. Looking at still frames of film director Terry Gilliam's plans for his Don Quixote adaptation was relatively uninspiring, but once animator Chaim Bianco recreated them as if we were getting to see them sketched in real time (with sound effects of pencil on paper), they took on new life.[11] Now the audience could experience them from Gilliam's point of view. I used the same strategy in my film *Finding Tatanka*, taking scans of typewritten letters and notes from my father and turning them into living, breathing documents via Jonathan Swartz's animation.[12] This gave us license to add rhythm to the typing (spurting out particular sentences and phrases together while pausing elsewhere for effect) and to make the audience feel as if they were present for the moment of its creation.

▶ **LOWER THIRDS**

There are two major categories of information being delivered to an audience in a film: the visual and the aural. But within the visual category there also exists the possibility of using text.

Lower-third titles can be a great way to quickly and efficiently introduce someone. Instead of characters having to verbally identify themselves onscreen ("Hi, my name is Jenny Matthews, and I'm an epidemiologist at the University of Wisconsin . . . "), we can use a lower third to silently convey this information. As with everything else, selectivity and specificity are key. If we're not careful, we will be giving the audience information they don't need and cluttering their experience.

One of the first decisions to be made is whether a subject needs identification at all. Most documentaries have secondary and tertiary characters who may show up for only one or two brief appearances, and they usually don't merit being identified by name. Leaving ID's out for nonessential characters reduces clutter, and is also a clear way of identifying to the audience who is a main character and who is not.

In *The Bad Kids*, only three characters get ID cards, and they are identified by first name only: Joey, Jennifer, and Lee. This designates them as the main stars of the film, letting the mosaic of other characters blend together without asking the audience to remember their names. In *Precious Knowledge*, a similar strategy was used: only three students were identified by name, and only their first names were used: Crystal, Pricila, and Gilbert. Other students were not identified, and while characters like teachers, administrators and politicians *were* identified, these people existed in a different category because their full names and institutional affiliations were included.

Why do this? An argument could certainly be made that by removing the students' last names from the title, they are being objectified and/or denied their full identities. In response, many documentary filmmakers might argue that they're just attempting to amplify the subject's status as a *character*, someone who becomes slightly mythical and larger than life, à la Prince, Beyoncé, or Batman. Knowing a character by their first name only invites us to identify them more strongly within the universe of the film itself.

When choosing what to put on the second line of a lower-third title—the one marking their affiliation, qualifications, and/or relationship to the other subjects—choose carefully. Even this seemingly straightforward decision comes with great consequences for the film. The rule of thumb here is to be judicious, and to get the information across in the most compact way possible. In *The World According to Sesame Street*, for instance, the employees of Sesame Workshop are never identified with the words "Sesame Workshop," but rather with their title alone. Cooper Wright is given the title of "V.P. International Co-Productions," for instance, because the context of the film makes the fact that he works for Sesame Workshop obvious and therefore unnecessary to spell out.

FIGURES 13.12–13.13 Single-word title introductions to main characters in *The Bad Kids* and *Precious Knowledge*

Also, think strategically about what role you want every character to play in your film. By identifying Michael Tucker as not only a bookstore manager but also an "Industry Analyst" in my film *Indies Under Fire: The Battle for the American Bookstore*, I gave his comments more authority and turned him into an unbiased observer of the drama unfolding onscreen (see Figure 13.14). At the time he may have spent 90% of his time in real life being a bookstore manager and only 10% being an armchair analyst, but all of his quotes in *this* film are commentary on the state of the bookselling business, so for our purposes he's an analyst.

Remember also that ID cards are yet another tool that the filmmaker can utilize to advance the audience's arc of understanding. In Sarah Polley's *Stories We Tell*, she identifies all subjects by their first names only, which allows her to temporarily obscure the fact that some of her siblings grew up with a different father, and to build strategically to the moment when she wants to reveal it. In *Racing Dreams*, director and coeditor Marshall Curry identifies most of his central characters with their full names, but young racer Brandon Warren's grandfather is simply identified as "Phil." Curry explains that this was partly to cut down on details—"the less extraneous information you can put on the screen the better"—but also to avoid getting into the complicated dynamics of their blood relationship. "Phil's last name is Petty, and he is not Brandon's birth grandfather," says Curry. "Brandon's dad is Phil's stepson, but all of that was complicated so by sticking with the first name we avoided having to explain it."

FIGURE 13.14 Lower-third title in *Indies Under Fire: The Battle for the American Bookstore*

ID cards can even create punchlines, as in a scene from *Sons of Ben*. In an interview clip, Bryan James' wife declares reluctant acceptance of her husband's decision to get involved with a fledgling supporters' club for a yet-to-be birthed soccer team, just as long as he "[doesn't] become president." In the next clip, James himself recalls the moment when she told him this: "I do remember her saying, 'If there's one thing I never want you to be, it's president of a supporters' club.'" After a pregnant pause of Bryan looking sheepish and a bit uncomfortable, up comes the title card: "Bryan James, President, Sons of Ben," a moment that gets a laugh at every screening.[13]

When crafting the *style* of your lower third it's worthwhile to engage a graphic designer, but for temp work a few guidelines pertain:

▶ **Make the first line look different from the second line.** Usually the name is set in a larger font than the identifying title; it's also common to put the top line (but not the bottom) in all caps. Do not, however, put the two in different fonts, as this can create stylistic chaos.

▶ **Make the style feel organic to the theme and content of the film itself.**

▶ **Fade in/fade out sometime in the first few seconds after you cut to the subject.** There are a few films that use cuts rather than fades for lower thirds, but this does attract attention to them in a way that is usually not desirable. There are also films such as the 2015 documentary *Peace Officer* that use hard cuts to black, with the titles fading on over black rather than over picture. This technique gives the lower thirds a percussive, stylish feel even if it makes it slightly harder for the audience to remember the name, since the person and their ID card are never onscreen at the same time.

How many times does one need to remind the audience of the identity of the people onscreen? There are no hard and fast rules about this, and you will see different filmmakers take different strategies. Some films only give each character a single card the first time they are onscreen, and leave it at that. Other films will put a second or third card in to remind the audience of the character's name if there is a long stretch of time between their appearances.

It should be noted that titles are not used universally in all documentaries. Take again the case of Frederick Wiseman, who has never used title cards to identify characters in any of his over 40 films. Titles are a way for the film to provide easy context for the audience, as well as to legitimize the characters via the titles that they hold. But Wiseman's films are often subtle *critiques* of the institutions he trains his camera on; denying his characters titles is one more subtle but powerful way of leveling the playing field by making the audience scrutinize their behavior without preassigning hierarchies and roles.

▶ LOCATION CARDS

As with lower-third cards, the first order of business with location cards is to consider whether your film really needs to identify the location of a scene at all. Is there another, more subtle way of getting across this information that does not require the somewhat obtrusive intervention of a title card?

In *The Central Park Five*, wrongfully convicted Antron McCray is finally released from a New York State prison after six years. As we see shots of greenery through a bus window, he says, "I just wanted to get out of New York [and] I had a cousin that lived in Maryland." We then see a shot of a row of houses (presumably in Maryland) as he concludes, "I kind of liked Maryland" and tells us about how he immediately found a job there. No title ever appears onscreen because it would be duplicating the information coming from the voice-over, and because Maryland doesn't end up figuring strongly in the overall story.

Consider also the case of the opening to *The Waiting Room*. Seeking to establish the location of the hospital ER room that will be the setting for the entire film, it begins with a shot taken from a public bus, which cuts to a shot of another bus wiping frame to reveal a sign that reads, "EMERGENCY." Following this, the camera follows a man who slowly walks toward the hospital, which is identified in large letters on top of the building in the background: HIGHLAND HOSPITAL. A group of people head toward the hospital, and we then see a shot of the hospital's interior with a news rack in the foreground that is slightly out of focus but clearly reads, "Oakland Tribune." In this brief introduction, the film has managed to give us both the general location (Oakland, California) and the specific site (the emergency room at Highland Hospital) without having to put any titles onscreen.

The music documentary *Can't Stand Losing You: Surviving the Police* uses a similar technique, also in the opening scene. Guitarist Andy Summers is seen going through his morning routine: playing some guitar, doing yoga, going for a swim. We don't know his location until we see in close-up the masthead of the newspaper he opens as he sits down for coffee: "Los Angeles Times."

If such shots are unavailable or impossible to arrange (or would take too much running time to include), using a title card can be beneficial. But consider very carefully which locations actually need title cards, and what the audience will gain from this information.

In *The Invisible War*, many locations are identified onscreen simply with the state ("Ohio" or "Kentucky") because there's nothing in the content of the footage that demands further specification. When the content of one scene benefits from extra specificity, the film provides it. For example, the fact that Trina McDonald's abuse happened in a remote location is an integral part of the details of her story so the title given at the beginning of the scene reads, "Adak Island, Alaska." "It was an isolated duty station," she states, "[and] they were in charge and we were .... like cattle."

FIGURES 13.15–13.16 Andy Summers opens up the newspaper in *Can't Stand Losing You: Surviving the Police*

▶ SUBTITLES

The artful, strategic use of subtitles is another underappreciated element in the documentary. A subject whose words are key to the narrative development of the film and who speaks in a different language will have to be subtitled. In addition, any lines that are unintelligible for any reason (e.g., the speaker's English is poor or the background audio is very loud) should be subtitled. These words at the bottom of the screen don't just appear there by magic; in better documentaries, their timing and content are quite carefully crafted.

There are certain conventions that should be followed, according to veteran subtitle artist Henri Béhar:

▶ Use a non-serif font.

▶ No more than 40 characters per line and two lines per card.

▶ Make sure the font size is large enough to be read clearly from across the room.

▶ Use an outline or drop shadow effect to create contrast against bright backgrounds

▶ Avoid keeping a subtitle on the screen over a cut, if possible.

▶ Place subtitles at precisely the moment when the first word of the line is being spoken. Sometimes this rule conflicts with the rule about never leaving a subtitle on over a cut and adjustment must be made.

▶ Use italics for offscreen dialogue, if desired.

Even with these constraints, this leaves you considerable discretion about interpretation. Deliberately manipulating the translation just to heighten the drama is a recipe for disaster, but there are always opportunities around the edges to make the character's words more clear and/or more poetic. For instance, in the opening statement made by Marcelo Ayala at the start of the 2001 documentary *Beyond the Border* I edited, he describes his motivation for trying to cross from his native Michoacán, Mexico, to the United States:

When I was nine years old, I began to imagine what the United States was like.

My brothers would visit, and they would send packages in the mail.

And in those packages were clothes and I loved the clothes.

I don't know, I imagined something beautiful.

A place with jobs that were probably difficult, but with a greater chance to live well.

If you listen to the dialogue in Spanish, Marcelo's closing line is actually, "pero con más posibilidades de ganar más dinero," which literally translates as "but with more

but with a greater chance to live well.

FIGURE 13.17 Subtitles in *Beyond the Border*

possibilities to earn more money." By changing "earn more money" to "live well," we made the line more compact and also changed the meaning slightly, burnishing it with the soft glow of aspiration. "Live well" means essentially the same thing as "earn more money," except that it is slightly less specific so it feels more in tune with the motivations of the character, who has an optimistic but vague idea of what it will mean to work in the United States. This is similar to the way that the phrase "God got tired of us," uttered by one of the Lost Boys of Sudan, was changed to the more poetic *God Grew Tired of Us* as the title of the film.

Language translation is not equivalent to converting meters to feet, or Fahrenheit to Celsius, because a language has all of the history of a culture bound up in it. Thus, it's often the case that the literal translation of the words will give an *inaccurate* understanding of what is meant, and one has to use a different saying to get at the true meaning (or to get closer to it). When Béhar was translating the film *Boyz in the Hood* into French, he came upon the line where the Laurence Fishburne character criticizes the company his son is keeping by saying, "What are 'y'all, Amos and Andy? Are you Stepin and he's Fetchit?" Behar determined that there were simply no equivalent cultural figures in France and that the audience would be confused by references to figures they were unfamiliar with, so he subtitled it as, "*Vous jouez a quoin, Laurel et Hardy? Il set Abbott, est Costello?*" There was no easy way of getting at the racial undertones of the statement.

Placement is another issue worth discussing. When an interview clip with a new character appears on the screen, it is usually more advantageous to bring on the lower-third title identifying them at the beginning of the clip, then wait to introduce the subtitles until after the lower third has left the screen. The subtitles will need to catch up with the dialogue, of course, but now the audience has the smooth experience of first knowing who the speaker is and then hearing what they have to say, and can digest the information in a straightforward way.

▶ NOTES

1 Another great Walter Murch quote comes to mind: "Most movies use music the way athletes use steroids. There's no question that you can induce a certain emotion with music—just like steroids build up muscle. It gives you an edge, it gives you a speed, but it's unhealthy for the organism in the long run." Michael Ondaatje, *The Conversations: Walter Murch and the Art of Editing Film* (New York: Knopf, 2004), p. 122.

2 This scene from *My Kid Could Paint That* begins at 2:49.

3 This music cue from *Food, Inc.* can be found at 22:07.

4 How long this remains the case is an open question. Now that video filters used to simulate the look of "old, scratchy" footage have become so convincing and ubiquitous, it's possible that this "look" will increasingly be seen as a purely stylistic choice rather than a true link to a previous era.

5 Sylvie Lindeberg's account of the production of *Night and Fog* is contained in the book, *Concentrationary Cinema: Aesthetics as Political Resistance in Alain Resnais' Night and Fog*, Giselda Pollack and Max Silverman, eds. (New York: Berghahn Books, 2012), pp. 60–61. Indeed, the nighttime tracking shot of the entrance to Auschwitz and "the pan of the Kapo's room, the vertical tracking shot of a puppet and the long bleak shot of the huge pile of women's hair preserved in Block 4" were all shot by Resnais. The tracking shot is at 7:55; the pan of the Kapo's room is at 19:25; the shot of the puppet is at 16:00; the hair shot is at 25:36.

6 It could be argued that the whole of *Nanook of the North* is one giant reenactment. As Flaherty acknowledged in the title cards that accompany the film's introduction, the film was made to "take a single character and make him typify the Eskimos," and Flaherty's accounts of making the film include notes about his collaboration with "Nanook" (real name: *Allakariallak*.) "Nanook" can be seen acknowledging the camera in many scenes, and gamely playing along with Flaherty's attempt to memorialize his romantic view of Eskimo life.

7 The segment runs from 1:15:18 to 1:23:48 in the fifth episode of *O.J.: Made in America*.

8 This moment occurs at 1:19:01.

9 This reenactment occurs at 1:06:00 in *20 Feet from Stardom*.

10 The first segment runs from 1:46 to 2:01. The second segment runs from 2:02 to 2:17. The third segment runs from 2:48 to 3:03. The fourth segment runs from 3:56 to 4:18.

11 These animated versions of Gilliam's original storyboards can be seen in the opening montage at 2:01, and in two other segments: one at 12:48 and another at 14:47.

12 These typewriter segments can be found at 23:01, 26:55, 31:38, and 36:45, and animated handwriting segments done in the same style can be found at 27:17 and 28:44 in *Finding Tatanka*.

13 The "punchline" moment comes at 8:59.

14 Atom Egoyan and Ian Balfour, eds., *Subtitles: On the Foreignness of Film* (Cambridge, MA: MIT Press, 2004).

14

Working with Time

As you continue to work on your cut, you have the opportunity to define your film's relationship to time. You and the director are building a world of your own making in your documentary, and you can stretch time in any direction you choose. Rhythm, pacing, and dynamics: these are crucial to your film's success.

▶ MARKING TIME

Before we go any further, we must bring up one crucial paradox that permeates documentaries: they are, by definition, about things that have already happened, but the audience will experience them at a place and time that is always *in the present*. In order to stick to our intention of bringing our viewers as close as we can to the experience of our characters, we have to work carefully around this contradiction.

Use of the Present Tense

Most documentaries operate with a slight fudge in the way they deal with time, in that they use the *present tense* when referring to their characters. In *Burden of Dreams*, one of the very first lines of narration reads, "In November, 1979, [Werner] Herzog builds a camp for cast and crew in the dense tropical rainforest near the Ecuadorian border. The geography is perfect..." Note that it read "*builds*" (not "built") and "*is*" (not "was"). Later on, the narration jumps us forward in time: "In April 1981, Herzog's new leading man Klaus Kinsky arrives at the Iquitos airport, and the filming of *Fitzcaraldo* starts all over again." Many documentaries also adopt this same strategy of using the present tense when putting title cards onscreen.

This orientation towards time also applies to the guts of the film itself. In certain cases it may be possible to change a "was" to an "is" for off-camera lines, for instance, and we used this technique liberally in some segments of *Lost in La Mancha*. If you look carefully, you'll see that we even did it once *on camera* when it couldn't be helped. Describing the chaos of the film production, Bernard Buix states, "nobody is able to give an answer"[1] even though his lips say, "nobody *was* able to give an answer." This completes the illusion that he's discussing the events within a few hours of their occurrence rather than at some far distant moment with the comfort of reflection, and the brief visual "lip flap" is too subtle for most audiences to catch.

Absolute Markers of Time

It's common practice in documentary to put title cards onscreen marking objective moments in time. A scene can begin with a card on the bottom of the screen marking it as "January 2018," for instance. The important thing to note about these tools is that they only carry meaning within the context of the narrative. Does this date carry meaning *for the story*? If not, we may want to omit it. It is often advantageous to omit time references that are too specific because they immediately date the film and can cause the audience to put undue attention on historical details at the expense of a scene's emotional value.

In *Startup.com*, for instance, we are informed at semi-regular intervals via title cards about how many people the company GovWorks.com employs.[2] Never does the film link these figures to an exact date, opting only for months stripped of their year. "May: 8 Employees," it says near the beginning of the film, "August: 30 employees," "October: 70 employees," "January: 120 employees," "April: 200 employees," and so on. For the final dispiriting figure of "50 employees," the film opts for a relational marker of "Six Months Later," perhaps conceding the fact that audiences rarely remember exact dates and figures in a film.

In *Lost in La Mancha*, we crafted a "ticking clock" structure in which time is marked in relationship to the start of shooting on Terry Gilliam's ill-fated 2000 production of *The Man Who Killed Don Quixote*. Given that the first third of the documentary centers on the many problems that plagued the preproduction of the film, this title card information is carefully calibrated to coincide with an increasing feeling of tension and fear. Thus, the film begins with the marker of "Eight weeks before production," then "Six weeks before production" several scenes later, and progressing to "Four weeks before production," "Two weeks before production" "One week before production" (whose importance is further emphasized by its placement over black rather than picture) and finally "Production Day One," when the ill-fated shoot finally begins. Note that in this case the only nonrelational marker of time is at the outset of the film when we're informed that it takes place in "Madrid, August 2000." Any extra information would be superfluous and distracting.

The Subjective Experience of Time

Time has a rational, objective measure to it—we all live in the same clearly designated days, hours, and minutes—but our experience of it is often wildly subjective. We've all had the experience of hours "flying by" when we're in deep concentration, or just a few seconds stretching on for a seeming eternity in the middle of a moment of trauma. Since we want our film to take a point of view, we can exploit the subjective possibilities of time.

Consider a harrowing sequence from *The Central Park Five*, the 2012 film that recounts the experience of the group of African American men in New York City who were coerced into confessing to a rape and beating that they did not commit. After laying out the set of events that occurred on the Wednesday evening of the crime, a shot of a Harlem apartment building is shown with the words "Thursday, 12:00pm" over it.[3] "There's a loud knock at the door," remembers Antron McCray, who then describes being taken down to the police station with fellow innocent Raymond Santana for questioning. Over an exterior shot of the precinct office, McCray begins to recount an ordeal in which he is repeatedly asked to tell what he knows about the crime, and is repeatedly attacked when he professes ignorance. At this point, we begin seeing reenactment shots of a shabby interrogation room, a lone cigarette burning in an ashtray.

- ▶ Camera tilts up from the cigarette in the ashtray to show an analog clock on the wall that reads 6:44.

- ▶ McCray: "Then he asked me to tell my story again. This time yelling at me, all up in my face, pointing at me, poking me in my chest. It just kept going on and on and on."

- ▶ Close-up of the clock, showing 10:50, with the second hand passing in real time.

- ▶ McCray: "We stopped a few times 'cuz I was crying."

- ▶ Extreme close-up of the clock, showing 10:51.

- ▶ McCray: "I had no protection. My father didn't do anything. I was scared."

- ▶ Time-lapse close-up of ashtray containing a lit cigarette.

- ▶ Santana: "Hours have passed."

- ▶ Wider shot of ashtray.

- ▶ Santana: "Time kept going by."

▶ Close-up of the clock, showing 4:14.

▶ McCray: "They kept asking questions."

▶ Extreme close-up of the clock, showing the number 2 as the second hand passes.

▶ Santana: "No food, no drink."

▶ Extreme close-up of the clock, showing the number 3 as the second hand passes.

▶ McCray: "I didn't eat. I didn't get no sleep."

▶ Santana: "And I didn't know when it was gonna end."

As you can see, the film here uses reenactment to show the audience the *subjective* experience of time as Santana and McCray might have experienced it. Though the film-makers have been careful to keep to the facts (the interrogation took place between 12 noon and shortly after 4 a.m. of the following day), they have made those hours pass arbitrarily amidst a disorienting haze of cigarette smoke, intimidation, and insults. In the space of one cut (see Figures 14.1 and 14.2) more than four hours pass, but at other

FIGURES 14.1–14.2 Time passes subjectively in *The Central Park Five*

times the second hand creeps by agonizingly slowly and it seems to take an eternity for two minutes to tick away.

▶ RHYTHM

As we saw in the structural diagrams of *The Hunting Ground*, *The World According to Sesame Street*, and *The Waiting Room*, a film has an overall strategy to how it is segmented. This segmentation is strongly correlated with (but is not the same as) the overall *rhythm* of the film. If this were a piece of music, what time signature would it be in? If it were a novel, how long would its chapters be? What kind of beat pulses at the heart of this film? Where do the big pauses land, and how many are there?

Into the Arms of Strangers is methodical and delicate, using the measured speaking rhythms of the interviewees who anchor the film as its guide. An average of once every four minutes or so, the film goes into a moment of repose, dropping the voices out and letting a segment of music play over archival images. These moments often mark a significant development in the narrative, whether it's the moment when the children start leaving Berlin on the train or the commencement of hostilities in World War II,[4] and they also provide a rhythmic break. "I prefer to think of them as chapter breaks," says the film's editor Kate Amend. "We needed some breathing space to let the audience reflect on what they just experienced before we moved on to the next story."

As we saw earlier, *The Waiting Room* is divided into many small segments (23 in all, each lasting between one and four minutes) telling the stories of its main characters, all woven into a tapestry of footage of other patients, doctors, and nurses. But it also has three small moments of repose when the film as a whole takes a break for an interlude. Each of these functions as a subtle act break in between the different sections of the film; they take place at 29, 60, and 76 minutes into the 81-minute film, dividing its running time into two roughly equal sections of about 30 minutes each and a final one of 18 minutes, plus one small coda before the closing credits. In the first interlude, we see time-lapse footage of the busy waiting room followed by a few shots of doctors retrieving food for their next shift. In the second, we see nighttime exteriors of the hospital ER room, as if the evening has passed into the wee hours. In the last, near-empty shots of the waiting room are shown (see Figure 14.3), followed by a time-lapse of the sun rising over the hospital. Each montage feels like a small pause in the action that also marks that moment of the evening in a particular way. Though the film was shot over a two-month period from over 175 hours of raw footage, these interludes successfully establish the conceit that we are witnessing the events of a single 24-hour period.

A film can also establish rhythms that become a core part of its identity, as in some of the work of James Benning. *El Valley Centro*, for example, consists of exactly 35 shots, each lasting exactly 2 minutes and 30 seconds. Filmed in California's mostly rural Central Valley, each shot is of a different landscape, and in each one we slowly come to appreciate the way that human and animal activity can develop over the course of

FIGURE 14.3 A moment of repose in the third interlude in *The Waiting Room*

a single 150-second shot. Over the course of the film, we become more attuned to the rhythms of the activity *within* the shot.

Whatever the story you're seeking to tell, look for ways to provide a rhythm to your film through the use of musical interludes, moments of repose, explicit title card chapter markers, and other devices.

▶ PACING

When it comes to the pacing of individual scenes, it's crucial to understand that there are no absolutes. A shot of four seconds' duration can feel extremely quick in one film, while it could be an eternity in another. It all depends on what the *film* has defined as being "slow" or "fast." In the quickly paced *Startup.com*, there is an early scene in which Kaleil Tuzman retreats from a conversation with his colleagues to make a final decision about what to name his nascent startup. He exits frame with the statement, "I'm going to go meditate on this," and the film then cuts to his colleague waiting for him, a laptop open on his lap. Exactly two and two-thirds seconds later, we see Kaleil reappear and inform his partners of his decision.[5] Could he really have "meditated" in the span of less than three seconds? Yes! It feels completely natural, given the brisk pace that the film has established.

Contrast this with the pacing of *The Iron Ministry*. The film begins with over three minutes of a black screen, interrupted only by the white-on-black title card for 10 seconds. Under this we hear the slow development of a thunderous, screeching, propulsive sound. What is it? In the shots that follow our patience is rewarded as we slowly come to realize that we are aboard a train. If we can be trained to be patient for 3 minutes without any picture at all, then the 90 seconds that it takes for a character to light his tobacco pipe later in the film doesn't feel long at all, and the scenes that play out at a more "normal" pace feel brisk.

Thus, there is an overall pacing established at the outset that sets the tone for the whole film. When considering the pacing for an individual scene, it's best to start by looking to the internal rhythm of the raw footage. What is the emotional and rhythmic tenor of the action? While the wonders of editing to sculpt these factors are undeniable, the results are often better if we work to *accentuate* rather than to manufacture. Tons of cutting with no purpose is confusing, because the form is saying one thing while the content says something else.

A great example of cutting to accentuate naturally occurring rhythms is a brief scene from *The Bad Kids*.[6] Black Rock High school student Guillermo is getting advice from Ms. Hill about letters of recommendation, and she delivers her bullets of advice in a hurried staccato. She is upbeat and exudes generosity, but the speed of her delivery also indicates urgency. Cutting this scene down was simply a matter of deciding which of the several points she made that we wanted to include, and accentuating her rhythm by removing some of the details to make it feel like a series of even more breathless commands.

▶ DYNAMICS

Webster's Dictionary defines "dynamics" as "variation and contrast in force or intensity." This sounds rather dry, but its implications for documentary film editing could not be greater. If we use dynamics to our advantage, every moment will feel sharper and more distinct because it will be set off from other moments in specific and powerful ways. When something makes an impact, it not only achieves its wallop by the brute force of the blow, but also because it was louder/more destructive/more emotional than anything that came before it. The same goes for the poignancy of a quiet or precious moment. As Edward Dmytryk states in his 1984 book *On Film Editing*, "Cutting to a close-up when no enhancement of emotion is necessary is not only wasteful, it diminishes the value of the subsequent close-ups. *Overuse of the close-up diminishes its effect*" (italics mine).

If you want a prime example of the power of dynamics, look no further than the masterful Lixin Fan documentary *Last Train Home*, edited by Fan, Mary Stephen, and Yung Chang. The film follows the tragic story of a Chinese family whose parents work most of the year in a far-flung province to try to give a better life to their kids. It features an amazing rendering of the father's character: stoic and proud, he rarely speaks a word (see Figure 14.4). But as the film progresses, the strain and stress caused by this difficult situation read clearly on his face. At the film's climax, he finally lets loose a tirade of anger and insults at his daughter, whom he considers immature and ungrateful.[7] The scene is shocking and disturbing precisely because he has spoken so little to this point.

Dynamics are also at work in the continuity and contrast between scenes, and many veteran documentary editors speak about the importance of finding ways to inject humor into their (often very serious) films. Humor can help with character identification and give the audience a welcome rest from an otherwise sobering experience. For instance, *Peace Officer* opens with dark, grainy footage of a SWAT team carrying out a deadly raid

FIGURE 14.4 Zhang Shanghai (left) is the picture of stoicism throughout most of *Last Train Home*

in which they kill a man unnecessarily, and the seriousness of the topic—abuse of police power—is successfully established. But the next scene takes place in bright daylight, and features protagonist Dub Lawrence gamely describing how he deals with raw sewage on a daily basis as a pipe repairman now that he has retired as sheriff of Davis County, Utah.

Regular doses of levity punctuate the seven-part Netflix series *The Keepers*, edited by Kate Amend, Mark Harrison, and Helen Kearns, which investigates the murder of a nun and the related sexual abuse scandal at a Baltimore parochial school. The subject matter is unrelentingly grim, so it makes a huge difference to take a small break from the story every 10–15 minutes to watch one of the investigators lament her poor cooking skills as she lifts her burnt dinner from the oven, or to meet a new character by letting her babble about her obsession with her dogs. These small moments may have nothing to do with the story, but they provide a welcome pause and serve as a palate cleanser before moving on to the next disturbing revelation.

▶ PAUSES

At every cut point, there is always some amount of space between the last word or action of the outgoing shot and the first word or action of the incoming shot, with a space of a few frames on either side of the cut. This spacing is something we have absolute control over as editors, and the exact number of frames we choose to include can speak volumes. (Please see the video tutorial on "Pauses" on the *Documentary Editing* companion website.)

If we think about a documentary film sequence as a paragraph, and the succession of clips that make it up as individual sentences, we can begin to understand how this works. The distance between each clip would tend to be relatively small, with the few frames coming at the end of each clip acting as a period. But at the end of the paragraph we want to put emphasis on the last thought to indicate that we will now be moving on to a new topic in the next paragraph, so a longer pause is merited. This can be accomplished by inserting an extra flourish of music at the tail of a particular section or cutting to a concluding moment of verité. Sometimes just introducing an extra-long pause after the character in question finishes speaking can do the trick.

Pauses can also convey other subtle meanings. Sometimes, an extra pause can cause us to question the validity or integrity of what we've just been told. At 48:45 in *The Cove*, Hideki Moronuki, the deputy director of the Fisheries Agency of Japan, makes a categorical denial that any health risks pertain to the consumption of dolphin meat despite the manifest evidence to the contrary, and the small pause at the end of the clip asks the viewer to put more scrutiny on his statements. In a similar vein, in the first episode of the true crime series *The Jinx*, the camera holds an extra-long time on the tail of one of Robert Durst's interview bites.[8] There is nothing literal to be gained in this moment, but as Durst flashes his weird, creepy smile, our suspicions of him as a possible murderer can only be magnified (see Figure 14.5).

In other contexts a pregnant pause can allow the emotions of a moment to swell and marinate, creating extra emotional resonance. A look of tearful silence speaks volumes after Kurt Fuchel makes his final statement in *Into the Arms of Strangers: Stories of the Kindertransport*.[9] He reflects on the bittersweet experience of returning at the age of 16 to Berlin to live again with his birth parents, whom he has not seen in nine years. Speaking in a swirl of conflicting emotions about the surreal moment of leaving the place he now called home to be reunited with a family he no longer knew, he states, "Whereas most of the kinder never saw their parents again, I not only had mine back, I also had another set of parents as well—what more could one ask for?" The moment shows his deep gratitude along with a powerful sadness, which creeps over his face as the shot plays out.

FIGURE 14.5 Robert Durst flashes a creepy smile in *The Jinx*

Sometimes, a pause doesn't really exist but can be manufactured. We did just that in the 2009 art biopic *Con Artist* when painter/art provocateur Mark Kostabi fidgets before the camera's gaze at the close of his most revealing interview yet. The film has shown us the history of Kostabi's insatiable desire for media attention as well as the slimy depths he's willing to go to to get it, but now he expresses something close to contrition. "I want to be loved," Kostabi states. "Is it insane to desire to be loved?" In the seconds that follow, he looks off camera with something close to longing, and it lends the moment a surprising poignancy.[10] In the raw footage the moment was less striking, because director Michael Sladek can be heard immediately asking the next question off camera. By replacing the audio with room tone silence, we made the pause take on a completely different meaning. (You can see the transformation of the raw footage into the final product in the "Pauses" video on the companion website.)

Such a pause can also be manufactured by cutting away from the subject to something else, then cutting back to the subject in a moment of repose. In Sarah Polley's *Stories We Tell*, her brother laments having to say goodbye to their mother after she lost custody of them. "I remember when mom used to drive us home," he states with a sad look on his face. "When she said goodbye to us . . . she would cry and cry, and we'd be crying and . . . we didn't want her to leave because we wanted to be with her." After a quick cut to reenactment footage of two small kids, the film cuts back to him as he sits with a silent look of sadness and longing on his face.[11]

▶ TRANSITIONS

Transitions between scenes are a key part of any documentary. These "in between" moments can be a way to build style into the foundation of your film. But before you charge off in search of a sexy visual motif, let's remember that the simplest and most effective transition between scenes is often a simple cut. One should always exploit the potential of the pause (see previous section) before looking for anything more elaborate. Should this prove insufficient, there are several other options.

The Fade or Cut to Black

When you are trying to signal a significant shift in your film, a fade or cut to black can provide an extra bit of punctuation that a simple pause cannot. If you've finished closing out an entire "chapter" of the film and are about to turn to a new idea, going to black can be quite effective. Consider a crucial transition in *Precious Knowledge*.[12] A mariachi song plays over an energetic montage showing excited students and motivated teachers in one of the Ethnic Studies programs at Tucson High School. Teachers are teaching, students are learning, and for the first time in the film it seems like academic achievement is happening for real. The montage concludes with a musical flourish and a title card touting impressive statistics for the program's success. Now the picture fades to black and settles there for slightly less than one second, giving a soft landing to this montage and subtly indicating that this chapter of the film is over.

Suddenly there is a hard cut to bright animated graphics and aggressive music from a local news broadcast, whose anchorwoman barks, "State Superintendent Tom Horne wants to *end* Ethnic Studies programs in the Tucson Unified School District!" This cut works precisely because of how abrupt it is, and how much it clashes with the soft landing of the previous section. In both form and content the film is announcing a sharp conflict.

But pauses in black can be dangerous. By letting the audience see a blank screen, you are potentially reminding them of the artificiality of the story and of the fact that they are *watching a movie*. Instead of giving them the next story point, you stop to give them a moment of absolutely nothing. Thus, these kinds of pauses should be used judiciously. In my opinion, more than two or three in the course of a feature film is too many. Exceptions, of course, abound—we used numerous fades to black in the jazz biopic *Jimmy Scott: If You Only Knew* because they so nicely complemented Scott's own patient, behind-the-beat vocal stylings—but these exceptions prove the rule.

The Flash to White

A variation on the fade to black is the flash to white, where one scene concludes by dissolving to a completely white screen and then dissolving back from white to the next scene. As with the fade to black, there must be a good reason to make this transition, especially because it resembles the editing style of disposable shows like *Access Hollywood*. One film where this motif is used quite successfully is Abigail Disney and Kathleen Hughes' *The Armor of Light*. There are 10 total flashes to white in the film; each one is used to transition from one character's story to a different one, but never just to get from one location to the next. This film also has a thematic justification for such a device, given its title. Minister Rob Schenck, a gun control advocate who fights an uphill battle to change the minds of his fellow evangelicals on the issue, paraphrases Paul the Apostle as saying, "Let us cast off the works of darkness—fear, ignorance, hatred, vengeance—and put on the armor of light."

Other Transitions

There are myriad graphical possibilities when creating transitions. If you simply reach into the grab bag of effects on your NLE and pick one out at random you will end up with transitions that bear no relationship to the tone and style of your film, but with some careful thinking you can create transitions that will match. In *Wordplay*, the popular 2006 documentary profiling *New York Times* crossword puzzle editor Will Shortz, scene changes are often accomplished with one image being pushed off the screen horizontally or vertically by another image (like the individual blocks of a crossword puzzle), and though it looks a little dated today it does have an organic relationship to the subject matter. In the 2016 series *Soundbreaking: Stories from the Cutting Edge of Recorded Music*, the filmmakers created their own graphic transition that is used continuously throughout the series. Colorful and brief with abstract flashes of light washing over the frame, it looks like a variation on a traditional film flare. Over the course of six to seven frames, the outgoing image is partially superimposed with the flare, and then disappears again once the cut has been accomplished (see Figures 14.6–14.11). Given that *Soundbreaking* is often celebrating the miraculous sonic objects achieved with analog audio equipment "back in the day," the effect feels fitting.

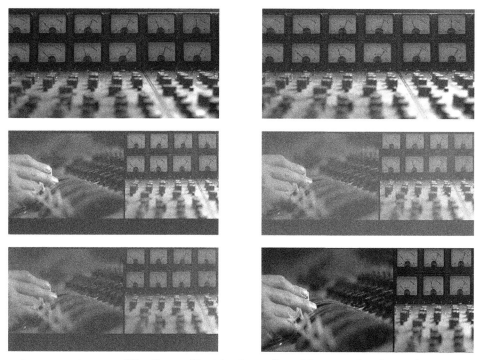

FIGURES 14.6–14.11 Film flare effect in *Soundbreaking: Stories from the Cutting Edge of Recorded Music.* Note that a cut is made on the third frame, but is masked somewhat by the hazy glow of the flare that blooms and then subsides over the course of the six-frame transition.

Look for opportunities to create transitional devices of your own, especially ones that can be accomplished with *footage* rather than fades to black or white. *The Central Park Five* has a terrific transitional shot that is worth highlighting. The opening nine minutes of the film firmly root the eponymous teenagers in the unique culture of their Harlem neighborhood, but the film now needs to transition us to Manhattan where the crime was committed. We see a telephoto shot of Harlem; the camera then tilts up and pans to the right, passing Central Park and finally revealing the skyscrapers of Manhattan.[13] This is an exceedingly simple transition, but it's impactful and elegant as well. Instead of just doing a straight cut to Manhattan, the film actually takes us from one place to the next *visually* so we feel a strong sense of the geographical and cultural distance between them. This reinforces the point made elsewhere in the film about how different the two boroughs were, and how unfamiliar some of the boys were with Manhattan.

The documentary *20 Feet from Stardom*, directed by Morgan Neville and edited by Doug Blush, Kevin Glauber, and Jason Zeldes, also has a brilliant transitional shot that moves us from a section with the Ikettes (who performed with the Ike & Tina Turner Revue) to the British rock scene of the late 1960s.[14] A riveting archival footage performance from the Ikettes concludes and, as we hear the crowd cheering, the film cuts to a different archival shot (or is it reenactment?) of them exiting a building in their matching blue dresses, as seen from a moving car. After the women leave the frame, the color quickly drains out of the picture, and then there is a cut to a black and white tracking shot of the same velocity in England, where we immediately see a British Bobby policeman directing traffic and hear Claudia Lennear say, "The English rock scene was just a phenomenon. . . " Quickly and effortlessly, we have made an extremely cinematic transition to a different locale.

▶ NOTES

1 This moment occurs in *Lost in La Mancha* at 1:12:17.

2 It's interesting to note that while these numbers follow closely with what the narrative is telling us about the success of the company, the match is not exact. When the figure of "233 employees" flashes across the screen, this is already at a point when the company has significant problems and is in danger of collapse, so the audience is invited to interpret the number as evidence of a bloated payroll instead of healthy growth.

3 This sequence runs from 27:42 to 29:40 in *The Central Park Five*.

4 These moments occur at 39:00 and 1:09:40, respectively.

5 This moment takes place at 8:00 in *Startup.com*.

6 This scene begins at 1:09:41.

7 This moment occurs at 1:07:34 in *Last Train Home*.

8 This long pause occurs at 29:43 in the first episode of *The Jinx*.

9 This moment occurs at 1:45:50.

10 This moment occurs at 31:17 in *Con Artist*.

11 This moment runs between 50:56 and 51:19 in *Stories We Tell*.

12 The montage begins at 20:12 and the fade to black occurs at 22:28.

13 This transition shot can be found at 8:55 in *The Central Park Five*.

14 The transition occurs at 30:18.

PART IV
The Refining Process

15

Feedback and Revision

▶ **EVALUATING THE WORK AND TAKING DIRECTION**

In the life cycle of every cut (be it a scene, sequence, or an entire film), there comes a moment when you have to take a step back to evaluate the work. Set the monitor up to display full screen, sit a little further away from it than you normally would, crank the volume up a bit, and turn down the lights in the room. Try to put yourself in the shoes of someone watching it for the first time. What do you think of it? Be honest with yourself.

You're likely to have lots of things to fix. Pacing will be awkward, concepts and narrative beats will be unclear, sound edits will be jumpy. Make a thorough set of notes and get back to work. After making modifications you're soon going to need some feedback from the director.

When doing so, it's crucial to see all ideas as valid even if they go against one's first instincts. As Kim Roberts says, "I've had enough experience now that even if a director has an idea that I think probably is going to fail, I'm going to try it. Because every now and then it succeeds and I'm totally wrong."

Geoff Richman expands on this idea by relating it to the fundamental issues of documentary editing:

> Everyone has opinions; of course as an editor you have a lot of strong opinions about how things should be put together, and so does the director. But no one's really right or wrong until you put it up on the screen in the context of the other scenes, and suddenly the opinions become reality or fact. It may work or it may fail, but if you're

not open to seeing the result then you're not going to be a good editor. There's a reason the edit is months or years long, because you need that time to see how every single revision actually plays on screen.

It's silly to even think of it as "bad ideas" or "good ideas" because you could argue that every idea is one that doesn't work until you reach picture lock. Until you have your final edit, every cut that you did that isn't in the final film isn't the right edit, but *you need every idea along the way to get to the next idea*. That's why if you don't entertain as many ideas as possible, you just won't just find the right path. And by trying ideas that you are against, it forces you to do the things that you would never, by definition, do on your own. And that idea—the bad idea—may lead to the next breakthrough.

This last point is a crucial one. Documentary editing is a long, arduous process that is built on the need for revision. Because of the myriad possibilities inherent in the raw footage, a workable structure and flow is built only partially by design. Mostly it is built through trial and error.

Sometimes the power of the director's vision is seen when giving notes on particular scenes. In *The Bad Kids*, there is a crucial scene early in the film in which the lead character Joey is going over his progress with his teacher Ms. Alexander. In my first edits, one could sense the tension between them, but it remained a relatively generic scene about a student who was underperforming and a teacher who was endeavoring to intervene. The scene was good but not great, and it lacked spark.

At one point in the raw footage Ms. Alexander says, "Joey, you need almost 30 credits in English, [and] you need to be doing these essays every credit check if you're serious about graduating," to which Joey tersely responds, "That sucks." Co-director Keith Fulton directed me to look at that particular moment of interaction and to think about it as the fulcrum point of the scene. I hadn't even included it in my first cuts of the scene and never saw it as being very important, but now that my attention was focused on it, I saw an entirely new set of dynamics at play. Joey was not only struggling but also being somewhat rude, which reflected both his frustration with his own lack of success and his basic distrust of authority. In recutting the scene around this one interaction (and looking for reaction shots to focus and amplify the emotion), the scene improved in several ways. First, emphasizing the "30 credits" line increased the size of the problem that Joey had to overcome, and thereby increased the level of satisfaction for the audience when they *did* see him make strides toward his goal. Second, it foreshadowed Joey's downfall in a subtle way by showing the self-pity that would eventually consume him. Third, it increased the level of conflict between the characters which made the scene more dynamic. Lastly, it drew our attention to the persistence of the teachers by showing that they will stick with a kid even when his first response is to reject the help that is being offered. The entire complexion of the scene changed because of one incisive note from the director.

▶ WHY HOLD A ROUGH CUT SCREENING?

At a certain point your ability to see whether an idea "works" or not will become somewhat fuzzy. An editor who has watched a scene 200 times inevitably becomes dulled to its effects, and after a while your ability to judge the overall effectiveness of what you've done becomes limited. "Weeks or months into the work, you accumulate these reasons why things have to be a certain way," says Geoff Richman. "It's almost impossible not to fall into the trap of becoming too comfortable with your edit."

Behold, the rough cut screening! Showing the film to an audience is an amazing tool for recentering your perspective, identifying what's being communicated effectively and what is not.

"Oftentimes those screenings are instructive for me to just sit there and feel the movie with other people, feel how it is playing and listen to how they're responding," says Aaron Wickenden. "You can immediately tell which jokes are landing, where the cut feels too tight, where people are shifting in their seats and getting bored." Then once the discussion begins, you quickly learn more. "You screen it to an audience and they'll quickly tell you all these other problems that you weren't even aware of, or just tell you it doesn't work," says Geoff Richman. "All the assumptions you made before without even knowing it, they all go out the window."

▶ TIPS FOR A SUCCESSFUL ROUGH CUT SCREENING

To get the best results from a rough cut screening, try following these basic guidelines:

- ▶ **Select your audience carefully.** If the cutting is still in the early going, you may want to choose a small audience of trusted "filmmaker types" rather than members of the general public because they will be better able to handle the harsh edges of a truly "rough" rough cut. If your film is a little further along and you have reasonably smooth audio transitions and the like, opening it up to a wider range of people is important because both experts and "civilians" have valuable insights to offer.

- ▶ **Select four to eight people.** Too few people will give you a sample size that's too small, but too many makes it impossible to have a meaningful discussion.

- ▶ **Give everyone a pad of paper and a pen.** Ask people to write down any thoughts that occur to them during the screening.

- ▶ **Leave just enough light in the room for people to write down notes.** The room should be nearly dark, just a little brighter than a theater setting.

- ▶ **Allow a few minutes after the film finishes for the audience to write down their thoughts and/or fill out a questionnaire before starting the discussion.**

It's important to have them fill this out *before* the discussion begins, because the discussion will start to change people's minds about the film and to make them question their own opinions. But their reactions were their reactions, and you want to know what they were. Your questionnaire can have a few specific questions regarding some of the issues you're most concerned about, but it should also have basic ones like, "What did you find most compelling" and "Where were you confused or bored?"

▶ **Prepare for harsh criticism.** The experience of seeing your cut ripped apart can be enormously frustrating, and it's important not to get defensive or else your audience may back off from giving you their most honest feedback. "You have to steel yourself for criticism and make sure not to argue," says Marshall Curry. "Even if I'm seething inside, I just smile and say "ah, yeah, that's *interesting*."

▶ **Take detailed notes.** Designate the assistant editor to be the scribe, or take notes yourself; make sure all comments are captured accurately. Some editors like to make an audio recording of the discussion for reference.

▶ **Beware of one or two people dominating the discussion.** Just because someone is more vocal doesn't make their opinion more valuable. If this starts to occur, try to shift the discussion back to quieter members or to another topic. A discussion about the film can easily get sidetracked onto one or two issues if you're not careful.

▶ INTERPRETING NOTES

After your screening has concluded, you will likely have a slew—if not an outright avalanche—of notes to consider. It may also be at this point that you reach a low point in your confidence. Much of what you thought was working isn't working at all, and your audience had to work to say nice things about it. If you feel like the film is terrible, has no saving grace whatsoever, or that you might as well just pack up your things and go home, join the club. Every documentary editor has been there, and most editors will tell you that there is at least one soul-shattering crisis of faith on every film they've cut.

Remember our principles: *trust in process* and *always be prepared to walk away from an idea that isn't working.* As Marshall Curry says:

There are points where it is going to be terrible, where you have been working on it a long time and it will not make sense or work emotionally. But you have to keep from getting rattled and realize that that is a part of the process. Push away the existential fear that maybe you don't know how to edit, or that the movie is a bad idea or whatever. It is just a matter of identifying problems and solving problems, over and over again. You just have to be willing to listen to criticism and throw away things that aren't working and just keep moving every day. Slowly, over time, your cut is going to get better and better.

"Despair? That's on every film, *every* film," says Geoff Richman:

> The minute you're high-fiving in the editing room because you've solved every problem, that's when you screen it to an audience, and it's always the case where it's like splashing cold water in your face. You can get to the point where it's overwhelmingly frustrating and you just have to hold it firmly in the back of your mind that this is the process. You still feel overwhelmed and frustrated but you can take some solace in the fact that it happens on every single film. That's why the edit is nine months long.

The next moment in the process is deciding how to handle the feedback you've just been given; that is, which notes to address and which to ignore. One valuable rule of thumb is to see which notes are coming from multiple audience members, and which are one-off anomalies. "When you're getting consistent notes," says Aaron Wickenden, "pay attention to those rather than things where somebody has a very specific note that nobody else has and that you've never heard before." This is not because you're trying to focus-group your film to death, but rather because it represents a reliable indication of what the film is actually communicating to its audience. Human perception is a complex phenomenon; it's possible for anyone to have an anomalous reaction to almost anything. But when multiple people are telling you that a particular section was confusing, or that a particular character is really fascinating, this is easier to rely on.

Those who have been at this awhile have also come to live by a helpful aphorism: listen to the problems, but not necessarily to the solutions. Your audience knows what they just saw and how they felt about it, but they may not be able to identify *why*. As Walter Murch discusses in his book *In the Blink of an Eye*, the concept of "referred pain" is valid here.[1] Your patient (the audience member) knows that something hurts, but they're not necessarily the best authority on the *source* of the pain. It could be that a particular scene isn't working because the pacing is off, but it could also be because the main character hasn't been set up well enough in the *previous* scene. As Mary Lampson explains:

> When people say things, you have to figure out why they're saying it. Oftentimes the reason they say it isn't what they tell you. It's something that happened 15 minutes earlier . . . so I actually take every single note, even the ones that I call stupid, really seriously. And I'm very clear that this isn't about an audience's solutions, it is about what the problems are. I rarely listen to anybody's solutions—I'm very suspicious of people who right away go to solutions.

Another thing to be wary of is the influence of external factors on the reaction of your audience. Every now and then you may have a screening that is very low energy, or may feel "off" somehow, and sometimes it's because of factors beyond your control. As Marshall Curry relates, "We had a screening right after Obama won the election and we were getting all these positive notes, almost no negative ones, even though we knew the film still had problems. We had to discount that screening a bit and assume that Obama's election had something to do with it."

Armed with a list of notes to address, you now head back into the cut with a renewed sense of perspective. Some notes will be easy to solve—a montage that needs tightening, a piece of music that doesn't work—but many will be head-scratchers. How do we avoid confusing people with too much information at the beginning while still providing needed background? Is one entire subplot unnecessary, or have we just failed to properly explain its relevance? One school of thought on how to prioritize is to go ahead and take care of the easy problems first. Any note that has a quick and obvious solution is worth getting out of the way because it's low-hanging fruit, and could help solve the other problems in a small way since every issue is interrelated.

From here, you can tackle the bigger stuff. What happens if you take out two whole scenes that seem to be cluttering up the mix? How about constructing a new backstory for one of your primary characters who is underdeveloped? Having created a copy of your sequence and archived the old version for reference, you should feel free to experiment and play, working over ideas to try them out and see how they work.

One thing to remember is that at this stage, you need to rewatch things through relatively frequently after you recut them. The film is a living, breathing organism, and adjustments in one area can have unintended consequences, both positive and negative, in another. Determining the effect of one change versus another requires viewing the entire thing from the top on a regular basis.

It can take anywhere from several days to a few weeks to work out all the ideas from a rough cut screening to their conclusion. Once you and the director feel that the cut has reached a new plateau and your critical senses are starting to dull again, it's time to have another screening.

It is impossible to overemphasize just how much persistence is necessary in order to arrive at a film where the kinks are fully ironed out, the characters are dynamic and engaging, and the narrative is working on all cylinders. By the time an editor has reached the final order of their scenes, there will likely have been hundreds of different iterations, usually in a two-steps-forward, one-step-back sort of progress. Continuous reshuffling is common and necessary.

One encouraging phenomenon is that the productivity of your time spent on structural changes does tend to improve as the cut marches forward. As Geoff Richman explains:

> Once you get six months into the edit and you see the clock starting to run out, it can be really frustrating because you have the sense that things are going to move at

the same pace that they did for the first six months and that you just won't finish the film. But it's not true at all. For me, I find on every film that the final weeks of the edit are exponentially more productive than anything that came before. So, you arrive at this six or seven month point in an eight month edit, and things are still not working and it seems like it's going to take another six months, but then one thing clicks into place and it causes 10 other things to click into place, and then 40 things click into place and then the film is a completely different film than it was two weeks earlier.

▶ CLARITY IS KING

While I am wary of feel-good maxims and suspicious of the supposed wisdom handed down from corporate titans, there was real wisdom in the marketing slogan chosen by Steve Jobs for Apple's first marketing brochure in 1977: "Simplicity is the ultimate sophistication." By all accounts, Jobs was constantly asking his engineers and industrial designers to minimize options and clarify user experience, and Apple's current design guru Jony Ive recently reiterated Jobs' philosophy when he stated, "You have to deeply understand the essence of a product in order to be able to get rid of the parts that are not essential."[1]

This is precisely the intention an editor needs to adopt at this stage of the process. Every extra nonessential element in your film must be excised so that the essential elements can do their job as efficiently as possible. For the sake of the sanity of your audience, remember Walter Murch's advice: "Do the most with the least," and *simplify, simplify, simplify*.

▶ TRIMMING SCENES DOWN

There's nothing worse than watching a movie and feeling like you know exactly where it's going because it's following such a familiar route. Even after months of editing, you still may have some scenes that are too long because you have become blind to them by watching them so many times, or because you've moved them into a new location in the cut where the setup for the scene is now being provided through other means. It is thus wise to follow screenwriter William Goldman's oft-quoted dictum, "Get in late and leave early." Instead of showing us elements of a scene that are obvious or plodding, drop us into it with just enough context to make it understandable, but little enough to make it intriguing.

Take an early scene from *The Armor of Light*. In an early section of the film showing several horrific mass shootings, a uniformed police officer, looking shaken, makes a chilling statement at a press conference: "He apparently told the kids to line up in front of the blackboard ... " The officer takes a considered pause, and the film then moves on with its story without letting him finish his sentence.[2] Taken on its own the statement is nearly meaningless, but given its placement we have plenty of context to fill in the blanks for ourselves. The officer's sentence has a bizarrely poetic flavor to it, and the deed seems even more shocking by the absence of further details.

Or take the moment in *Happy Valley* when Penn State football coach Joe Paterno dies.[3] The event is marked not by any words to this effect, but by a single shot of a hearse driving in a funeral procession through a cemetery. Paterno's likeness is never shown, his voice is not heard, and we are never explicitly told he has died, but we know exactly has happened and the film benefits from a light touch.

Beyond just cutting the beginnings and endings of scenes, inspect the core by giving your scenes this basic smell test:

▶ **Is it obvious?** If so, leave it out.

▶ **Is it interesting?** If not, leave it out.

▶ **Does it advance the story, build our understanding of the issue, or build one of the characters in a meaningful way?** If not, leave it out.

▶ **Can it be shortened without damaging it?** Consider doing so.

▶ CUTTING SCENES TO REMOVE REDUNDANCY

One of the enemies of good storytelling is needless repetition. An audience does not want to be lectured at, and telling them the same thing over and over again is one of the quickest ways to lose their attention. Thus, one of the first steps we can take is to look at our cut and see whether there are any scenes that are "duplicates"; that is, they both cover the same dramatic territory. It can be painful to cut one of these scenes if it is dynamic, emotional, and taut when viewed on its own, yet if it simply repeats the same territory covered by another scene then it is hurting the film, not helping it.

We had this issue with two scenes of Jennifer seeking consolation over her father's lack of supportiveness in *The Bad Kids*. Both were riveting, but they also had too many similarities to ignore. In one, she brings up the issue with her principal, Vonda Viland, and in another she bursts out crying during an academic counseling session with one of her teachers. The second scene had the obvious advantage of being more spontaneous and urgent, so we used it first. Then we cut the scene with Vonda way down and used it as a cue for Vonda to reveal something important about *her* own background. This way the problem is introduced in one scene, and the "solution" is offered in the second; also, the focus shifts from Jennifer in the first scene to Vonda in the second. Using shortened, nonredundant versions of both scenes reinforced the idea that the care of the students was a group effort, with multiple teachers and administrators intervening in different ways.

▶ CUTTING SCENES TO IMPROVE NARRATIVE OR EMOTIONAL LOGIC

There are other reasons why you might need to cut a scene from your film. Sometimes a scene's emotional logic just doesn't track with what we know about a character from other scenes. The editing has set them up in a particular way to emphasize certain elements of their story and/or certain aspects of their personality, and then a scene comes along that disrupts that balance in a fatal way. While complexity is something to strive for, a scene that feels *contradictory* can be problematic.

In *The Bad Kids*, one of the most affecting scenes we cut was one in which 17-year-old Joey visits his principal Vonda in her office. He is clearly strung out: he shields his eyes from the modest lamps that light the room and his voice has moved an octave higher, the result of meth use. He says very little, but watching him in this state is both horrifying and mesmerizing. He is a young man clearly headed toward an early demise, and this scene was always considered one of our most compelling.

Unfortunately, the actions that Vonda had already taken to try to get him into treatment were not possible to include in the preceding scenes for unrelated reasons, so when Vonda responds to him by suggesting that he return to school full-time, it plays as "off," if not downright irresponsible. It seems like she should be getting him to a treatment center on the double rather pleading with him to return to class. Every time we watched it, we kept wanting the scene to work but had to conclude that it didn't. We took it out.

▶ NOTE

1   Walter Murch, *In The Blink of an Eye: A Perspective on Film Editing*, 2nd ed. (Los Angeles: Silman-James Press, 2001), p. 52.

16

Fine Cut to Final Cut and Beyond

After multiple rounds of revision, hopefully your overall structure is functioning smoothly. Your lead characters are compelling; your narrative arc is clear; and your audience is not confused about any major issues. You are "over the hump" and can now focus on the *details* of your cut with renewed focus and vigor. In order to move forward, every aspect of the cut must be thoroughly inspected to make sure it is there for a reason.

▶ REMOVING UNNECESSARY PAUSES AND UTTERANCES

By the time you reach picture lock, every single moment of dialogue, including the silences, must be tightly and purposefully edited. As Marshall Curry explains:

> In the final stages I go through and question every clip, every bite, every breath, to make sure it truly needs to be in there. I tell myself to imagine that we had to cut five minutes out of the film. Where would we get that? And would those cuts make it better or worse? Sometimes a breath is really nice, and keeps the pacing natural and real. But sometimes a breath is just a breath and it can be removed. I look for places where I can pull out six frames or even two frames. Sometimes a stutter is interesting or revealing, but sometimes it is just messy and should come out.

When the source of the dialogue is off-camera, you have carte blanche to clean it up: you can remove all those "umm"s, "uh"s and other unwanted utterances at will. When your subjects are on camera your options are somewhat more limited, but the prior section on making use of cutaways should be revisited for ideas on how use them as efficiently as possible.

▶ INSPECTING AND IMPROVING CUTAWAYS

Author Jay McInerney spoke in 2016 about the influence of his mentor Raymond Carver on his writing. "One of the things I remember most distinctly," said McInerney, "was Ray turning to me one day and saying, 'Why are you using the word *earth* here? What you really mean is *dirt*. Why don't you just say, *dirt*? You're seeking a grandiosity that you don't need. Say what you mean, and say it in the most direct way you can.'"[4]

Think about how this advice applies to cutaways. Up until now, you may have chosen your cutaways primarily for their functionality. (Does it cover the required number of frames? Has it served to oil the gears of your scene so it plays more smoothly?) Now is your chance to reinspect each one and make sure it holds up to a new standard: is it absolutely the best that it can be? Here are a few reasons to reject a cutaway in favor of a better one:

- ▶ **Poor camera work.** (Shot jerks unnecessarily, etc.)

- ▶ **Poor composition.** (It's just not satisfying.)

- ▶ **Too generic.** (Fails to add something specific to the mix.)

Take a look at the ending of the three-scene sequence from the documentary *Small Farm Rising* shown at the end of the "Cutting a Verité Dialogue Scene" tutorial available on the companion website. Fledgling Crow Farm co-owner Ian is on the phone, bargaining with a customer over the price of the heads of romaine lettuce that they're selling. There is a bit of tension in the air because Ian may lose this customer if he doesn't lower the price enough. The strain shows on Ian's face, but take a close look at the multiple cutaways to his co-owner Lucas, for each one conveys something very specific. The first one is there to cover a break in the sync dialogue, but there is a wistful quality to the expression on Lucas' face that adds something more, as if he's saying to himself, "It's all up to fate now . . . " The second reaction shot happens right as the price is being mentioned, and the look of expectation on his face significantly amplifies the tension that's already been built up. The third one comes as Ian is extolling the quality of their product, and Lucas nods his head in agreement as if to say to himself, "Whether you buy it or not, buddy, we know that our lettuce is the best." All of this adds up to a scene that is significantly richer than if the cutaways were purely functional.[5]

▶ MOVING BACKWARDS: OVERCUTTING AND HOW TO AVOID IT

Near the end of the process you may start to question the value of many sections and details that once seemed vital. Some of this skepticism is healthy, but some of it is dangerous. There is a very real peril at this stage of the game that you will start to make scenes shorter than they need to be, and that you might remove elements that have genuine value. It's important to stay vigilant about this and to avoid over-cutting your film. Remember Mary Lampson's advice about the dangers of oversimplification in our section on experimentation: you can easily lose valuable idiosyncrasies in the service of trying to streamline a film. In the same interview, she cautioned that, "I've seem films that have lost their heart in the "cleaning up" stage. Just because every tiny thing doesn't fit into a perfect little box doesn't necessarily mean that it's bad."

The best method to avoid overcutting is to remember to take long breaks—a day or two at a stretch, or a week—and to keep in consultation with your director and other members of the team, who can talk you out of poorly considered ideas. Doing a rough cut screening for an audience and seeing it afresh is also a good idea; it can remind you of the value of the bits of the film which are now starting to seem tired.

▶ PICTURE LOCK AND BEYOND

At long last, you will come to the glorious moment known as "picture lock." All the many possible avenues for the film's structure have been explored, everything has been checked twice and thrice, and you and the director(s) have concluded that the film is finished. Congratulations! Expect to feel exhausted, relieved, and maybe even a little sad that it's all over.

But it's not quite over! Once picture lock is achieved, there are still crucial finishing tasks to be accomplished, and the editor must make sure that everyone who is taking the film forward from here—the sound editor and mixer, the colorist, and the person supervising the final conform—has what they need to complete their work. What follows is a short overview of the process; for a much more detailed view, check out Scott Trundle and Tasha Trieu's book *Modern Post: Workflows and Techniques for Digital Filmmakers*.

The Sound Mix

Most editing rooms lack the sound baffling and high-quality speaker setups of professional mixing environments, and most NLEs lack subframe editing capabilities, so you should hand off the sound editing and mixing to a professional.[6] They will take all of the work you've done to this point and rebuild it from the ground up. Every cut and dissolve will be inspected and reworked, and sophisticated noise reduction and EQ will be applied.

This means that you need to provide the sound editor with the various tracks organized to their specifications via an AAF or OMF file. It's best to check with the audio editor, but a standard configuration might look like this: Tracks 1–4: dialogue/production sound; Tracks 5–6: narration; Tracks 7–10: sound effects; Tracks 11–14: background/ambience tracks; Tracks 15–18: music. Remember that the sound editor won't have a visual reference for any of your individual audio tracks, which is why this kind of organization is crucial. If they have to contend with sound effects sitting in the music track and narration in the ambience tracks, it can create needless extra work for them to sort out.

You will also be expected to provide an output of the finished film with slate, countdown, 2-pop, tail pop, and burn-in timecode.

Color Grading and Conforming

To move forward you need to understand how the conform is going to be accomplished. Is the color grading going to happen at the same facility as the final conform? Will any material that was shot by a camera with a lower resolution or a different frame rate be spit out in its original format for the post house to work with separately from the other files, or will you be using the transcoded version of those files that you may have edited with? Figure out whether the titling work you may have done is going to be used, or whether it will be redone from scratch in the conform. (Titles have to be put on last, because otherwise the whites will no longer look white once each shot has been colored differently.) If you're going to use the titles you created, how will they be given to the post house doing the conform?

The ultimate name of the game here is *communication*. It's an editor's job to provide detail and clarity to the professionals who will be handling these operations, so make sure to ask questions and make sure that everyone is speaking the same language. Your color-grading artist will need your AAF or XML file that was exported from the NLE (ask them what settings they suggest), plus the hard drive that has all of the original video files. Make sure that the AAF or XML is linking back to the full-resolution files (not the proxy files, if you've been using them).

▶ NOTES

1   Walter Isaacson, "How Steve Jobs' Love of Simplicity Fueled a Design Revolution." *Smithsonian Magazine*. Smithsonian.com. September 2012. Web.

2   This short news clip plays at 12:29 in *The Armor of Light*.

3   The hearse scene takes place at 41:43 in *Happy Valley*.

4   Interview with Terry Gross, Fresh Air, August 5, 2016.

5   It is also interesting to note that these reaction shots were all taken completely out of context from different moments in the conversation. When Lucas nods in agreement in the raw footage, he's not thinking about the lettuce at all, but agreeing with Ian's assessment that they fight like brothers.

6   Final Cut Pro X is a notable exception; it has subframe audio editing capabilities.

PART V
Seeing It All Come Together
Analyses of Four Films

▶ **INTRODUCTION**

The best way to learn about documentary editing is to edit a documentary. Nothing substitutes for the trial-and-error process of putting a film together, especially if you have talented mentors who are willing to give constructive criticism. But you can also learn a great deal by watching finished films. By analyzing a documentary in depth, one can uncover its structural underpinnings and learn from the specific choices that it makes. As a gesture in that direction, I've included analyses of four films in this final section: the features *My Kid Could Paint That* and *An Inconvenient Truth* and the shorts *Skip* and *Hotel 22*.

My Kid Could Paint That is a complex drama that required the director and editor to confront rich storytelling questions about point of view, observational versus participatory framings, and character development. The editorial challenges of *An Inconvenient Truth* are simpler: how can we keep an audience interested in a 90-minute lecture by a former politician? It contains lessons about how to liven up material that is fundamentally static and uncinematic, and how to think creatively about how to build a narrative into a topic that doesn't seem to have one.

Skip is a charming interview-based short that is a lesson in how to build mystery and narrative development into a story that was shot entirely *after* the events in question had played out. *Hotel 22*, by contrast, has no interviews at all, and is built entirely on verité footage; its patient, elegant design holds lessons in how the search for patterns in footage can yield strong results. Both shorts have subtle internal rhythms that give them strong identities, and carry some great lessons in dynamics.

17

Analyses of Two Feature Documentaries

▶ *MY KID COULD PAINT THAT* (2007)

Directed by Amir Bar-Lev

Edited by Michael Levine and John Walters

My Kid Could Paint That is a 2007 documentary that tells the story of Marla Olmstead, a 4-year-old girl whose abstract paintings begin selling for tens of thousands of dollars on the New York art market. The film, as rendered by its director Amir Bar-Lev and editors John Walter and Michael Levine, contains a fascinating narrative about what happens when the true authorship of the paintings is questioned; it also becomes a meditation on authenticity, meaning, and value in modern art. But perhaps its biggest accomplishment from an editorial perspective is how it deftly manages the inclusion of the director in the narrative, and how it navigates the complexities of participatory filmmaking. It is also a master class in how to craft characters with clearly defined perspectives and points of view.

Of the many perils that participatory films risk, perhaps none is greater than the sense that the decision to include the filmmaker as a character is an arbitrary or narcissistic one. When a director gets involved in the story that he or she is investigating, it must feel to the viewer like that involvement was necessary and/or inevitable. Thus, the motivations of the character of the director have to be managed just as precisely as that of any other character, if not more so.

The reality of the situation as experienced by Bar-Lev was intense and volatile. After having spent over six months filming and developing personal ties with Marla and her parents, he was thrown for a loop when a *60 Minutes* segment raised troubling questions about whether the parents may have helped paint the works and masterminded an elaborate deception. Struggling with the conflicting priorities of his own personal relationship with the Olmsteads versus his commitment to the truth of the story, Bar-Lev developed a case of insomnia severe enough to require medical treatment, and started having frequent dreams about the Olmsteads. In one, the family was keeping him in a glass room and watching him at all hours before an assassin shot him dead.

Of course, the true power dynamics were actually operating in reverse, with Bar-Lev in a position of authorial control over how he would tell the story of the Olmsteads. "How should I depict the Olmstead family if I didn't know for sure whether Marla did the paintings?" he asked himself in a fascinating piece he wrote for The Huffington Post.[1]

> I had 100 hours of tape I needed to cull down into a 90-minute film. The inclusion of a possibly cagey facial expression, the exclusion of a peculiar off camera aside—these cuts would point my audience toward conclusions, and these conclusions would have real-world consequences for the Olmsteads. Was I really evaluating these questions with sober journalistic detachment, or was my perspective colored by my feelings of friendship—or, for that matter, my desire to make a dramatic movie?

Bar-Lev tried to follow his initial plan, which was to make the film with an *observational* frame; that is, an uncomplicated window onto a story that simply reveals itself to the audience. This would involve removing all traces of himself from the footage, removing his offscreen interactions with the subjects and deleting all but the most crucial offscreen questions. And yet the circumstances of the situation kept getting in the way. As he noted in his Huffington Post article:

> The documentary screen appears to us a lot like the picture frame must have seemed to audiences of representational paintings one hundred years ago: a window into another reality. But is the screen really a window, and are the things it seems to show

us the real world, or constructions? The more I struggled with my own "canvas," the more truthful it felt to draw attention, at least in a small way, to the act of depicting itself. To pretend *My Kid Could Paint That* is simply a window into the life of a family would be like pretending that a painted mountain was a mountain, and a painted figure a person."

Bar-Lev had a big problem, however. To simply introduce himself as a character half-way through the film at the moment when the *60 Minutes* segment aired would create an untenable narrative, because it would be introducing a new character—and a brand new "participatory" frame—way too late in the story. This was clear to Bar-Lev and his editors, so they first sought to set up Bar-Lev as the narrator of the entire film, beginning with a voice-over segment on the history of art. Yet this proved to be unsatisfying, because it kept stealing too much of the spotlight away from the real subjects of the film, and created a heavy-handed tone. So they kept searching for ways to accomplish the task.

That task was made even more difficult by the fact that since Bar-Lev never anticipated putting himself in the narrative, he shot very little footage of his interaction with the Olmsteads. In essence the film was shot with one camera, but what was needed was a second camera, showing him in the frame along with the family.

This is exactly how the film begins, with a wide shot of Bar-Lev approaching the Olmstead's modest home in Binghamton, New York. As he sits down on the front porch with Marla and her younger brother, the perspective quickly shifts to footage taken with Bar-Lev's own camera, which points up into Marla's face. He chats amiably with her, hoping that Marla will discuss her new panting, but Marla is having none of it. "You have to *play*, Amir, you can't just do the camera," she says, giggling with delight. With this quick scene, Bar-Lev is instantly introduced to us as a curious observer of the Olmsteads who has also developed personal ties to them.

But how did he find the footage for this introductory scene? Answer: he shot it *late* in the process, *after* editing revealed that he would need to be present in the film from the beginning.

As the film progresses, it makes subtle editing choices that cleverly keep Bar-Lev alive as a secondary character in the first half, present but unobtrusive. One way it does this is by including a couple more low-key scenes of him and Marla interacting together in her home. In one early scene, Bar-Lev has the camera on the floor as Marla works on a puzzle, and he good-naturedly tries to coax some answers out of her. "So what's the name of your new painting?" he asks. "How do you know when you're finished with a painting?" Marla is uninterested in answering, and instead wants Bar-Lev's help in putting together the puzzle. The scene ends with her saying, "Amir, I can't do this all by myself, you should help!" At which point Bar-Lev says, "Alright," and cuts off the camera so he can grant her request.

Note the function of the scene: Bar-Lev gains no useful information from the inter-action, so it's not about learning the answers to his questions or giving any narrative information. But it brings Bar-Lev into the mix as an active presence, shows the grow-ing relationship between him and the family (which will make its later dissolution more dramatic) and also helps set up a major theme of the film: money and celebrity as cor-rupting influences on Marla's innocence. Marla is just a little girl, and just wants to play rather than to have to answer questions from an outsider. As local Binghamton journalist Elizabeth Cohen asks rhetorically at one point, "doesn't every child deserve a childhood? Isn't that one of those inalienable rights, to just be a child?" The film adroitly shows that Marla's parents have very different views on the possibility of the fame and fortune that may flow from Marla's talents, with the mother much more protective of her daughter and the father more cavalier about their decision to thrust their daughter into the spotlight.

The other scenes containing Bar-Lev in the first half operate in a similar way. Instead of framing him out of the story by scrubbing the footage of his presence, he's slightly *more* present than usual. His questions to other interviewees are often heard offscreen in full, for instance. When he brings *New York Times* art critic Michael Kimmelman into the film, we hear Bar-Lev ask, "Michael, how did you get personally involved with the story of Marla?" rather than simply letting Kimmelman explain.

Then, as events unfold, the editing brilliantly depicts Bar-Lev as being inexorably *drawn into* the drama (as opposed to actively inserting himself into it). Cohen, the journalist, narrates the immediate fallout to the damaging *60 Minutes* story, expressing sympa-thy for the parents as we see their faces fall in real time as they watch what they had assumed would be a story celebrating her daughter's achievements. "They really were in over their heads," Cohen says sympathetically. Then she goes on: "*and they must feel a little nervous now about you, I mean, it is kind of similar*," referring to Bar-Lev as another figure from the media who could turn out to damage their reputation.

Seven minutes later, after we see some of the fallout from the *60 Minutes* story, Cohen again acts as the catalyst for bringing Bar-Lev into the mix, this time more explicitly than ever. "From the very beginning, you were kind of a wildcard," she muses as we see footage of Bar-Lev entering the Olmstead's home, "because you weren't from a network, you weren't going to be putting them on the evening news—you were a guy who just wanted to make his own film. What attracted you to it?" she asks. This is the moment where we finally hear Bar-Lev explain what's been going on in his mind as all of the drama he's been filming has played out. Again, using Cohen as the catalyst for Bar-Lev's presence justifies it in a way that makes it feel utterly organic.

The film then builds up to a highly dramatic final scene, in which Bar-Lev finally con-fronts the parents on camera regarding his doubts about the provenance of the paint-ings. We have seen with our own eyes the striking difference in the level of refinement and maturity between the only painting that was ever captured on camera from start to finish and the rest of her oeuvre, which Bar-Lev cannot ignore. Though the confrontation comes almost in the form of an apology, it is nonetheless devastating to the Olmsteads. The film ends with Sheila (Marla's mother) reacting to Amir's distrust with dismay, sadness, and anger. As the tears start to flow, she gets up and abruptly leaves the interview, aware that her emotions will be perfect for Amir's film. "Documentary gold," she says disgustedly as she leaves. Because of the way Amir has positioned his own character, we can see both the exploitative nature of his project as well as the good reasons for his misgivings.

My Kid Could Paint That is also notable for the rigor it applies to the way its central characters are depicted, and the roles that they play. For a story that had so much publicity, there were doubtless dozens of possible players that could have been included in the drama, but the film culls things down to just eight, each of whom have a clear connection to the drama and a consistent role to play.

- ▶ Marla Olmstead: Star of the show, but a bit of a cipher. She enjoys painting, but really just wants to have fun.

- ▶ Zane Olmstead (Marla's younger brother): A minor character, but clearly desirous of all the attention Marla's getting.

- ▶ Sheila Olmstead (Marla's mother): Protective of Marla and ambivalent about the entire prospect of putting Marla into the spotlight, yet also a bit of a cipher. She protects her family's honor, but it's unclear what kind of a relationship she has with her husband given the disparity in their views.

- ▶ Mark Olmstead (Marla's father): Friendly and chatty, he is gung-ho about the possibility of Marla as a child prodigy earning big bucks. Intriguingly, he is also an amateur painter. Does he have secrets that he has not told his wife about the nature of his involvement with Marla's paintings? The film gives us tantalizing bits of information that makes this interpretation possible, including the fact that each of the parents has opposite work schedules and are thus rarely home at the same time during the week. His reaction to the *60 Minutes* story seems a little off, but is that explainable by the fact that he was in the highly unnatural position of being filmed at the time?

- ▶ Elizabeth Cohen (local Binghamton journalist): Writer of the original newspaper story about Marla, and the voice of conscience for the film. Again and again, she frames the issues in moral terms. She warns the family that if she runs her story it may have potentially negative as well as positive consequences, and continues to discuss her misgivings about the family's choices with respect to their daughter.

- ▶ Michael Kimmelman (art critic for the *New York Times*): Writer of the first national newspaper story about Marla, which set off the craze about her work, and the voice of authority about modern art's relationship with issues of authenticity and "genius." He always appears "above the fray," commenting with authority on issues from a historical/cultural perspective.

▶ Anthony Brunelli, gallery owner: Clearly an opportunist, he is the organizer of Marla's gallery shows, and gleeful promoter of the juicy tale of Marla as a child prodigy. He bails on his gallerist career and returns to painting full-time after the debacle, and seems to have some scruples in the end.

▶ Amir Bar-Lev, filmmaker: Initially interested in a story about modern art, he ends up being dragged into a major controversy over the authenticity of his subject's paintings. Ambivalent and self-aware, he exposes his own impure motives as the maker of a documentary with an unexpectedly juicy twist.

It's crucial to note that each of these people is of course a multifaceted individual with myriad interests and proclivities, and complex life histories. But for the sake of the documentary, they each play a specific and constrained role. Marla's mother does not comment on the finer points of art history, just as *New York Times* art critic Michael Kimmelman does not opine on child-rearing. Each character has a direct, organic connection to the story as a whole, and is consistent in their point of view. This is not to say that they are one-dimensional. In fact, there is great complexity to be found here. But without structure, rigor, and exclusion (of irrelevant details, minor characters that distract from the main narrative, etc.), there is no film.

Bar-Lev never definitively answers the question of whether Marla painted all of her own paintings without help, and the film is much better for the absence of any kind of final statement. The actions onscreen have laid out the contradictions as clear as day, and it's up to us to come to our own conclusions.

▶ AN INCONVENIENT TRUTH (2006)

Directed by Davis Guggenheim

Edited by Jay Cassidy and Dan Swietlik

Released in 2006, *An Inconvenient Truth* is the Academy Award–winning environmental documentary featuring former Vice President Al Gore's lecture on the dangers of climate change. Stop right there and you will find one undeniably painful word in that sentence: *lecture.* A lecture is something that you endure, not enjoy. (*"Don't lecture me . . . " "I don't need a lecture from you . . . " "He lectured on and on. . . "*) And given the highly visual nature of the film medium, a filmed account of a politician delivering a speech from a stage has the potential to be excruciatingly dull. But *An Inconvenient Truth* shows us how specific documentary editing and directing techniques can be brought to bear on such material in order to transform it into a compelling cinematic experience.

It's worth noting how the film, which spawned a 2017 sequel, came to be. Producer Laurie David saw Gore give an abbreviated version of his slideshow in New York in 2004 and was "floored." "[His] presentation was the most powerful and clear explanation of global warming I had ever seen,"[2] she stated, and she made it her mission to produce it as a film. She assembled a team, including fellow producer Lawrence Bender and line producer Lesley Chilcott, and enlisted documentarian Davis Guggenheim to direct. Thus from the outset it was clear that the lecture, which Gore claimed to have already given over 1,000 times to different audiences around the world, would be the centerpiece of the film. Gore had already developed a finely honed presentation, complete with humorous asides and personal anecdotes, and it was a combination of his persuasive rhetorical skills, charisma, and solid grasp of the facts that seemed to be so powerful in person, and which, it was decided, should be preserved in the film.

As Guggenheim noted:

> If you want to [get into] the science of global warming, there are lots of better ways—you can read voluminous books—but this is a way to really experience the full profound time with Gore. And I thought, if we give people time with Gore then we get them hooked, and they can take the rest of the journey on their own.

The film does two major things in the service of turning the lecture into a satisfying film. First, it makes the lecture more cinematic by frequently leaving the lecture hall behind and entering a world of animations, charts, and verité segments. Second, it turns Gore into a true character by transforming his experience of attempting to get his message out to the world into a narrative of its own. In segment after segment, we break away from Gore's rhetoric to small scenes filling in the gaps of his history of activism on the issue and showing the personal roots of his interest. This helps build audience identification with Gore so that we are not only being taught about global warming, but also made to root for him on his quest to teach *other* people about it.

Figure 17.1 shows a structural diagram of the film. Note that it consists of a very compact introduction, followed by 22 segments and a credit sequence/call to action at the end.

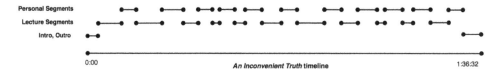

FIGURE 17.1 Structural diagram for *An Inconvenient Truth*

These 22 segments oscillate back and forth between lecture segments and personal segments. This mix keeps the flow of information to the audience from ever becoming static, and enlists the audience as partisans, cheering Gore's quest to convince the world (including us) of the importance of the issue. Gore is portrayed as *a man on a mission* who is delivering a vital message about the urgency for action on climate change.

In the following sections I will analyze the intro segment in detail, and then dissect how a sample lecture segment and a sample personal segment function.

Intro Segment

The intro, a mere 3 minutes and 52 seconds in length, sets up the framework for the entire rest of the film. It begins with four shots depicting an almost impossibly idyllic riverside scene, with the sun's rays reflecting off a river onto the underside of the bright green leaves of a tree, with the serene sounds of Michael Brooks' synth-and-piano score playing in the background. As we watch the water flow past at a soothingly slow rate, Gore's voice announces itself, relaxed and calm, with long pauses between the sentences.

> You look at that river gently flowing by. You notice the leaves rustling with the wind. You hear the birds; you hear the tree frogs. In the distance you hear a cow. You feel the grass. The mud gives a little bit on the river bank. It's quiet; it's peaceful. And all of a sudden, it's a gear shift inside you, and it's like taking a deep breath and going, "Oh yeah, I forgot about this."

With "supercapitalism" making leisure time ever more scarce for a majority of Americans, this is a little fantasy that many people would like to indulge in.[3] Gore is inviting us to view nature as a respite from everyday life, and making its survival feel like not only a moral good *(we should do something to save it)* but also an individual, personal good *(I want to be by that river right now)*. If the film is going to be about saving the planet, then one can see the advantage of starting with a visceral experience of what the planet offers.

On the last piano phrase, we cut to a close shot of an Apple laptop computer on a table, Gore's hands hovering above it with his audience visible but out of focus in the background.[4] An image of the Earth is seen on the laptop, and we then zoom into a much closer shot so that the edges of the laptop disappear. Gore begins speaking as three cutaway shots of audience members (all enthralled) are shown.

> This is the first picture of the Earth from space that any of us ever saw. It was taken on Christmas Eve 1968 during the Apollo 8 mission . . .

Right as he's about to launch into his second sentence, we cut to three more audience reaction shots, only these are in China, and a recording of his voice from a *different* lecture is heard.

> . . . within relatively comfortable boundaries. But we are filling up that thin shell of atmosphere with pollutants.

Finally we see him finishing the lecture in a *third* location to the sound of generous applause. He steps toward the crowd and greets his audience, who have smiles on their faces, happy to have the privilege of meeting the former vice president as they snap pictures. This mini-section concludes with one more shot of Gore from behind, a spotlight bathing him in angelic light, as he walks through a tunnel that will bring him to the venue for the lecture that we will witness for the next 87 minutes. The message of this little sequence is clear: this guy is a rock star, performing in multiple venues worldwide, and you definitely want to hear what he has to say.

But note what the film has held back. In all of these shots, we only see Gore from *behind* or from a disadvantaged profile shot. In order to provide a bit of narrative suspense, it has denied us a full shot of his face in order to be able to reveal it in the following shot.

Starting his lecture, Gore gives one well-timed opening line ("I'm Al Gore [and] I used to be the next president of the United States," and we finally get to see his face. After some laughter and applause he follows with a second self-deprecating joke: "I don't find that particularly funny . . . "

Now a montage of media images from the 2000 presidential election are shown: beginning with shots of adoring crowds lining the streets as seen from inside of a campaign bus, a series of clips depicts Gore on the campaign trail, looking hopeful, confident, and idealistic. Next, as if returning to that same vehicle but in the present day, we see Gore open his laptop in the back of a limousine. He looks at it seriously. "I've been trying to tell this story for a long time and I feel as if I've failed to get the message across," he says in voice over with a certain amount of regret, and then looks meaningfully out the window. Cut to a shot of blocks of ice floating on the sea in the Antarctic, moving the same direction and at approximately the same speed as if he were seeing them outside of the limo window. The music intensifies and goes from mildly dramatic to threatening as seven more shots follow the same tonal trajectory: gorgeous sun-dappled forest, water rushing by in a snow-capped stream, closer shot of snow from the same stream, cracked earth, smoke belching from a refinery, wider shot of smoke belching from a refinery, *a wildfire burning out of control . . .* Cut back to an extreme close-up of Gore (the closest yet), looking worried as he continues staring out the window of the limo.

In a very short amount of time, the film has managed to:

▶ Humanize Al Gore as someone who is humble. ("I've failed to get the message across.")

▶ Make Al Gore into the consummate underdog, with unfinished business he must now attend to. (He's traveling the world spreading his message, despite the setbacks.)

▶ Visually present a nightmare scenario of environmental devastation *as seen through Gore's eyes*. (The visual montage buttressed by the musical score.)

Now all that's left to do is embellish the message already delivered and introduce the title. After Gore says, "I was in politics for a long time, I'm proud of my service," we see disturbing images from Hurricane Katrina, as New Orleans mayor Ray Nagin pleads for help from the federal government. The clips play full screen before they are revealed to be images from Gore's own laptop: he's viewing them and using them as part of his slideshow presentation. The shots of Gore keep getting tighter and tighter, the last one showing one eye in extreme close-up. Gore gives one final line that sets up the film's title ("there are good people who are in politics who hold this at arm's length because they acknowledge it and recognize it as a moral imperative to make big changes") as Nagin gives one final impassioned plea ("and let's fix the biggest damn crisis in the history of this country!") and Gore is seen through the window of his limo. We see his body but not his face, which is obscured by a reflection in the window. As the object obscuring him moves aside his face is finally revealed and the title of the film appears onscreen: "An Inconvenient Truth."

Lecture Segment

Immediately following the intro, the lecture begins. The lecture is the core of the film, so it's worth digging into its details to see how it uses the continual presentation of fresh visual information to retain the audience's interest in the subject matter and to give the feeling of this being a real, live event, rather than a staged one.

First of all, it's important to note that we join the lecture as it's *already in progress*, an interesting choice that helps build the illusion that the presentation is actually something that existed independent of the film's production. (It was, of course, specifically staged for the purposes of shooting *An Inconvenient Truth*, complete with an elaborately planned lighting setup, a video wall, and a sympathetic crowd. The audience is lit so that they can be seen nearly as well as Gore himself, a situation that might be distracting for the audience but works well for using their reactions as a cue for how we're meant to respond to Gore.)

Next, let's note how even within the lecture segments, the film continually shifts between the two basic types of material: shots of Gore and the audience in the auditorium as he delivers his speech, and full-screen images of charts, graphics and animations. Note in the chart shown in Figure 17.2 how the first lecture segment plays out. "LEC" stands for lecture shots (Gore speaking onstage) and "GRAPHICS" stands for graphics and animations.

As you can see in the column on the right, a variety of shots are employed, from a sweeping wide shot used in the beginning to establish the geography of the room to close-ups of Gore and the audience members. Shifting between these angles helps keep the lecture shots fresh, even as they're also being broken up frequently by the graphics shots. Also note how in the longer shots (like the ones that are 13–14 seconds in duration) there is movement in the frame via a digital zoom, which is accomplished in the editing room. This keeps things feeling "alive" and active even though there is no cutting. It should be stressed that shots of longer duration like these can be strikingly effective because they allow the audience to focus on *one* visual idea as the narrative or concept is being developed via the words.

As the lecture segments develop and evolve over the course of the film's running time, the ratio between lecture shots and graphics shots moves gradually toward the latter, and among the graphics material the ratio of still frames to video material also moves toward the latter. For instance, the first 80 seconds of the third lecture segment contain not a single shot of Gore. Thus, the lecture segments gradually become more visually complex, mirroring the increasingly intense emotional content, as the film drives forward toward its final pitch for action.

Personal Segment

To discuss the personal Gore segments let's focus on the second one, which deals with his son's death.[5] Gore has just finished wrapping up the first big chunk of his slideshow presentation about the dangers of global warming. "Ultimately this is not so much a political issue so much as a moral issue," he says with conviction. "If we allow that to happen," he asserts, pointing to a scary looking spike in carbon dioxide emissions projected for the year 2055 on the enormous video screen behind him, "It is *deeply* unethical."

At this point Gore stops talking and the personal Gore segment begins. We pan up from the surface of a desk to Gore's hands on his laptop, and then cut to his face as he tweaks his slideshow document. Gore continues to speak, but this time in a measured, almost confessional voice: we are now getting the *private* Al Gore. "I had such faith

SHOT LENGTH	WORDS	IMAGES
:02	. . . and they lost radio contact	LEC Medium shot of audience member.
:02	when they went around the dark side of	LEC Close-up of a row of audience members.
:03	the moon and there was inevitably some suspense.	
:07	Then when they came back in radio contact they looked up and they snapped this picture,	LEC Medium close-up of audience member. LEC Very wide high-angle tracking shot of Gore speaking, revealing most of the audience.
:14	and it became known as Earth Rise. And that one picture exploded in the consciousness of the human kind. It led to dramatic changes. Within 18 months of this picture the modern environmental movement had begun.	GRAPHICS Shot of Earth Rise picture (still). Zooms in very slowly.
:06	The next picture was taken on the last Apollo mission, Apollo 17.	LEC Medium-profile shot of Gore with audience in background.
:09	This one was taken on Dec. 11th, 1972 and it is the most commonly published photograph in all of history.	LEC Wide shot of Gore in front of video wall, with picture beside him.
:04	And it's the only picture of Earth from space that we have	LEC Close-up shot of Gore speaking.
:13	where the sun was directly behind the spacecraft so that the Earth is fully lit up, and not partly in darkness. The next I'm going to show you has almost never been seen.	GRAPHICS Close-up shot of Earth picture, almost filling the frame. Shot is static for three seconds, then zooms in.
:12	It was taken by a spacecraft called the Galileo that went out to explore the solar system, and as it was leaving Earth's gravity it turned its cameras around	LEC Medium close-up shot of Gore speaking. GRAPHICS Time-lapse animation of Earth spinning.
:11	and took a time-lapse picture of one day's worth of rotation here compressed into 24 seconds. Isn't that beautiful?	

FIGURE 17.2 First lecture segment from *An Inconvenient Truth*

in our democratic system . . . I actually thought and believed that the story would be compelling enough to cause a real sea change in the way Congress reacted to that issue," he says as we see a black-and-white picture of him on the Capitol steps, presumably after pressing his case before his fellow senators. "I thought they would be startled and they weren't." We now see four slow-motion video clips in succession of him testifying before Congress, looking determined but slightly defeated, as he waxes philosophical in the voice-over:

> The struggles, the victories that aren't really victories, the defeats that aren't really defeats... they can serve to magnify the significance of some trivial step forward, and exaggerate the seeming importance of some seeming massive setback.

The film is putting his present mission in the context of his past efforts and elaborating on the sense of humility we saw in the introduction, yet as the shot dissolves to what looks like a black-and-white still photo of the sun our curiosity is piqued: what are we looking at?.

The succeeding shots answer the question. The camera zooms out as we discover that the "sun" shot is really the bright flood light of a parking lot, which dissolves to a newspaper headline that reads: "Senator Gore's son, 6, hit by car near stadium, condition serious." Speaking slowly, Gore narrates:

> April 3, 1989. My son pulled loose from my hand and chased his friend across the street. He was six years old. The machine was breathing for him. We were possibly going to lose him.

We see black-and-white shots of a hospital ward. The shots are empty of people, as if taken in the wee hours of the morning when all hope seemed to be lost. It's interesting to note how effortlessly these shots (which are likely from a stock photo library or were shot as reenactment) manage to fit into a very personal story, because they simulate the relatable experience of spending an agonizing night in the hospital, wondering about a loved one's fate.

Then we hear the conclusion of the story:

> He finally, uh, took a breath. We stayed in the hospital for a month, it was almost as if, uh, you could look at that calendar and, *whoosh*, everything just flew off. Trivial, insignificant. He was so brave, he was such, such a brave guy.

Here it's interesting to note how the filmmakers leave in some of the imperfections of Gore's speech, including two "uh"s and the double utterance of the word "such." In a different segment this might be a bad move, but in a section of such tender emotions it serves to further humanize the politician. We cannot help but smile when the film cuts to a picture of Gore smiling at his son, who sits up in his hospital bed looking triumphantly well.

Now the segment comes full circle, as it cuts back to an image of Gore testifying at another hearing.

> It just turned my whole world upside down and then shook it until everything fell out. My way of being in the world, it just changed everything for me. How should I spend my time on this Earth?

Now the music starts with a pulsing electronic bass, as if Gore's motor has been started again. "I really dug in," says Gore. "Trying to learn about it much more deeply," the pace quickening. We see shots of ice sheets in the Antarctic and shots of the Amazon River from a helicopter as he says, "I went to the South Pole, the North Pole, the Amazon." Gore is looking down on the Amazon from the helicopter now. "Went to places where scientists could help me understand sides of the issue that I didn't really understand in depth."

We then see three gorgeous black-and-white archival images of Gore's young son, the last of them with Gore whispering something intimate in his ear.

> The possibility of losing what was most precious to me . . . I gained an ability that I maybe didn't have before, but when I felt it, I felt that we could really lose it.

Here the film cuts back to that first image from the intro, the one of the peaceful river scene, and activates all of the emotions generated in that earlier segment. Gore then finishes his final line of the segment, delivered in a reverent near whisper: "What we take for granted might not be here for our children . . . "

Let's think about what this segment has accomplished. With one simple story about his son's accident, it has managed to increase Gore's reliability by sharing an intimate moment that any parent could identify with and it also, crucially, ties that experience to the cause of saving the Earth. It has done so in a gentle pattern of raising subtle questions à la Kate Amend's "show, then tell" method by subtly making the audience work to search for a payoff to a small question. And it has let the visuals say things so that they don't need to be said in narration (i.e., the specifics of the son's accident, which are revealed via the newspaper headline). Just as crucially, it has let us take a break from the relatively more static and less cinematic lecture segments, which we are now ready to rejoin as the segment concludes.

Conclusion

The raw materials of *An Inconvenient Truth* are pretty simple: extended multi-camera footage of a lecture on a stage, extensive audio interviews with Al Gore, various bits of verité and B-roll footage of Gore telling stories on his family's farm and delivering lectures around the globe, archival materials from Gore's past, and stock and archival images from Gore's slideshow. The editor and director preserve the integrity of the original lecture while breaking it up into bite-sized chunks that keep it from getting too didactic. All of the personal material about Gore is condensed into discrete sections, each of which revolves around a different personal anecdote. The back-and-forth nature of the structure allows each type of material to reinforce the other, and as we learn details of Gore's history he turns into a more and more credible lead character, who we root for as he fights against the forces of ignorance and intransigence worldwide. Gore himself has actually been a somewhat controversial figure within the environmental movement at times, getting criticism for everything from the large utility bill on his Tennessee mansion ($30,000 yearly by some reports) to the 2003 sale of his Current TV network to Al Jazeera, which is funded by the oil kingdom of Qatar,[6] but none of that is included here. Instead, a pleasing portrait of a do-gooder is presented. Gore seems infinitely more comfortable crusading against climate change in this film than he did as a candidate on the campaign trail back in 2000, and much of this is undoubtedly due to the editing. From the luxurious pauses that are included in the more reflective moments of the film to the highly effective use of graphics throughout, *An Inconvenient Truth* manages to take a lecture and turn it into a real film.

▶ NOTES

1   Bar-Lev, Amir. "The Blog: My Kid Could Paint That." *The Huffington Post.* huffingtonpost.com. August 31, 2007. Web.

2   Blair, Elizabeth. "Laure David: One Seriously 'Inconvenient' Woman." *All Things Considered.* National Public Radio. npr.org. May 7, 2007. Web.

3   Robert Reich, *Supercapitalism: The Transformation of Business, Democracy, and Everyday Life* (New York: Vintage Books, 2008).

4   The film is also a highly effective ad for Apple; Gore is seen crisscrossing the planet with his MacBook Pro always in tow.

5   The segment about Gore's son's near-death begins at 24:52.

6   Tapper, Jake. "Al Gore's 'Inconvenient Truth'?—a $30,000 Utility Bill." *ABC News.* abcnews.go.com. February 26, 2007. Web.

18

Analyses of Two Short Documentaries

▶ **SKIP (2011)**

Directed and edited by Fielder Jewett

Skip is a nine-minute short film made in 2011 by Fielder Jewett, who was then an undergraduate student at Wesleyan University.[1] It is a funny and touching portrait of Alfie "Skip" Consavage, a self-described "big, dumb Polack" who wins the lottery one day after working for decades as a self-employed welder in Ridgefield, Connecticut. The editing builds an assured rhythm that oscillates between voice-over segments and verité segments at the same time that it also shifts back and forth between comedic and poignant moments. It uses images of specific objects to build characterization, uses dynamics in interesting ways, and creates a powerful "arc of experience" for the audience.

The film begins with an arresting quote from Skip over a close-up shot of him welding something at a work bench, his reflective welder's helmet hiding his face. "In my life, to make money, I've crawled inside septic tank trucks," he says in a working-class Connecticut accent. "I dated a girl once who said she used to take her clothes off as a stripper, I said 'No big deal, I swam in your shit, which is worse?' How many people can say they've been in shit, and literally mean that?"

Right from the beginning, we are set up to understand Skip as a colorful character who has some funny stories to tell. We have also been made curious by the fact that we can't see his face, setting up a reveal in the next scene. The main title appears, gracing the screen in fancy cursive, and provides an ironic stylistic contrast to his verbal content and gives us a subtle cue that it's okay to laugh.

Our curiosity about what he looks like is satisfied as we now see Skip sitting alone in his truck, sipping coffee from a large Styrofoam cup. If there were any doubts about his name, it's shown in the embroidered lettering on his workman's shirt. As the shot plays on, it holds on him so we can get a good look at his kindly face, then slowly pans down to two lottery scratcher cards prominently visible in the foreground in the passenger seat. Clearly and simply, the film is telling us that these objects have some kind of meaning. But what is it? This is the central question of the film. Next is a cutaway to a pack of Virginia Slims cigarettes on the dashboard, a detail that makes this seemingly crude character even more quixotic and adorable.

Returning to a scene with dialogue, Skip talks to us as he drives. "I've been doing this so many years, I don't know what else I'd do," he says matter of factly. "I mean, if I had 10 million dollars then I could do whatever I want. Yeah, then maybe I'd think of something else but . . . " Skip trails off.

The combination of the scratcher tickets we just saw and the line about the 10 million dollars confirms Skip as a guy who has jackpots on his mind, and who has a somewhat resigned attitude about life. "I hate traveling," he continues. "On Sundays, my daughter is like, 'Let's go down to Norwalk to the Polish deli.' I don't even want to drive a half hour to go to Norwalk, you want me to fly eight hours to go to another country? What, are you nuts?" Skip chuckles. This gives us some further character information, defining Skip as a guy who is somewhat cheerfully set in his ways, and we also learn that he has a daughter (but not, as we will soon see, a life partner).

Now that the film has set up a narrative hook via our curiosity about the lottery tickets, it shifts to showing us scenes from his daily life and filling in the backstory. After a short scene in which Skip stops to consult his map in search of the right address, he walks up to the stoop of a modest house, his butt crack clearly showing between his too-small work shirt and his sagging jeans. This shot is satisfying precisely because it is a detail that is *not* overtly pointed out to us, but is available for us to see if we're paying attention. He has a short interaction with an old man at the door, and then begins making measurements on the steps so he can build a railing. The measuring work takes some time, but the film has given us enough to be curious about that we're satisfied just to be observing what seems to be a typical day in Skip's life.

Back in the car, the theme of Skip as a man who has come to accept his lot in life is expanded.

> When I was a kid they used to say, 'you're a dreamer, you're a dreamer.' I said, 'I want to go down to Florida to look for sunken treasure, or one day I want to own a castle like that, or I'm gonna do this or that.' Everybody dreams different things but then reality sets in after a while—you gotta work, you gotta make a living, you know, blah blah blah.

This last line is given with a touch of resignation in Skip's voice, and the shot plays with an elongated pause after he finishes speaking so that we glimpse some sadness on his face.

We then settle on a shot of his messy garage, part of Skip's figure visible in the doorway to his office. A Mickey Mouse clock ticks away on the wall. Abruptly, the film cuts inside the office as Skip strikes a match and lights a Virginia Slim. Lest the film spend too long in a serious mode, it shifts back again to a comedic one as he starts talking to us with a smile on his face: "Now if cigarette companies could advertise smoking, they'd have me all the time, I'd be the new Marlboro Man. I'd be the Virginia Slim [sic] man," he says with a hearty chuckle.

We're now inside Skip's office for the first time (literally the closest we've gotten to his private space), and as the camera pans over old pictures on the wall of Skip as a young boy and a teenager we hear him muse about his life.

> I was born and bred to work. My dad used to say, 'You're a big dumb Polack.' So you just worked hard. As far as having a future for myself, yeah I wanna have a girlfriend, a house, go places, get laid three times a day, who cares? But it's now and here, so you do what you can now and here, and tomorrow will take care of itself.

The emotional tenor of the film is again oscillating back to the serious/poignant side, and his resignation is creeping back in.

After we liven the mood with a shot of Skip making huge fireballs in his garage with the help of an aerosol spray can, he then narrates a section which brings one of the film's most touching moments. "If you're judging a book by its cover, my cover is two pieces of solid steel with rocks glued to it," says Skip, making a subtle reference to the railings that he's working on for the old man.

> I pound things, you see sparks flying, I get cuts and bruises. [But if] you open it up, if you ever get to the inside, you're going to see the finest little tiny rice tissue paper with the most majestic writing on it you can find, if you ever get inside there.

At this precise moment of tender self-reflection, we are seeing a slow-motion effect applied to Skip raising, then lowering again, his big welder's hat.

It's important to note how the editing has helped increase the emotional impact of this moment. This is one of only three slow-motion shots in the film, so it stands out since it's used selectively. And what is the shot of? Fittingly, it's of Skip protected by a huge impenetrable mask, which he then flips away to reveal his vulnerable face, and then puts back in place again. The slow motion turns the moment into a more poetic one and the symmetry between the visual metaphor (mask blocking his face) and the spoken words is perfect.

Breaking away from the reverie, we see Skip assembling a bunch of dirty dollar bills at his messy desk, then pumping gas into his truck at a gas station. As he is seen inside the convenience mart putting down money on Powerball, he begins speaking again.

"I've been gambling my whole life, one way or another. People ask, 'Can you afford it?' Well, the money I take it's just pocket money. Yeah, I should have taken some of the money and put it aside for my future, this and that, but today is today." He scratches off the coating on one of his scratchers, then moves onto the second one. No luck.

Now all of the themes that have been put into play in this short film are coming together. We see Skip as a man who wants more than he's got, even though he's also a man who seems to have an even-keeled perspective on his own life. We sympathize with him, and also want him to have more than he's got. "I don't know if I'm gambling to win," he says. "I think I'm gambling because at the end of my day it's something to do, and yeah if you win you feel better, if you lose, fu** it, move on, tomorrow's another day." At this point the film has taken the portrait of Skip as far as it can go with the available material.

* * *

Suddenly there is a cut to a piece of archival footage from a local news station. "Talk about having a pretty good day, just ask Alfred 'Skip' Consavage of Ridgefield," booms the announcer. In the short clip, we succinctly learn that Skip won $1 million, and we see him holding a big oversized check. We are shocked and joyed by the revelation.

The film has obviously used its assets in a strategic way, building Skip up as a guy who gambles, and who would very much like to win, but has probably not won yet. Director Jewett, who edited the film himself with editorial advice from Katja Straub, builds the news of the prize into a huge reveal that changes our entire outlook on the main character, even though all of the footage was actually shot *after* he won.

But lest we feel that this is just a cheap editing trick, everything we learn in the remaining third of the film confirms that the man with $1 million in lottery winnings is exactly the same man he was before he won. Skip becomes even more lovable because his essential outlook on life has not changed.

After the TV news clip of him winning, Skip muses about the moment when he found out that he had won as we see him continuing to work in his garage. "I've been to plays where all of a sudden everything stops and everybody stands up and applauds or something. *That moment right there, it was just a moment . . .* " Perfectly matching these words, Jewett has a second slow-motion shot to use over it: Skip opening the door to his garage from the inside and being bathed in a beatific, heavenly light that washes out most of the frame.

Lest the tone get too reverential and sappy, Skip brings us back to earth. "The next day, I went back to work," he says matter-of-factly. His coarse language resumes as he describes his workplace. "Most people look at this place, it's a garage, it's nasty. But this is my home, like it or not. A dirty metal place with red hot sparks burning your dick." Skip is now revealing the fact that his life has not changed very much since winning the lottery, and that his everyday work has meaning to him.

Returning to verité, we see Skip handling the big oversized check that we saw on TV. The magic of the moment he described earlier is indeed over, as we now see it as a simple prop that is cluttering up his desk. He waves it around, noting that he hasn't decided whether or not to put it up on the wall yet.

"Prior to this money, I had no retirement plan, I had nothing saved," says Skip over a shot of him in corner of his garage, sunlight streaming through a fan vent in the corner.

> My retirement plan was going to be 'work till I die.' You get the social security, enough to live on, try to find something. If nothing came up and I couldn't survive, you kiss a train going 60 miles an hour. That was my retirement plan. I kept thinking, somewhere something good's gotta happen to me.

We are starting to realize now just how much Skip really did need the money, and in the film's most emotional moment he says, "So many people have come up and thanked me, just to say, 'It's nice to see somebody like you win.' That's cool." Tears well up in Skip's eyes as he says it. "Does anybody *deserve* anything in this world? You work for it, then you get paid, that's how I look at it. Somewhere down the line God said, 'Okay.' "

This statement is the closest Skip has come to articulating a complete philosophical statement on his life. He seems to feel that he followed the rules laid out for him by society, worked hard, and "did the right thing." He is lucky, but also somehow cosmically deserving. And yet, he still goes to work.

Making the last oscillation in tone, the film shifts for the final time from the emotional/philosophical back to the deeply practical. Over shots of Skip parking his truck in his garage, we hear him talk about his schedule for the rest of the day.

> My plan this afternoon is: my oven needs to be cleaned. Because tomorrow my daughter and I are baking, and I know my oven needs a good cleaning. I might stop in Walmart; I bought some pants that were a little too small, I gotta return them and get slightly bigger ones. That's what I'm doing this afternoon.

As a final wrap-up statement, Skip says the following to us on camera, with a wistful but satisfied tone: "I gamble money, I lose, I gamble money, I lose, I gamble, I lose, I gambled . . . I *won* today. That's all. I won today. But life goes on, you know? Life goes on. And you gotta go right back to work."

* * *

Narratively, the film hooks us in the second shot with the tease about the lottery tickets, then pauses to build up his background and his character. By rearranging the flow of information into a satisfying "arc of audience experience," it makes us wait until about two-thirds through the film for the revelation about winning the $1 million prize. The level of emotionality also has an arc, slowly growing throughout the film up until the moment when the tears reach Skip's face. The film follows an oscillating pattern back and forth between verité scenes and "evidentiary" ones, as well as between comedic scenes and more emotionally poignant ones.

The overall pace of the film reflects Skip's attitude toward life. Instead of talking in a gushing monologue, there are well-chosen pauses between each one of his anecdotes, even when we're not switching back and forth between verité and narrated segments. The pauses are at one with Skip's own physical rhythms, which are of a man who approaches life with a somewhat resigned but relaxed attitude, taking every day as it comes.

Connective tissue between the scenes helps move the film along smoothly. For example, the word "Skip" is seen on the screen in two successive scenes: first in the title card and then again on his work shirt in the shot directly after it. And right after he uses the phrase "tomorrow's another day," the TV announcer follows in the next shot with, "talk about having a pretty good day!"

Geographically, the film starts outside in public space, and slowly moves inside toward Skip's private space. The more emotional moments only happen once the private space has been revealed. The slow-motion shots are used with discretion, and saved for moments where the emotionality of the scene merits them.

▶ *HOTEL 22* (2014)

Directed and edited by Elizabeth Lo

Hotel 22 is an award-winning eight-minute documentary by filmmaker Elizabeth Lo, produced at the Stanford University Documentary Film and Video Program with support from the Sundance Institute, and featured on the *New York Times* Op-Docs website.[2] Upon first look, the raw footage for this film about a 24-hour bus line in Silicon Valley must have seemed rather dull. Lots of it is of people sleeping, not exactly the most scintillating subject matter. Compounding the issue is the fact that it takes place in such constrained quarters. But Lo, who edited the film herself, found a way to break her clips down into highly refined categories and build a pattern out of them. That pattern brilliantly showcases the relatively small amount of dialogue and makes it sing, while turning the background of the bus line into a strangely beautiful and hypnotic backdrop.

Stark in its tone and patient in its pacing, the film shows how footage of relatively mundane activities can be elevated by strong cinematography, a deft use of editing dynamics, and solid structure. The film has no narrative development to speak of, and no main characters, but makes excellent use of its observational footage and delivers an experience that has a definite arc.

The film begins with a disclaimer that reads:

The following video contains language that will be offensive to some viewers.

While this is just a standard warning, it also functions as a subtle teaser. It's like a less sensationalistic version of the disclaimer that ran at the head of A&E's *Intervention* show: "The following program contains disturbing images, *viewer discretion advised*," which was read in a serious but unmistakably seductive tone of voice. The warning serves the same function as the teaser montages featured in many television documentaries, as mentioned in Chapter 12: it promises drama, buying time with its audience. The early minutes of the film are slow ones as the film sets about establishing its measured pace, and it is impossible not to wonder when the offensive language will occur.

The disclaimer out of the way, the film begins with the following two title cards, which are a case study in concision. Each one is displayed for under four seconds and together they offer everything we need to know to make sense of the images we are about to see.

> In Silicon Valley, Line 22 is a 24-hour public bus.

> Each night, it is a popular route for the homeless.

It should be said that the downside of offering this information right away is that it *tells* the audience what it's about to see before showing them anything at all. Yet the upside—greater context and intelligibility—ultimately wins out.

The film begins with a stark shot of a figure slumped over on a public bench at night. Seen from behind, the person's head is hidden from view amidst the pitch-black background, so we have no way of determining their age or sex, but this is part of what makes the image so intriguing. Instantly we are working to understand what we're seeing, and the fact that the following shot of the same figure as seen from the side reveals little more continues the intrigue. Perhaps the anonymity of the image is precisely the point: this person, shielding themselves from the cold by crouching for warmth and closing the hood on their sweatshirt, could be anyone, and is a stand-in for the homeless in general.

This pair of shots becomes part of the first of eight sections that make up the film (see Figure 18.1). The first and last sections contain title cards over black, the first one reading "8:35pm" and the second one reading "8:28am," effectively bookending the film and making us feel that we have witnessed a complete 12-hour period.

In between, the film consists of four movements, each consisting of footage shot inside the bus and containing a passage of speech in which someone makes a declaration or a request. Three interludes provide pauses between the movements and contain shots of the *outside* world passing by (see Figure 18.1).

The "speeches" that define the four movements are staggered in intensity to create an arc. The first is delivered as audio only, as we hear the bus driver warning passengers of

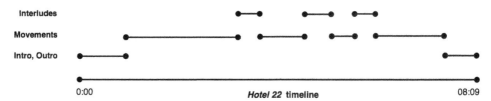

FIGURE 18.1 Structural diagram for *Hotel 22*

the rules (no feet on the seats, etc.). This first movement is the most sedate and contains the fewest cuts, as it establishes a patient, hushed rhythm for the rest of the film. The shots are wider than in the movements to come, grounding us in the geography of the bus before later zeroing in on individuals.

The second movement ups the ante, showing us a passenger beseeching the bus driver to turn up the heat on the bus. ("Why don't you put the heat on, brother? You won't hear another word from me if you put the heat on.") There is some anger in his voice and his words are coarse, but the man is not physically threatening, and argues his point like a lawyer making his case to a judge.

The third movement is the most intense, as we witness a sudden outburst of crude hate speech. A passenger standing next to the exit lets loose a string of racial obscenities, and when an African American man in the foreground briefly objects, he, too, is shouted down. The man in the foreground stays seated, seemingly resigned to hearing the other man out.

Finally, indicating that closure is at hand, the fourth movement again gives us the voice of the bus driver in a forceful declaration that the bus is coming to its final destination. "Wake up, wake up!" he barks. "Everybody's getting off now!"

As stated above, three small interludes are sandwiched between the movements, providing pauses and indicating the passage of time. As we look out on a small series of shots of the dark suburban streets, the world floats by in montage.

Thus the film oscillates back and forth between speech and silence, and between verité editing (in the movements) and subtle montage editing (in the interludes). The effect is a soothing one that seems to mirror the experience of riding the bus all night long, with its lulling engine noise punctuated by regular stops and the occasional interruption of the peace by words blaring from the bus's PA system or by an outburst from a mentally ill passenger. A woman is twice heard offscreen singing a lullaby.

There's a wonderful shot that closes the fourth movement that is extraordinarily effective at conveying the overall message of the film. A man rises out of his seat with extreme difficulty, his face contorted in an intense grimace until he reaches a standing position. He then grabs his walking cane and begins to shuffle off, resigned to another day of the same old thing. This is the general mood of the population on the bus: disgruntled, in pain, but resigned to their powerlessness.

▶ NOTES

1   *Skip* can be viewed at https://vimeo.com/40269913, and via a link on this book's companion website.

2   *Hotel 22* can be viewed at: www.nytimes.com/video/opinion/100000003473921/hotel-22.html, and via a link on this book's companion website.

Appendix A
List of Films Cited

13th (2016). Directed by Ava DuVernay. Edited by Spencer Averick.

20 Feet from Stardom (2013). Directed by Morgan Neville. Edited by Doug Blush, Kevin Klauber, and Jason Zeldes.

The Act of Killing (2013). Directed by Joshua Oppenheimer. Edited by Nils Pagh Andersen, Charlotte Munch Bengtsen, Ariadna Fatjó-Vilas, Janus Billeskov Jansen, and Marido Montpetit.

Aging Out (2004). Directed by Roger Weisberg, Maria Finitzo, and Vanessa Roth. Edited by Sandra Christie and Christopher White.

American Movie (1999). Directed by Chris Smith. Edited by Jun Diaz and Barry Poltermann.

An Inconvenient Truth (2006). Directed by Davis Guggenheim. Edited by Jay Cassidy and Dan Swietlik.

The Armor of Light (2015). Directed by Abigail Disney and Kathleen Hughes. Edited by Andrew Fredericks.

Aspen (1999). Directed and edited by Frederick Wiseman.

At Berkeley (2013). Directed and edited by Frederick Wiseman.

The Bad Kids (2016). Directed by Keith Fulton and Lou Pepe. Edited by Jacob Bricca and Mary Lampson.

Best of Enemies (2015). Directed by Robert Gordon and Morgan Neville. Edited by Eileen Meyer and Aaron Wickenden.

Better This World (2011). Directed by Kelly Duane De La Vega and Katie Galloway. Edited by Greg O'Toole.

Beware of Mr. Baker (2012). Directed by Jay Bulger. Edited by Abhay Sofsky.

Beyond the Border (2001). Directed by Ari Palos. Edited by Jacob Bricca.

Born into Brothels (2004). Directed by Zana Briski and Ross Kauffman. Edited by Nancy Baker and Ross Kauffman.

Boxing Gym (2010). Directed and edited by Frederick Wiseman.

Boyz in the Hood (1991). Directed by John Singleton. Edited by Bruce Cannon.

Burden of Dreams (1982). Directed by Les Blank. Edited by Maureen Gosling.

Can't Stand Losing You: Surviving the Police (2012). Directed and edited by Andy Grieve.

Capturing the Friedmans (2003). Directed by Andrew Jarecki. Edited by Richard Hankin.

Cartel Land (2015). Directed by Matthew Heineman. Edited by Matthew Hamachek, Matthew Heineman, Bradley J. Ross, and Pax Wassermann.

The Central Park Five (2016). Directed by Sarah Burns, Ken Burns, and David McMahon. Edited by Michael Levine.

Chronicle of a Summer (1961). Directed by Jean Rouch and Edgar Morin. Edited by Néna Baratier, Francoise Colin, and Jean Raven.

Con Artist (2009). Directed by Michael Sladek. Edited by Jacob Bricca and Michael Sladek.

Control Room (2004). Directed by Jehane Noujaim. Edited by Julia Bacha, Lilah Bankier, Charles Marquardt and Alan Oxman.

The Cove (2009). Directed by Louie Psihoyos. Edited by Geoffrey Richman.

Coven (2000). Directed and edited by Mark Borchardt.

The Cutting Edge: The Magic of Movie Editing (2004). Directed by Wendy Apple. Edited by Daniel Loewenthal and Tim Tobin.

Daughter from Danang (2002). Directed by Gail Dolgin and Vicente Franco. Edited by Kim Roberts.

Detropia (2012). Directed by Heidi Ewing and Rachel Grady. Edited by Enat Sidi.

Don't Look Back (1967). Directed and edited by D. A. Pennebaker.

El Valley Centro (1999). Directed and edited by James Benning.

Feed (1992). Directed by Kevin Rafferty and James Ridgeway. Edited by Sarah Durham.

Finding Tatanka (2014). Directed and edited by Jacob Bricca.

Finding Vivian Maier (2013). Directed by John Maloof. Edited by Aaron Wickenden.

The Fisher King (1991). Directed by Terry Gilliam. Edited by Lesley Walker.

Fitzcaraldo (1982). Directed by Werner Herzog. Edited by Beate Mainka-Jellinghaus.

The Fog of War: Eleven Lessons from the Life of Robert S. McNamera (2003). Directed by Errol Morris. Edited by Doug Abel, Chyld King, and Karen Schmeer.

Food, Inc. (2008). Directed by Robert Kenner. Edited by Kim Roberts.

Glengarry Glen Ross (1992). Directed by James Foley. Edited by Howard Smith.

God Grew Tired of Us (2006). Directed by Christopher Quinn and Tommy Walker. Edited by Geoffrey Richman.

Grey Gardens (1976). Directed by Ellen Hovde, Albert Maysles, David Maysles, and Muffie Meyer. Edited by Susan Froemke, Ellen Hovde and Muffie Meyer.

Grizzly Man (2005). Directed by Werner Herzog. Edited by Joe Bini.

Happy Valley (2004). Directed by Amir Bar-Lev. Edited by Dan Swietlik, Brian Funck, and David Zieff.

Harlan County U.S.A. (1976). Directed by Barbara Kopple. Edited by Nancy Baker, Mira Bank, Lora Hays, and Mary Lampson.

Hell and Back Again (2011). Directed by Danfung Dennis. Edited by Fiona Otway.

High School (1969). Directed and edited by Frederick Wiseman.

The Hill (2012). Directed and edited by Lisa Molomot.

Honor Diaries (2013). Directed and edited by Micah Smith.

Hoop Dreams (1994). Directed by Steve James. Edited by William Haugse, Steve James, and Frederick Marx.

Hospital (1970). Directed and edited by Frederick Wiseman.

Hot Girls Wanted (2015). Directed by Jill Bauer and Ronna Gradus. Edited by Brittany Huckabee.

Hotel 22 (2014). Directed and edited by Elizabeth Lo.

How to Draw a Bunny (2002). Directed and edited by John Walter.

The Hunting Ground (2015). Directed by Kirby Dick. Edited by Doug Blush, Derek Boonstra, and Kim Roberts.

(i hate myself :) (2013). Directed by Joanna Arnow. Edited by Max Karson and Joanna Arnow.

If a Tree Falls: A Story of the Earth Liberation Front (2011). Directed by Marshall Curry. Edited by Marshall Curry and Matthew Hamachek.

Iraq in Fragments (2006). Directed by James Longley. Edited by James Longley, Billy McMillin, and Fiona Otway.

Indies Under Fire: The Battle for the American Bookstore (2006). Directed and edited by Jacob Bricca.

The Interrupters (2011). Directed by Steve James. Edited by Steve James and Aaron Wickenden.

Into the Arms of Strangers: Stories of the Kindertransport (2000). Directed by Mark Jonathan Harris. Edited by Kate Amend.

The Invisible War (2012). Directed by Kirby Dick. Edited by Doug Blush and Derek Boonstra.

Iraq in Fragments (2006). Directed by James Longley. Edited by James Longley, Billy McMillin and Fiona Otway.

The Iron Ministry (2014). Directed and edited by J. P. Sniadecki.

Jimmy Scott: If You Only Knew (2002) Directed by Matthew Buzzell. Edited by Jacob Bricca.

The Jinx (series, 2015). Directed by Andrew Jarecki. Edited by Zachary Stuart-Pontier.

Juvenile Court (1973). Directed and edited by Frederick Wiseman.

The Keepers (series, 2017). Directed by Ryan White. Edited by Kate Amend, Mark Harrison, and Helen Kearns

Knight of Cups (2015). Directed by Terrence Malick. Edited by A. J. Edwards, Keith Fraase, Geoffrey Richman, and Mark Yoshikawa.

Koyaanisqatsi (1983). Directed by Godfrey Reggio. Edited by Ron Fricke and Alton Walpole.

Last Train Home (2009). Directed by Lixin Fan. Edited by Lixin Fan, Mary Stephen, and Yung Chang.

Life Itself (2014). Directed by Steve James. Edited by Steve James and David E. Simpson.

The Long Way Home (1997). Directed by Mark Jonathan Harris. Edited by Kate Amend.

Lost in La Mancha (2002). Directed by Keith Fulton and Lou Pepe. Edited by Jacob Bricca.

Man on Wire (2008). Directed by James Marsh. Edited by Jinx Godfrey.

Meet the Patels (2014). Directed by Geeta and Ravi Patel. Edited by Matthew Hamachek, Billy McMillin, Dhevi Natarajan, Geeta Patel, and Ravi Patel.

Millhouse (1971). Directed by Emile D'Antonio. Edited by Mary Lampson.

Murderball (2005). Directed by Henry Alex Rubin and Dana Adam Shapiro. Edited by Conor O'Neill and Geoffrey Richman.

My Kid Could Paint That (2007). Directed by Amir Bar-Lev. Edited by Michael Levine and John Walter.

Nanook of the North (1922). Directed and edited by Robert Flaherty and Charles Gelb.

Naqoyqatsi (2002). Directed by Godfrey Reggio. Edited by Jon Kane.

Near Death (1989). Directed and edited by Frederick Wiseman.

Never Been Kissed (2016). Directed and edited by Stacy Howard and Elen Tekle.

Night and Fog (1956). Directed and edited by Alain Resnais.

O Brother, Where Art Thou? (2000). Directed by Joel Coen. Edited by Ethan Coen, Joel Coen, and Tricia Cooke.

O.J.: Made in America (2016). Directed by Ezra Edelman. Edited by Bret Granato, Maya Mumma, and Ben Sozanski.

Peace Officer (2015). Directed by Brad Barber and Scott Christopherson. Edited by Renny McCauley.

The Pearl (2016). Directed by Jessica Dimmock and Christopher LaMarca. Edited by Fiona Otway.

Planet Earth (2006). Directed by Alastair Fothergill. Edited by Andy Netley, Stuart Napier, David Pearce, Andrew Chastney, Martin Elsbury, Jill Garrett, Jo Payne, and Thom Sulek.

Point and Shoot (2014). Directed and edited by Marshall Curry.

Powaqqatsi (1988). Directed by Godfrey Reggio. Edited by Iris Cahn and Alton Walpole.

Precious Knowledge (2011). Directed by Ari Palos. Edited by Jacob Bricca.

Primary (1960). Directed and edited by Robert Drew.

Pure (2008). Directed and edited by Jacob Bricca.

The Queen of Versailles (2012). Directed by Lauren Greenfield. Edited by Victor Livingston.

Racing Dreams (2009). Directed by Marshall Curry. Edited by Marshall Curry, Matthew Hamachek, and Mary Manhardt.

Rashomon (1950). Directed and Edited by Akira Kurosawa.

Rivers and Tides: Andy Goldsworthy Working with Time (2001). Directed and edited by Thomas Riedelscheimer.

School's Out: Lessons from a Forest Kindergarten (2013). Directed and edited by Lisa Molomot.

Sherman's March (1985). Directed and edited by Ross McElwee.

Skip (2011). Directed and edited by Fielder Jewett.

Sleepwalk with Me (2012). Directed by Mike Birbiglia and Seth Barrish. Edited by Geoffrey Richman.

Small Farm Rising (2012). Directed by Ben Stechschulte. Edited by Ben Stechschulte, James D'Amico, and Jacob Bricca.

Sons of Ben (2015). Directed by Jeff Bell. Edited by Jacob Bricca and Glen Gapultos.

Soundbreaking: Stories from the Cutting Edge of Recorded Music (series, 2016). Directed by Maro Chermayeff, Jeff Dupre, and James Manera. Edited by Alexandre Landreau, Nancy Novack, Samuel D. Pollard, Howard Sharp, E. Donna Sheperd, and Jay Keuper.

Star Wars: Episode IV: A New Hope (1977). Directed by George Lucas. Edited by Richard Chew, Paul Hirsch, and Marcia Lucas.

Startup.com (2001). Directed by Chris Hegedus and Jehane Noujaim. Edited by Pedro Pablo Celedón, Chris Hegedus, Erez Laufer, and Jehane Noujaim.

Stop Making Sense (1984). Directed by Jonathan Demme. Edited by Lisa Day.

Stories We Tell (2012). Directed by Sarah Polley. Edited by Michael Munn.

Super Size Me (2004). Directed by Morgan Spurlock. Edited by Stela Georgieva and Julie Lombardi.

Taxi Driver (1976). Directed by Martin Scorsese. Edited by Tom Rolf and Melvin Shapiro.

Tell Me Do You Miss Me (2006). Directed by Matthew Buzzell. Edited by Jacob Bricca.

The Thin Blue Line (1988). Directed by Errol Morris. Edited by Paul Barnes.

This Changes Everything (2015). Directed by Avi Lewis. Edited by Mary Lampson and Nick Hector.

Titicut Follies (1967). Directed and edited by Frederick Wiseman.

True Conviction (2017). Directed by Jamie Meltzer. Edited by Jeff Gilbert.

Underground (1976). Directed by Emile D'Antonio. Edited by Mary Lampson.

Waiting for "Superman" (2010). Directed by David Guggenheim. Edited by Jay Cassidy, Greg Finton, and Kim Roberts.

The Waiting Room (2012). Directed by Peter Nicks. Edited by Lawrence Lerew.

White Earth (2014). Directed and edited by J. Christian Jensen.

Why We Fight (series, 1942–1945). Directed by Frank Capra and Anatole Litvak. Edited by William Hornbeck and William A. Lyon.

Wordplay (2006). Directed by Patrick Creadon. Edited by Doug Blush.

The World According to Sesame Street (2006). Directed by Linda Goldstein Knowlton and Linda Hawkins. Edited by Kate Amend, Johanna Demetrakas, and Alicia Dwyer.

Zoo (1993). Directed and edited by Frederick Wiseman.

Appendix B

Case Studies of Schedules for Feature Documentaries

▶ *LOST IN LA MANCHA* **(7 MONTHS)**

On *Lost in La Mancha*, the verité-heavy documentary that I cut in 2001 about director Terry Gilliam's failed attempt to make his adaptation of *Don Quixote*, we had a relatively small amount of footage (well under 100 hours) to work with. Directors Keith Fulton and Lou Pepe focused my efforts by stringing out their favorite selects into a small seven-hour reel, and I began from there.

The easiest part of the editing was cutting the verité scenes that would eventually become the core of the film, and these ended up constituting about a third of the 89-minute run time. This work went quickly, while it took longer to build the opening third of the film and the final section.

All in all, it took about 12 weeks to reach our first full rough cut, and this was followed by another 9 weeks to get to a fine cut. At this point the film was mostly done, with two or three more weeks of work to be done with final smoothing. Thus, this verité-heavy film with under 100 hours of raw footage took a total of 24 weeks to edit, spread out over a somewhat longer period because of short breaks and hiatuses.

▶ *THE BAD KIDS* **(9 MONTHS)**

There were approximately 230 hours of raw footage on this verité film about a group of students dealing with the crippling effects of poverty at a continuation high school in the Mojave Desert. Our fantastic assistant editor Bill Hilferty had started several weeks before I came on, ingesting, logging, and organizing all the footage into a well-organized Final Cut Pro project, which included several select reels. I spent the first six weeks in "play" mode: viewing footage, making notes, coming to an overall impression of the strengths and challenges of the footage, and starting some select reels of my own. The next six weeks were spent coming to a very rudimentary rough edit which was meant to show an initial sketch of what the film could be. At this point directors Keith Fulton and Lou Pepe started working with me much more closely, and month four brought us to a complete (though very long and messy) rough cut. Two and a half months more were then spent getting this rough cut down to a shorter length and working out many of the story issues, which included an eight-day visit to the Sundance Documentary Edit and Story Lab, where we workshopped the film. Editor Mary Lampson came on for six weeks during the home stretch to work on some of the issues still at play, and both of us then worked together for the final two weeks to come to the locked picture cut.

All in all, I edited for a total of 18 weeks spread out over seven months; Mary worked for six weeks over two months. The edit thus took approximately nine months to get to picture lock.

▶ PRECIOUS KNOWLEDGE (13 MONTHS)

The edit for this 2011 documentary on the banning of Ethnic Studies programs in Arizona public schools began in mid-October of 2009 and was picture locked just before Thanksgiving of 2010. This 13-month period included several breaks, ranging from a few days to several weeks each, to allow additional shooting to take place and to facilitate thoughtful reflections on how to proceed with the complex story. Thus, my total number of weeks worked was far less than the 13 months might indicate. Additional editing was also performed on many segments by Lisa Molomot, and director Ari Palos also served as assistant editor by setting up the Final Cut Pro project and organizing the dailies even before the 13-month period began, and by continuing to refine sequences and look for additional footage as needed.

▶ TELL ME DO YOU MISS ME (3 MONTHS)

This 2006 documentary on the indie rock band Luna was part travelogue, part concert documentary, part low-key personal drama. The speed with which we completed post-production was an anomaly. This was partly due to the fact that director Matthew Buzzell completed the entire organization and setup of the project himself by synching and organizing all the footage (a large portion of which was live concert footage) before the clock started running on the edit. He picked his favorite live performances of songs, which helpfully limited the amount of footage we were considering.

The main reason we were able to complete it so quickly was that the narrative content of the film was relatively small. Instead, the film played out as a series of stylish sketches about life on the road as a mid-level rock band, with a mild drama brewing in the background between the two guitarists. While we skipped some cities in our rendering of the band's travels, we did not alter the real-life timeline of events, and really only had to find the "best bits" among the footage. We spent six furious weeks cutting the majority of the film together in Los Angeles. I worked a few more weeks from my home, and assistant editor David Fine was brought on near the end to cut some final elements including the song that plays over the end credits.

Appendix C
Documents You Will Need

SUB INSPECTOR SANDHYA
head Women's Help Line

SUB INSPECTOR KRISHNA
former head of Help Line

Nautiyalji
office manager

HELP LINE CONSTABLES

Pushpa Jha

Ranjana

Sunita

Mumta

Pushpa Arya

Meenakshi

Kamla

Rakhi

Neema

Amarlata

OTHERS

Seela
(friend of the constables)

Sub inspector Deepika
former head of Help Line

Sub Inspector Umesh
Sandhya's husband

FIGURE A.1 Cast of Characters document for *Marriage Cops*

Time Code And Scene Name	Precious Knowledge 01 Pricila Home Int Pricila Home 01-2 – 1-7	216 02 Pricila
	Are you good with the levels? Ya.	
05:44:06	What was common with all the people in that movie? THAT THEY ALL HATED THEIR PARENTS. They all hated their parents? WELL THE DIDN'T LIKE THEM, CUZ, WELL I THINK FOR, WELL THEY WOULD IGNORE THEM, LIKE THEY WOULD PRETEND THEY DIDN'T EXSIST AND FOR THE OTHER ONE LIKE FOR THE BAD KID "THE GANGSTER" WELL NOT THE GANGSTER BUT LIKE THE CRIMINAL UM HIS PARENTS WOULD LIKE BEAT HIM LIKE THEY DON'T GIVE HIM A LOT OF ATTENTION. AND FOR LIKE THE PRINCESS GIRL- THEY'D LIKE USE HER CUZ THE PARENTS WOULD BE FIGHTING SO THEY LIKE GET BACK AT EACH OTHER. Ahh the phone! That's what I hate most.	
	Int Pricila Home 01-3	
05.45.14 05.45.17	It was my mom. Your mom?! I want to talk to her. Do you know anyone who doesn't like their parents? I THINK THAT'S EVERY TEENAGER AT ONE POINT OR ANOTHER. WASN'T LIKE THEM BUT DOESN'T LIKE THEM AT THAT MOMENT. BUT YOU MEAN LIKE DAILY? LIKE EVERYDAY? Well like in general.	
05.45.38	MM NO. I MEAN WELL CRYSTAL HAS ISSUES WITH HER DAD BUT OTHER THAN THAT… This is pretty common. I know a lot of kids who don't like their parents. Seriously. A lot of teenage girls have problems with their day. When they're young they're very close but then when they're a teenager they don't like them telling them what to do. "I hate my dad! I hate my parents!" (LAUGHING) YA I mean that's why the "Breakfast Club" was a hit, people could identify with it. YA THAT'S WHY.	
05.46.35	Well I think you're different Pricila. Seriously, aren't you different? You don't hate your mom. NO, I MEAN THERE ARE INSTANCES WHERE WE IGNORE EACH OTHER AND WE ARGUE, BUT OTHER THAN THAT…BUT YEAH ITS REGULAR.	
05:46:46	Have you ever said you hate your mom? LIKE, TO SOMEONE ELSE? Yeah. NO I DON'T THINK SO. I'VE JUST SAID, I THINK I'VE SAID, "MY MOM IS LIKE MEAN" AND I'LL LIKE DESCRIBE WHAT SHE DID. "TOOK MY TV AWAY EVEN THOUGH I WAS WATCHING" YOU KNOW; I'LL COMPLAIN- I'LL DO THAT.	

FIGURE A.2 Interview transcript from *Precious Knowledge*. Note the timecode stamps on the left (there should be a time stamp at least once per minute) and the naming system that shows which clip(s) the page corresponds to. (In this case it starts on clip "Int Pricilla Home 01-2" and continues into clip "Int Pricilla Home 01-3".)

	A	B	C
1	Time Code	**SUNDANCE LAB CUT**	
2			
3		Probation officer visit with Joey	
4		The Bad Kids title card	
5		Counseling session Montage	
6		Desolate desert shots (includes next service 90 miles)	
7		VV Arrives at school early and works in office building dropout powerpoint (VV voice over)	New Day
8		Bus arrives at desert bus stop	
9		Joey and Stephen Jam Together ("I'm yours") in the morning before school	
10	01:05:01:08	Joey interior thoughts	
11		Bus ride to school (including Joey)	
12		VV Greets bus, recognizes joey "Hey you, look at me.."	
13		Intake session montage (Arianna, Joseph, Jeffrey) - add Program only works if you want it	
14		Joey intake session (No hiding, you're in charge)	
15		Joey walks in hall playing guitar	
16		Joey plays guitar in woodshop	
17		Hall Transition (with marcus and paige kissing)	
18		Hustle, Bustle, Urge to get credits montage (Including Joey talking to JC during a test and	
19	01:10:13:20	Mario flip bus driver off and Luke wants to beat up a kid discipline montage	
20		VV tells Joey the importance of a diploma	
21		Ambrosius calls student looking for them to get to school	
22		Lee tells class making 20 credits is too hard	
23		Lee talks with VV in Hallway - ready to give up and drop out	
24		Faculty meeting: Staff discuss Victor Ballester and Jessie Silva	
25	01:16:25:07	Evening valley town shots from mountaintop	
26		Lee "World is a dark place" interior thought	New Day
27		Lee and Layla discuss having first baby on the porch	
28		Lee and Layla push stroller	
29	01:18:38:00	Safe Dates: Discussion of Anger and Abuse	
30	01:20:32:22	Lee and Dennen talk - not giving up, still trying to graduate	
31		Dennen knife game in P3	
32		Joey teaches Jacob Guitar	
33		Wings of Desire #1	
34		Jennifer Interior thoughts	
35		Jennifer rotary club interview	
36	01:25:12:03	Jennifer talks to VV about her dad not wanting her to graduate early	
37		EOD Transition	
38		Bartz plays guitar alone under pavillion as students arive to school	New Day
39		Joey shreds on electric guitar	
40		Bartz tutors Joey in Math	

FIGURE A.3 Portion of a continuity document used on *The Bad Kids*

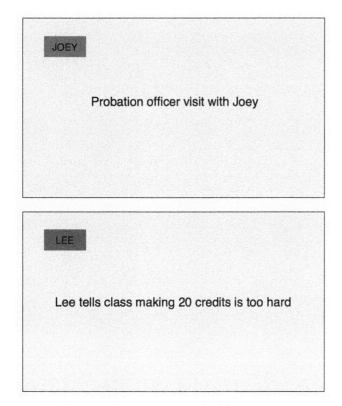

FIGURE A.4 Sample index cards from *The Bad Kids*

Index